AGRICULTURAL ACAROLOGY

AGRICULTURAL ACAROLOGY

By
Dr. Shubhrata R. Mishra
Deptt. of Botany
Vikram University
Ujjain (M.P.)
(India)

DISCOVERY PUBLISHING HOUSE PVT. LTD.
NEW DELHI-110 002

Published by:
Tilak Wasan
DISCOVERY PUBLISHING HOUSE PVT. LTD.
4383/4B, Ansari Road, Darya Ganj
New Delhi-110 002 (India)
Phone : +91-11-23279245, 43596064-65
Fax : +91-11-23253475
E-mail : parul.wasan@gmail.com
discoverypublishinghouse@gmail.com
web : www.discoverypublishinggroup.com

***First Edition:* 2013**

ISBN: 978-93-5056-316-8

Agricultural Acarology

Printed at:
Aditi Fine Art Press
Delhi

PREFACE

Most acarines are minute to small, but the largest Acari some ticks and red velvet mites may reach lengths of 10–20 millimetres. It is estimated that over 50,000 species have been described and that a million or more species are currently living. The study of mites and ticks is called acarology.

A procedure known as 'flagging' is an effective way to collect acarines especially ticks from vegetation. A white flannel cloth is tied to a stout stick and used to brush/sweep the vege-tation. Ectopa-rasitic acarines detach from the vegetation and attach to the moving cloth. The cloth is examined and any acarines found can be removed using the above stated procedure.

Mites (Acari or Acarina) are the most diverse and abundant of all arachnids, but because of their small size usually less than a millimeter in length and we rarely see them. The ticks are an exception, in that they are usually big enough to see, especially when they are filled with blood. There generally exists an uneasy truce between the insects pests and man , and this is termed as 'balance in nature'.

Cultural control is a preventive method which is inexpensive and may prove more efffective and efficient, if employed after acquiring a through knowledge of the life history and habits of a pest. Deep ploughing after harvesting the crop to expose the hiding and resting insects, the removing and destroying of the suitable and other trash, adjusting the time of sowing to avoid the peak incidence period, clean cultivation, the removal of alternative wild hosts, catch crops and suitable rotations are some of the important measures included under this method of control.

This book is the outcome of long innings of research work in library and Internet. I also consulted foreign authors' books on this topic. The editorial staff of this publication along with publisher also helped me in every possible way. I am highly indebted to all these resources for publishing this book on scheduled time in eye-pleasing format.

—Author

CONTENTS

CHAPTER – 1

Integrated Pest Management Tools

Integrated Pest Management (IPM) is being practised for a wide range of crops in all regions of the world. It is about an approach and not a set of techniques. The approach is universally applicable.

It does not necessarily involve sophisticated information gathering and decision making. The IPM approach can be introduced at any level of agricultural development. For example, improvement of basic crop management practices, such as planting time and crop spacing, can often be effective in reducing pest attack. It is a dynamic process. A useful beginning can be made with relatively limited specialized information or management input. Later, additional information, technologies, and mechanisms can be developed to enhance the effectiveness of the system.

In addition to crop production, this management also calls for non-chemical alternatives to post harvest loss prevention. This is particularly important as losses due to post harvest damage can be significant and use of chemicals on stored produce is a common cause of poisoning people.

CROP MANAGEMENT IN AGRICULTURE

Integrated pest management is an integrated approach of crop management to solve ecological problems when applied in agriculture. The term "integrated" was thus synonymous with "compatible." Chemical controls were to be applied only after regular monitoring indicated that a pest population had reached a level (the economic threshold) that required treatment to prevent the population from reaching a level (the economic injury level) at which economic losses would exceed the cost of the artificial control measures.

These methods are performed in three stages: prevention, observation, and intervention. It is anecological approach with a main goal of significantly reducing or eliminating the use of pesticides while at the same time managing pest populations at an acceptable level.

For their leadership in developing and spreading IPM worldwide, Dr. Perry Adkisson and Dr. Ray F. Smith received the 1997 World Food Prize.

CONCEPT OF SUPERVISED INSECT CONTROL

In the 1950s, when synthetic insecticides became widely available, entomologists in California developed the concept of "supervised insect control". Around the same time, entomologists in cotton-belt states such as Arkansas were advocating a similar approach. Under this scheme, insect control was "supervised" by qualified entomologists, and insecticide applications were based on conclusions reached from periodic monitoring of pest and natural-enemy populations. This was viewed as an alternative to calendar-based insecticide programmes. Supervised control was based on a sound knowledge of the ecology and analysis of projected trends in pest and natural-enemy populations.

Tools of IPM

Monitoring : Keep tracks of the pests and their potential damage. This provides knowledge about the current pests and crop situation and is helpful in selecting the best possible combinations of the pest management methods.

Pest resistant varieties : Breeding for pest resistance is a continuous process. These are bred and selected when available in order to protect against key pests.

Cultural pest control : It includes crop production practices that make crop environment less susceptible to pests. Crop rotation, cover crop, row and plant spacing, planting and harvesting dates, destruction of old crop debris are a few examples. Cultural controls are based on pest biology and development.

Mechanical control : These are based on the knowledge of pest behaviour. Hand picking, installation of bird perches, mulching and installation of traps are a few examples.

Biological control: These includes augmentation and conservation of natural enemies of pests such as insect predators, parasitoids, pathogen and weed feeders. In IPM programmees, native natural enemy population are conserved and non-native agents are released with utmost caution.

Chemical control : Pesticides are used to keep the pest population below economically damaging levels when the pests cannot be controlled by other means. It is applied only when the pest's damaging capacity is nearing to the threshold.

Supervised control formed much of the conceptual basis for the "integrated control" that University of California entomologists articulated in the 1950s. Integrated control sought to identify the best mix of chemical and biological controls for a given insect pest. Chemical insecticides were to be used in manner least disruptive to biological control.

It extended the concept of integrated control to all classes of pests and was expanded to include tactics other than just chemical and biological controls. Artificial controls such as pesticides were to be applied as in integrated control, but these now had to be compatible with control tactics for all classes of pests. Other tactics, such as host-plant resistance and cultural manipulations, became part of the IPM arsenal. IPM added the multidisciplinary element, involving entomologists, plant pathologists, nematologists, and weed scientists.

In the United States, integrated pest management was formulated into national policy in February 1972 when President Nixon directed federal agencies to take steps to advance the concept and application of IPM in all relevant sectors. In 1979, former President Carter established an interagency IPM Coordinating Committee to ensure development and implementation of IPM practices.

Applicability in Agriculture

The integrated pest management is applicable to all types of agriculture and sites such as residential and commercial structures, lawn and turf areas, and home and community gardens. Reliance on knowledge, experience, observation, and integration of multiple techniques makes IPM a perfect fit for organic farming without artificial pesticide application. For large-scale, chemical-based farms, IPM can reduce human and environmental exposure to hazardous chemicals, and potentially lower overall costs of pesticide application material and labour:

- *Monitor or sample environment for pest population:* How many are here? Preventative actions must be taken at the correct time if they are to be effective. For this reason, once the pest is correctly identified, monitoring must begin before it becomes a problem. For example, in school cafeterias where roaches may be expected to appear, sticky traps are set out before school starts. Traps are checked at regular intervals so populations can be monitored and controlled before they get out of hand. Some factors to consider and monitor include: Is the pest present/absent? What is the distribution—all over or only in certain spots? Is the pest population increasing or decreasing?

- *Proper identification of pest:* What is it? Cases of mistaken identity may result in ineffective actions. If plant damage due to over-watering are mistaken for fungal infection, spray costs can be incurred, and the plant is no better off.
- *Learn pest and host life cycle and biology:* At the time you see a pest, it may be too late to do much about it except maybe spray with a pesticide. Often, there is another stage of the life cycle that is susceptible to preventative actions. For example, weeds reproducing from last year's seed can be prevented with mulches. Also, learning what a pest needs to survive allows you to remove these.
- Conversely, there is a point at which action must be taken to control cost. For the farmer, that point is the one at which the cost of damage by the pest is morethan the cost of control. This is an economic threshold. Tolerance of pests varies also by whether or not they are a health hazard (low tolerance) or merely a cosmetic damage (high tolerance in a non-commercial situation).

  Different sites may also have varying requirements based on specific areas. White clover may be perfectly acceptable on the sides of a tee box on a golf course, but unacceptable in the fairway where it could cause confusion in the field of play.
- *Establish action threshold viz. economic, health or aesthetic:* In some cases, a certain number of pests can be tolerated. Soybeans are quite tolerant of defoliation, so if there are a few caterpillars in the field and their population is not increasing dramatically, there is not necessarily any action necessary.
- *Evaluate results:* How did it work? Evaluation is often one of the most important steps. This is the process to review an IPM programme and the results it generated. Asking the following questions is useful: Did actions have the desired effect? Was the pest prevented or managed to farmer satisfaction? Was the method itself satisfactory? Were there any unintended side effects? What can be done in the future for this pest situation? Understanding the effectiveness of the IPM programme allows the site manager to make modifications to the IPM plan prior to pests reaching the action threshold and requiring action again.
- *Choose an appropriate combination of management tactics:* For any pest situation, there will be several options to consider. Options include, mechanical or physical control, cultural controls, biological controls and

chemical controls. Mechanical or physical controls include picking pests off plants, or using netting or other material to exclude pests such as birds from grapes or rodents from structures. Cultural controls include keeping an area free of conducive conditions by removing or storing waste properly, removing diseased areas of plants properly. Biological controls can be support either through conservation of natural predators or augmentation of natural predators.

Augmentative control includes the introduction of naturally occurring predators at either an inundative or inoculative level. An inundative release would be one that seeks to inundate a site with a pest's predator to impact the pest population. An inoculative release would be a smaller number of pest predators to supplement the natural population and provide ongoing control.

Chemical controls would include horticultural oils or the application of pesticides such as insecticides and herbicides. A Green Pest Management IPM programme would use pesticides derived from plants, such as botanicals, or other naturally occurring materials.

Principles

An IPM system is designed around six basic components: The US Environmental Protection Agency (EPA) has a useful set of IPM principles:

1. *Acceptable pest levels:* The emphasis is on control, not eradication. IPM holds that wiping out an entire pest population is often impossible, and the attempt can be econmically expensive, environmentally unsafe, and frequently unachievable. IPM programmes first work to establish acceptable pest levels, called action thresholds, and apply controls if those thresholds are crossed. These thresholds are pest and site specific, meaning that it may be acceptable at one site to have a weed such as white clover, but at another site it may not be acceptable. By allowing a pest population to survive at a reasonable threshold, selection pressure is reduced. This stops the pest gaining resistance to chemicals produced by the plant or applied to the crops. If many of the pests are killed then any that have resistance to the chemical will form the genetic basis of the future, more resistant, population. By not killing all the pests, there are some un-resistant pests left that will dilute any resistant genes that appear.

2. *Preventive cultural practices:* Selecting varieties best for local growing conditions, and maintaining healthy crops, is the first line of defense, together with plant quarantine and 'cultural techniques' such as crop sanitation (e.g. removal of diseased plants to prevent spread of infection).

3. *Monitoring:* Regular observation is the cornerstone of IPM. Observation is broken into two steps, first; inspection and second; identification. Visual inspection, insect and spore traps, and other measurement methods and monitoring tools are used to monitor pest levels.

   Accurate pest identification is critical to a successful IPM programme. Record-keeping is essential, as is a thorough knowledge of the behaviour and reproductive cycles of target pests. Since insects are cold-blooded, their physical development is dependent on the temperature of their environment. Many insects have had their development cycles modeled in terms of degree days. Monitor the degree days of an environment to determine when is the optimal time for a specific insect's outbreak.

4. *Mechanical controls:* Should a pest reach an unacceptable level, mechanical methods are the first options to consider. They include simple hand-picking, erecting insect barriers, using traps, vacuuming, and tillage to disrupt breeding.

5. *Biological controls:* Natural biological processes and materials can provide control, with minimal environmental impact, and often at low cost. The main focus here is on promotingbeneficial insects that eat target pests. Biological insecticides, derived from naturally occurring micro-organisms (e.g.: Bt, entomopathogenic fungi and entomo-pathogenic nematodes), also fit in this category.

6. *Responsible Pesticide Use:* Synthetic pesticides are generally only used as required and often only at specific times in a pests life cycle. Many of the newer pesticide groups are derived from plants or naturally occurring substances like nicotine, pyrethrum and insect juvenile hormone analogues, but he toxophore or active component may be altered to provide increased biological activity or stability. Further 'biology-based' or 'ecological' techniques are under evaluation.

An IPM regime can be quite simple or sophisticated. Historically, the main focus of IPM programmes was on agricultural insect pests. Although, originally developed for agricultural pest management, IPM programmes are now developed to encompass diseases, weeds, and other pests that interfere with the management objectives of sites such as residential and commercial structures, lawn and turf areas, and home and community gardens.

Solutions to Pest Control

Integrated Pest Management is not an input or a technology *per se;* rather it is an approach that should be applied according to the local circumstances. It encourages farmers to find specific solutions to the pest problems they encounter in their fields based on understanding of agroecological principles, monitoring interactions among crops, pests and natural enemies of pests, and selecting and implementation of adequate control measures.

There is no "blueprint" for planning interventions in support of IPM in a particular setting. Many countries have ongoing activities related to IPM in the fields of research, extension and farmer training, often supported by foreign donors. It is worthwhile to examine the capacity and experiences of national or subregional organizations when planning project interventions.

Change of Farming Systems

Providing support to research is an important element of an IPM intervention strategy because there is still a lack of locally adapted solutions to pest problems. Additionally, new pests constantly emerge with the change of farming systems.

The integration of pest management technologies into a location-specific IPM approach is a classical example for a public good. Private companies invest in research and development of technologies that might fit into an IPM approach, such as biological control, reduced-risk chemicals etc. However, there are little market incentives to invest in knowledge management of farm resources because benefits can not easily be captured to repay capital investment. This is especially true when it comes to using low-external input and long-term strategies such as crop rotation, cultural management techniques, use of compost and other organic matter.

Countries with a well-established national agricultural research system often have programmes and associated staff with long-term experience and knowledge in biological control and other components of IPM. Many of those programmes came from a technology-centred perspective and work on issues related to individual pests or crops. They have faced two major constraints which limit their outreach capacity and the actual adoption of suggested solutions to pest problems by the farming community.

Firstly, many of those programmes have difficulties to pass disciplinary barriers and adopt a holistic, problem-oriented perspective which would include an orientation towards the socioeconomic conditions of farmers.

Secondly, because of weak research-extension linkages technologies developed in IPM research programmes are often not sufficiently disseminated and do not reach a large number of farmers. National extension programmes have been reluctant to take the IPM approach on board, because their modes of operation have been rarely conducive for a complex, situation-specific and knowledge-intensive approach like IPM.

Despite these constraints, continuous support to IPM research, especially for locally adapted pest management solutions is needed. Current research programmes that are funded through public organizations focus specifically on:

- Emerging new pests, some of them of global importance (*Example:* The whitefly has emerged as a pest that threatens cropping systems all over the world).
- Biological control and biopesticides (e.g. metarhizium for locust control).
- Host plant resistance, either through classical breeding methods or through techniques of genetic modification (e.g. *Bt* cotton, virus-resistant sweet potato).
- Use of IT in forecasting and scouting.
- Integration of various control methods into locally adapted IPM approaches.

Examples of important ongoing international IPM research programmes:

- The System-Wide Programme of the CGIAR (SP-IPM) bundles activities in international and national research centers according to the specific thematic focus.
- The IPM Collaborative Research Support Programme of US universities with counterpart researchers in a number of developing countries, supported by USAID, focuses on the pest management problems of horticultural export crops, peri-urban vegetables, olives, and some staple crops.
- CABI has a long record for developing biocontrol techniques and IPM approaches for many location specific pest problems.
- International Centre of Insect Physiology and Ecology is a leading research center in insect ecology and runs field research programmes which include many horticultural crops.
- Support to IPM extension and farmer training.

Over the past decade, a more participatory and farmer-based perspective on IPM has gained ground in a large number of countries. This perspective is being increasingly promoted by multi- and bilateral donor agencies as well as by NGOs. While in many countries there are pilot initiatives for farmer training which are scattered over many different regions and cropping systems, some countries have national IPM programmes for farmer training in IPM. For example, in 1993 the Philippine government established the kasakalikasan for provincial and municipal-based farmer training programmes. Other countries in South East Asia, such as Indonesia, Vietnam and Cambodia have run similar programmes for specific crops, e.g. rice.

There is unanimous support among all stakeholders that an IPM approach involves enhancement of the knowledge and skills of farmers. This can be done through a variety of measures, for example:

- Demonstration plots and trials as traditionally known in agricultural extension.
- Distribution of information via television and radio broadcast, newsletter, and internet services.
- Training of individual farmers or in groups.

The Farmer Field School (FFS) approach is increasingly considered and used in many countries. A closely related concept is the Farmer Participatory Training and Research (FPTR) approach promoted by CABI and others. International and national agricultural research centers are using FPTR to bridge the gap between research and implementation by farmers.

Farmer Field Schools

The concept of Farmer field schools comprises usually a season-long group training exercise for a group of farmers in an on-site location. Emphasis is put on agroecosystem analysis as a way to acquire environmental management knowledge in learning by doing approach. It have been used in many Asian countries to address pest problems caused by injudicious and over use of insecticides, especially in irrigated rice.

The approach has been promoted by the Systemwide Programme on IPM (SP-IPM) which is based at FAO and supported by the Bank. The Facility supports FFS pilot schemes in over twenty countries in Africa, Asia and Latin America. A large-scale IPM training programme that used the FFS concept was supported by the Bank in Indonesia from 1993-1999. While the capacity building effort in that project has reached over 600,000 farmers, there is still inconclusive evidence about the economic impact and the financial sustainability of the FFS concept as costs per trained farmer can be substantial.

Neem seeds and leaves contain many compounds which are useful for pest control. Unlike chemical insecticides, neem compounds work on the insect's hormonal system, not on the digestive or nervous system and therefore does not lead to development of resistance in future generations. These compounds belong to a general class of natural products called 'limonoids'.

The liminoids present in neem make it a harmless and effective insecticides, pesticide, nematicide, fungicide etc. The most significant liminoids found in neem with proven ability to block insect growth are: azadirachtin, salanin, meliantriol and nimbin. Azadirachtin is currently considered as *neem's* main agent for controlling insects. 'It appears to cause 90 per cent of the effect on most pests. It does not kill insects – at least not immediately – instead it both repels and disrupts their growth and reproduction.

Research over the past years has shown that it is the most potent growth regulator and feeding deterrent ever assayed. It will repel or reduce the feeding of many species of pest insects as well as some nematodes. In fact, it is so potent that a mere trace of its presence prevents some insects from even touching plants.'

Certain hormones are necessary for growth and development of insects. These hormones control the process of metamorphosis as the insects pass from larva to pupa to adult. Azadirachtin blocks those parts of the insect's brain that produce these vital hormones. As a result, insects are unable to molt. It is through these subtle hormonal effects that this important compound of neem breaks the life cycle of insects. The insect populations decline drastically as they become unable to reproduce.

Meliantriol and salannin act as powerful anti-feedants. Nimbin as well as nimbidin, an another neem component have antiviral property.

But, for all the uncertainty over details, various neem extracts are known to act as various insects in the following ways:

- Disrupting or inhibiting the development of eggs, larvae or pupae.
- Blocking the molting of larvae or nymphs.
- Disrupting mating and sexual communication.
- Repelling larvae and adults.
- Deterring females from laying eggs.
- Sterilizing adults.
- Poisoning larvae and adults.
- Deterring feeding.
- Blocking the ability to "swallow" (i.e., reducing the motility of the gut).
- Sending metamorphosis awry at various stages.
- Inhibiting the formation of chitin.

All these effects listed above are not equally strong or certain. Blocking the larvae from molting is considered to be neem's most important quality which can be used to eliminate many pest species. Neem products are harmless to most insect eaters, humans and other mammals, except certain marine life like crabs, lobsters, fishes and tadpoles.

Neem's Effects on Some Major Pests

Locusts (winged insects) are a great menace to crops and trees in Africa and Asia. The effects of ingredients and seed kernels of the neem tree on locusts and grasshoppers were studied in laboratory conditions, semi-field and field trials in Africa, Asia and Europe. There was very strong phagorepellent effect of neem oil on the desert locust and on the red locust.

The same applied to the variegated grasshopper. The results showed that neem oil and other products (aqueous seed kernel extracts, neem seed powder) can be applied against some important locusts and grasshopper species in farmer's fields with success.

Neem oil enriched with azadirachtin prevents locusts from developing into their migratory swarms that are so destructive to vegetation. Even doses equal to a mere 2.5 liters per hectare are enough to prevent formation of plagues of locusts. "Although alive, they become solitary, lethargic, almost motionless and thus extremely susceptible to predators such as birds."

Grasshopper nymphs are affected by neem in a similar way. By applying neem products to soil or by using seeds soaked with neem products can protect some crops from locusts for a week to a month.

Neem seed extract has been shown to retard the growth of several cockroach species. It kills the young cockroaches and inhibits the adults from laying eggs.

For Protecting Rice Crop

De-oiled Neem cake (the residual remaining after the oil has been pressed out of the seeds) and neem oil are quite effective against rice pests. Five applications of a 25 per cent oil emulsion sprayed with an ultra low-volume applicator can protect rice crops against brown plant hoppers. Neem products greatly reduce the tungo virus transmission efficiency of green leaf hopper in rice.

For Protecting Stored Crop

One of the traditional uses of neem in Asia has been for controlling pests of stored products. Farmers usually mix neem leaves with grain before keeping it in storage for several months. Neem leaves, oil or extracts acts as repellent against several insects such as weevils, flour beetles, bean-seed beetles and potato moths. Treatment of jute sack by neem oil or azadirachtin-rich-products prevents the penetration of pest like weevils and flour beetles.

Neem oil destroys bean-seed beetles (bruchids) – a variety of insects mostly attacking legumes – at the egg-stage itself. A mixture of neem leaves with clay and cow-dung develops pest resistant property so it can be used to make bins for storage of grain.

Experiments have shown that neem products are quite effective against European corn borer, a deadly pest which causes massive damage to corn and other crops in Europe and North America.

Neem is quite effective against armyworm, one of the most devastating pests of food crops in the western hemisphere. Azadirachtin in extremely low concentrations – a mere 10 mg per hectare – inhibits the pests.

Neem extract is useful against leaf miner, a serious pest in parts of North America. Neem seed extract works as well as available commercial synthetic pesticides. It has been approved by the US Environmental Protection Agency for use on leaf miners.

Protection of Crops

Neem in extremely useful as an anti-feedent and ovipositional repellent for protection of crops like tobacco, groundnut, cotton and sweet potato from the damages caused by tobacco caterpillar or tobacco cutworm, a serious polyphagous pest of several crops in India.

Neem products are quite effective against the larvae of a number of mosquito species which stop feeding and die after treatment. At present developing countries use expensive imported pesticides to control mosquito population. These countries can save a lot of money by using locally available simple neem products which are equally effective.

Simple techniques such as throwing crushed *neem* seeds into pools and ponds in the towns and villages can prevent mosquito breeding.

Experiments have shown that neem is also effective against fruit flies. Med fly, one of the most damaging horticulture pests, can be controlled by spraying *neem* solution under fruit trees. Neem has an advantage over the currently used pesticides.

Whereas the conventional pesticides kill fruit flies as well as their internal parasites, *neem* products on the other hand, leave the biological-control organisms unaffected; they only kill fruit flies. This reduces, in fact, eliminates adverse, unintended effects.

Neem is useful against gypsy moth, a pest which is causing severe damage to forests in parts of North America. Laboratory tests have shown that a very low concentration application of neem seed extract formulation, approved by the US Environmental Protection Agency, can kill gypsy moths.

Blowflies kill a large number of sheep in Australia. Experiments have shown that *neem* products can be useful in controlling blowflies. This opens up an interesting new line of neem application in animal husbandry.

It has been scientifically proved that, *neem* products can influence about 400-500 insect species.

So far we have concentrated on the effects of neem products on some of the important insects which cause severe damage to crops and animals. As can be seen from the discussion above, it is now established that neem and its products are highly effective against many pestiferous insects.

Non-insect Pests

Research in recent years has shown that neem is quite effective against non-insect pests also. Thread worms are among the most devastating agriculture pests. These nematodes are very difficult to control. Use of synthetic nematicides is not desirable as they cause toxicological effects. Research has shown that these pests are susceptible to neem products. Certain limonoid fractions extracted from neem kernels are providing active protection/defence against root-knot nematodes. Water extracts of neem cake are also nematicidal. Neem cake is already being used on commercial basis by cardamom farmers in south India.

Damage due to Fung: Attack

Fungi attack plants and trees in numerous ways and forms. They cause massive damage to important crops such as wheat, rice and corn. Several tests have demonstrated that neem acts as a fungicide. Should this prove widely applicable, it would have enormous positive effects on agriculture, environment and food supply with highly valuable effects like reducing poverty, increasing production etc. on a global scale.

Some tests have shown unusual and promising results neem-leaf extracts failed to kill the fungus *Aspergillus flavus* but completely stopped it from producing aflatoxin'. This is important because aflatoxin is a powerful carcinogen that is causing increasing concern regarding the world's food supplies.

Pest control, as practiced today in most developing countries relies mainly on the use of imported pesticides. This dependence has to be reduced. Although, pesticides are generally profitable on direct crop returns basis, their use often leads to the contamination of terrestrial and aquatic environments, damage to beneficial insects and wild biota, accidental poisoning of humans and livestock, and the twin problems of pest resistance and resurgence.

More than 500 arthropods pest species have become resistant to one or more insecticides. Resistance of the cotton bollworm, *Helicoverpa armigera*, in India and Pakistan, and of the *Colorado potato* beetle, *Leptinotarsa decemlineata*, in the USA to all available insecticides, and resistance of the diamondback moth, *Plutella xylostella*, to all classes of insecticides, including *Bacillus thuringiensis*, in Hawaii, Malaysia, the Philippines, Taiwan, and Thailand, illustrate the complexity of the problem.

Shifts in pest status-from minor to major, and resurgence of pests, such as white flies, caused by direct or indirect destruction of pests natural enemies are other unwelcome developments associated with pesticide use.

Crop Pests

Neem has had a long history of use primarily against household and storage pests and to some extent against crop pests in the Indian sub-continent.

It was a common practice in rural India to mix dried *neem* leaves with grains meant for storage. Mixing of *neem* leave (2-5%) with rice, wheat and other grains is even now practiced in some parts of India and Pakistan. Also, as early as 1930, neem cake was applied to rice and sugarcane fields against stem borers and white ants.

Some innovative farmers in Karnataka and Tamil Nadu States in India even today "puddle" green twigs and leaves in rice nursery beds to produce robust seedling and simultaneously ward-off attack by early pests-leafhoppers, planthoppers, and whorl maggots.

Controlled experiments confirmed that rice seedlings raised from seed treated with neem kernel extract or cake were vigorous and resistant to rice leafhoppers and planthoppers. Early observations that neem leaves were not attacked by swarming locusts were also confirmed in laboratory studies and attributed to neem's antifeedant activity against locusts.

Pest Control Potential of Neem

The pest control potential of neem in developing countries, however, remained largely untapped due to the advent of DDT and other and other broad-spectrum synthetic insecticides. Also, wide publicity given to slogans such as "the only good bug is a dead bug" and identifying traditional uses of neem as backward, gradually influenced people away from using *neem*.

It is only in the past decade, that the pest control potential of neem, which does not kill pests but affects their behaviour and physiology, has been recognized. Though subtle, neem's effects such as repellence, feeding and oviposition deterrence, growth inhibition, mating disruption, chemosterilization etc. are now considered far more desirable than a quick knock-down in integrated pest management programmes as they reduce the risk of exposing pests natural enemies to poisoned food or starvation.

In spite of high selectivity, neem derivatives affect ca. 400 to 500 species of insects belonging to Blattodea, Caelifera, Coleoptera, Dermaptera, Diptera, Ensifera, Hetroptera, Homoptera, Hymenoptera, Isoptera, Lepidoptera, Phasmida, Phthiraptera, Siphonoptera, and Thysanoptera, on species of ostracod, several species of mites and nematodes, and even noxious snails and fungi, including aflatoxin-producing Aspergillus flavus. Results of field trials in some major food crops in tropical countries will illustrate the value of neem-based pest management for enhancing agricultural productivity in Asia and Africa.

Pest of Stored Products

Post-harvest losses are notoriously high in developing countries. Worldwide annual losses in store reach up to 10 per cent of all stored grain, i.e. 13 million tons of grain lost due to insects or 100 million tons to failure to store properly.

Dr. R.C. Saxena has recently reviewed the potential of neem against pest of stored products grain legumes, maize, sorghum, wheat rice and paddy, potato tubers. At farm level storage and warehouses, the application of neem derivatives to bags and stored grains has provided protection against insect pests. Powdered neem seed kernel mixed with paddy (1 to 2%) significantly reduced infestation and damage to damage to grain during a three month storage period; the effectiveness capacity jute bag (100 x 60 cm) controlled 80% of the population of major insects and checked the damage to wheat up to six months. The treatment with untreated control. The neem seed extract treatment was as effective as that of 0.0005% primiphos methyl mixed with the grain. Using this technology in Sind (Pakistan) high benefit-cost ratios were obtained by small, medium, and large-scale farmers.

Effectiveness of Neem Oil

The effectiveness of neem oil alone or in combination with fumigation was evaluated against five major species of stored grain pests infesting rice and paddy grains in a warehouse trials conducted in the Philippines. Rice grain treated with 0.05 to 0.1 per cent neem oil or treated with neem oil after fumigation with 'Phostoxin', and stored for eight months had significantly less *Tribolium castaneum* adults than in untreated control.

Both kinds of neem treatments were as effective as the bag treatment with 'Actellic' at 25ug/cm^2 or grain treatment with Actellic at 0.0005 per cent, and suppressed the pest population by 60 per cent. The population build-up also was reduced when either fumigated or non-fumigated rice was stored in bags treated with neem oil at more than 1 mg/cm^2.

Rhizopertha dominica, Sitophilus oryzae, Oryzaephilus surinmensis, and *Corcyra cephalonica* were similarly affected by neem treatments alone or in combination with prior grain fumigation. Fumigation and Phostoxin were effective only for about two months against R. dominica, and for up to six months against other pest species, while neem oil treatments were effective up to eight months. Compared with the pest damage to untreated or fumigated rice, neem oil treatment significantly reduced the damage to rice grain.

At eight months after storage, weevil attacked grains in neem treatments were 50 per cent of those in the fumigated rice and 25 per cent of those in the untreated rice. Neem treatments also reduced the pest populations and damage in paddy.

In studies conducted in Kenya, the growth and development of 1st instars of the maize weevil, *Sitophilus zeamais*, was completely arrested in maize grain treated with neem oil at 0.02 per cent, while the weight loss of treated cobs was less than 1 per cent as compared with a 50 per cent reduction in weight of untreated cobs stored for six months.

While *neem* treatments cannot replace completely chemical pesticides used in stored products preservation, the amounts of pesticides needed could be reduced, thereby decreasing the pesticide load in food grains. With proper timing and innovative methods of application, their use could be integrated in stored products management.

Protecting Skin

Researchers have reviewed the effects of neem on hematophagous insects affecting humans and livestock. Application of a paste made from neem leaves and turmeric in 4:1 proportion to the skin cured 97 per cent of the patients suffering from scabies caused by the mite *Sarcoptes scabei* in 3-15 days.

Monthly sprays of ethanoilic extracts of neem or weekly bathing in azadirachtin-rich aqueous 1:20 'Green Gold' controlled the bush tick, *Ixodes holocylus*, and the cattle tick, *Boophilus microplus* in Australia, but were less effective against the brown dog tick, *Rhipicephalus sanguineus*. In Jamaica, neem kernel extract controlled ticks on cattles and dogs.

Neem products repel and affect the development of mosquitoes. Two percent neem oil mixed in coconut oil, when applied to exposed body parts of human volunteers, provided complete protection for 12 hour from bites of all anophelines. Kerosene lamps containing 0.01-1 per cent *neem* oil, lighted in rooms containing human volunteers, reduced mosquito biting activity as well as catches of mosquitoes resting on walls in the rooms; protection was greater against Anopheles than against Culex.

Effectiveness of mats with neem oil against mosquitoes has also been demonstrated; the vapourizing repelled mosquitoes for 5-7 hour at almost negligible cost. The sandfly, *Phleobotumus argentipes*, also was totally repelled by neem oil, mixed with coconut or mustard oil, throughout the night under field conditions in India.

Application of neem cake at the rate of 500 kg/ha, either alone or mixed with urea, in paddy fields in southern India reduced the number of pupae of Culex tritaeniorhynchus, the vector of Japanese encephalitis, and also resulted in higher grain yield.

Pest Resistance to Neem Materials

A few herbivorous insects, including Homoptera, Coleoptera, and Lepidoptera do survive on neem but, largely, it is free from serious pest problems. Although, Taylor indicated that insects may possibly adapt to limonoid rather quickly, but Vollinger demonstrated that two genetically different starins of *P. xylostella* treated with a neem seed extract showed no sign of resistance in feeding and fecundity tests up to 35 generations. In contrast, deltamethrin-treated lines developed resistance factor of 20 in one line and 35 in the other.

There was no cross resistance between deltamethrin and neem seed extract in the deltamethrin-resistant lines. Also, the esterase and multi-function oxidase enzyme activity did not change during the 35 generations. The diversity of *neem* allelochemicals and their combined behavioural and physiological effects on insect pests seem to confer a built-in resistance prevention mechanism in neem. However, wisdom demands that users should refrain from exclusive and extended application of single bioactive materials, such as azadirachtin.

BIOLOGICALLY-BASED INTEGRATED PEST MANAGEMENT

Biologically-based Integrated Pest Management (B-IPM) integrates, or combines, different management tools to provide better leafy spurge control than any single tool could produce.

The foundation for this B-IPM approach is biological control: Biocontrol agents like the host-specific leafy spurge flea beetle are integrated with other tools—such as multi-species grazing programmes, herbicides, reseeding, tillage, burning and clipping—to produce effective, affordable and ecologically sustainable leafy spurge control. B-IPM offers the flexibility landowners and land managers need to devise different management strategies for different situations.

Control Tools

A variety of tools can be used to manage leafy spurge. All of these tools can produce varying degrees of control; unfortunately, none offers "the perfect" solution.

1. Herbicides are the most commonly used control tool, and are the preferred tool for containing and preventing the spread of infestations.

   Disadvantage: Herbicides are expensive — the cost of treatment can exceed the value of the land and/or the economic return from the land. In addition, herbicides are not target specific and are subject to environmental restrictions.

2. Cultural and mechanical controls such as reseeding, clipping and burning can be used to give desirable grasses and plants a competitive advantage while reducing leafy spurge's dominance.

   Disadvantage: Cultural controls are generally not practical for large scale infestations, and no single tool offers the "perfect" solution.

3. Multi-species grazing can provide leafy spurge control while increasing ranch profitability by diversifying cattle grazing operations with sheep or goats.

   Disadvantage: Most ranchers do not have the equipment needed for sheep, or are not interested in sheep.

4. Biological control is another tool that can be used to manage leafy spurge and offers some advantages when compared to "traditional" management tools:

   (a) Biological control is economically sustainable. Leafy spurge biocontrol agents can usually be obtained or collected for free, and do not require a large investment of money or time to use or maintain. Other tools require a greater investment of resources.

   (b) Biological control is ecologically sustainable. Once established, leafy spurge biocontrol agents are self-sustaining — they'll always be there, working in the background to control leafy spurge.

   (c) In addition, biocontrol agents are not known to cause any adverse ecological consequences.

These factors make biocontrol an attractive alternative for long-term, sustainable leafy spurge management. In addition, biocontrol works well when used with other tools in integrated pest management strategies. It can be used in areas that are environmentally sensitive or difficult to access with sprayers, and as such, can often provide the perfect compliment to other management tools. But best of all, biological control is effective, affordable, sustainable, target specific and easy to use.

Disadvantages of Biological Control

Like other management tools, biological control is not a perfect solution to the leafy spurge problem. The biggest drawback is that biological control is not a "quick fix". In most cases, biocontrol agents will take several years to successfully establish a population and begin making a significant contribution to leafy spurge management.

In addition, no one biocontrol agent works in every situation. An agent that works well in one soil type, for example, may not work at all in another soil type. In the long run, more than one type of biocontrol agent may have to be used to achieve uniform control across a variety of different situations and land types.

TRADITIONAL AGRICULTURE AND IPM

In many countries of Africa, traditional methods are mostly seen as backward and outmoded. An extension worker in Africa, who has to inform a visitor about his impact, will show "model" farmers using fertilizers and pesticides, planting new varieties in rows, etc. However, if the visitor visits the extension worker's own field (or those of his family) he will conclude that the extension worker's family probably doesn't belong to the category of modern farmers. They mostly work the same way as their ancestors, and the extension worker cultivates his own fields completely differently from what he is telling his farmers.

In most of Africa, traditional methods of agriculture and plant protection are still dominant. In this study, We will try to answer the question if there are elements of these traditional systems which can be used in new integrated pest management systems. Most examples come from West Africa and especially Togo.

Traditional Follow Systems

It should be clear that in traditional fallow systems, plant protection methods were first of all preventive methods. Element of such preventive methods (besides of course the fallowing) were: choice of varieties, choice of field, mixed cropping, crop rotation, selection of seed and planting methods and storage. Examples will be given of each.

Choice of Field

A farmer in the Plateaux de Dayes, a highland, cocoa-growing area in Southeast Togo, gave a clear example of his knowledge about pests and diseases and their relation to his field. When he was asked why he didn't plant any cocoa in the lower parts of his fields or in the valley bottoms, he answered that the fruits of the cocoa trees turned brown in these areas.

What the farmer indicated was black pod disease, caused by Phytophthora palmivora, which is only infective if the leaves of the cocoa plant are wet for prolonged periods.

In the lower areas at the riverside, these conditions prevail more than in the higher located fields. State cocoa farms in Togo don't consider this and therefore need a heavy input of fungicides.

Traditional Varieties

Development agencies in northern Togo and Benin try to develop new semi-dwarf sorghum varieties which have a shorter 80-day vegetation period (most of the traditional sorghum varieties flower only after six months). The introduction of these new varieties caused, however, some problems. The new varieties flowered before the wild grasses and this caused enormous damage by birds. Even a bigger problem was that the new varieties, with their upright and compact panicles, were attacked in the field by storage pests, esp. *Sitophilus zeamais*. In a test of hundred heads of the new sorghum variety Noga White in Adjengre, Central Togo, an average of seven beetles per head was found.

The traditional varieties, however, weren't affected at all. These varieties ripen in the dry Harmattan period, in which the continuous dry and dust Harmattan winds blow. This is very unfavourable for insects. Also the hanging, open panicles are less attractive to birds and beetles. Furthermore, arguments against the new varieties are: (a) the lesser suitability for the preparation of local beer; and (b) the smaller stover production, as in the existing shortage of fuel wood in northern Togo and Benin the sorghum stems are very important in the kitchen. In southern Togo, a similar example with a newly introduced maize variety can be found.

Here the problem of storage pests (esp. *Sitophilus*) intensified since the husks were not long enough to be protective against these pests. Although, these examples should not give the impression that the introduction of new varieties can never improve the traditional systems, they show that it is necessary to adapt these varieties to the farmers' criteria.

One of these criteria is a reasonable resistance not only to field pests and diseases, but to storage pests. Too often, however, new varieties are developed elsewhere (e.g. in Mexico for maize) and are too quickly adopted and stimulated by government and extension.

Mixed Cropping

Mixed cropping can have a lot of advantages. In many cases the lessened problems with pests and diseases are mentioned. Unfortunately, such a general statement is not strictly true as also negative effects can be found.

Mixed cropping should, therefore, not be seen as the solution to plant protection problems. Still, some positive experiences can be found e.g. with maize-bean inter-cropping. Maize suffers less from stem borers and beans are less affected by thrips. In each specific situation possibilities for mixed cropping should be considered.

Method of Crop Rotation

Crop rotation is a well-known method of preventive plant protection. In northern Togo, however, farmers are used to planting mixtures of six-months millet, four-months millet and beans for several consecutive years. Still, this continuous planting of the same crops doesn't cause great damage by pests and diseases. Probably, this can be explained by the previous selection of seeds. However, it has also become obvious that this type of mixed cropping gives a dangerous weed, *Striga* spp. a chance.

Experiences in several West African countries show that the Striga infestation is more or less tolerable if a real rotation with single crops is used. A rotation of millet or sorghum in the first year should then be followed by a single cropped legume (groundnuts, bambara nuts, beans) in the second year.

Selection of Seed and Planting Methods

Farmers select the seed for the next year with precision. Besides yield characteristics, the seed of e.g. maize is selected on the basis of cob weight, length of the husks, and the absence of pests and diseases. Also, the storage of seeds is important: onions, dried tomatoes, okra, maize and beans for the next year are kept above the fireplace inside the house.

In the drier regions, the bambara nuts and the beans are shelled and mixed with ash. In addition, the planting of the seeds is important. Some farmers soak the maize seeds in water. By this slight pre-germination, the plants grow faster and develop an advantageous young growth which gives them generally a head start over other plants.

Not seldom the wet maize seeds are mixed with ash. According to the farmers, the dark colour prohibits the seed from being found by fowl and birds. Another method, less used, is to soak maize seeds in water mixed with e.g. neem tree leaves.

The germinating seeds absorb sane of the bitterness of this extract. This also makes the seed unattractive for termites, birds and fowl. Furthermore, the time of planting is important. In Togo's Plateau des Dayes, farmers don't plant maize after the end of April. Experience has told than that maize planted after this date suffers badly from stem borers.

Cement turns out to be hygroscopic and doesn't isolate very well, causing an increase in storage pests and diseases. Farmers use e.g. neem leaves to mix with their stored products. In northern Togo beans are mixed with fine sand (1:2 in volume). The farmers pound it lightly so that the beans are completely surrounded by sand. This results in a situation where beetles cannot move enough to copulate, and the sand damages their shields, which causes them to dry out.

Discussion

The above mentioned examples are all used by farmers. They are definitely very elaborate, not easy to improve, and should certainly be taken into consideration in "modern" integrated pest management. Most of the methods are preventive, but also some curative methods are known: for example:

(a) the spreading of harvested products in the sun, causing adult beetles to leave for more shadow and killing the non-adult beetles; and

(b) the digging of ditches with sharp vertical walls to trap grasshoppers.

Still, the traditional methods should not be overestimated. In some cases, the farmers are not aware of certain diseases and pests. One example is that farmers don't destroy cocoa pods infected by *Phytophthora palmivora.* They are not aware that these affected pods are a potential disease source for the following new pests such as the green spider mite and the mealy bug in cassava, *Prostephanus truncatus* in maize, and others. Also, farmers are confronted with decreasing fallow periods, causing extra problems with soil fertility and plant protection.

Therefore, the need for improvement is certainly present. In many countries, however, the improvement is sought in fertilizers, new varieties and pesticides. We should take care that the above, mostly preventive, methods are also included in "modern" IPM-systems. There are still many difficulties.

Why should an organised farmer then try to decrease his pesticide usage? In Togo, all efforts of the National Plant Protection Service and a GTZ-project to install a warning system for cotton pests were frustrated by these political decisions.

CHAPTER – 2

Integrated Mite Management

Mites are members of the order Acarina, which also includes ticks. Hundreds of species of mites occur in the United States. This module describes life histories and integrated pest management strategies for seven species that have been found to be of greatest concern in the National Park System. Six of the mite species in this package are in the family Tetranychidae which includes the mites commonly known as spider mites, while the seventh, the eriophyid mites, are in the family Eriophyidae.

All are extremely small, requiring a hand lens to determine their presence and numbers. Mites do not have a true head, wings, or abdomen. There are four pairs of legs and a pair of leg-like palps associated with the mouthparts. Mouthparts consist of a pair of needle-like stylets (chelicerae) used to pierce cell walls, allowing the mouth to suck up cell contents. This is important because the type of mouthpart creates the stippled appearance associated with Tetranychid mite injury.

The injury caused by Eriophyid mites is much more variable, and includes yellowed foliage, distorted foliage, or a variety of leaf and petiole galls. Mite-feeding injury is often confused with injury caused by insects or air pollution.

LIFECYCLE OF TETRANYCHID MITES

The lifecycle of tetranychid mites includes the following stages: egg, larvae, nymph (up to several nymphal instars), and adults. In some species, males are unknown and reproduction is believed to be parthenogenic. This means that females give rise to offspring without mating, enabling rapid reproduction and population increases. Because of the large number of generations in a single season, high infestations of mites can develop rapidly.

In general, mites deposit two to twenty eggs in a single day, the exact number determined by environmental factors and the species or strain involved. Silk production by mites varies from species to species, with some producing copious amounts of silk, others little or none.

Habitats for the mite species in this module consist mainly of the foliage of suitable host plants. Larvae and nymphs tend to feed on the underside of leaves, while adults and older nymphs feed on both undersides and tops of leaves as well as occasionally on buds and shoots.

Mites feed by rupturing leaf cells with a pair of needle-like stylets (chelicerae) and inserting the mouth parts to draw up the cell contents while the chelicerae are pushed deeper. Feeding causes small chlorotic spots to appear, which eventually coalesce. Stippling occurs and large portions of the leaf or the entire leaf becomes yellowed, bronzed, or whitened in appearance. Leaf injury on evergreens may last for several seasons; injury on other plants may cause premature leaf drop or may result in the death of the host plant.

Boxwood mite (*Eurytetranychus buxi* [Garman]). Adults are 1/32" long, yellow green to reddish brown. Eggs are yellow, rounded, with flattened ends. This species produces silk and is found throughout the United States on boxwood, specifically varieties of American and European boxwood (*Buxus sempervirens*). Japanese boxwood (*B. microphylla*) is rarely infested. The boxwood mite eggs overwinter on the undersides of leaves and hatch in mid-April.

Early nymphs feed on undersides of leaves, second instar mites feed on both sides of the leaf, and third instars move from leaf to leaf to feed. Adults feed on shoots and upper surfaces of leaves. Populations are highest from early spring to early summer, with a second peak in the fall.

Clover mite (*Bryobia praetiosa* [Koch]). Adults are brownish red to red, 1/16" in length. Eggs are brick red, the nymphs red. These mites are easily recognized under low magnification by their long front legs, which are over twice as long as the other legs, and by the featherlike plates on the body. This species does not produce silk, so the presence of webbing cannot be used as a sign of this pest. Distributed throughout the United States on suitable host plants, clover mites are also common indoors, frequently entering buildings in large numbers in the fall.

Clover mite eggs overwinter in cracks in concrete foundations, between the exterior and interior walls of buildings, and on the underside of the basal bark of trees. These mites also overwinter as adult females or in other life stages. Clover mites can become active at temperatures slightly above freezing. Eggs hatch in late winter or early spring; one generation is usually complete before mid-summer. Males of this species are unknown;

reproduction is parthenogenetic. Most eggs deposited by this generation aestivate until September, but some hatch in early summer and produce several small successive summer generations.

These mites feed on a wide variety of plants including clover, grasses, dandelion, iris, ivy, mallow, strawberry, peas, tomato, violet, and zinnia. A related species, the brown mite, feeds on tree foliage.

European red mite (*Panonychus ulmi* [Koch]). Adult mites are 1/32" long and velvety red, with four rows of curved hairs on back arising from tan or white humps (tubercles). Eggs and first instar nymphs are bright red; each egg has a single central stalk or hair. Second and third instar nymphs are dull green or brown. This species produces silk and thus webbing is seen at high population levels.

European red mites occur throughout the United States on suitable host plants. They feed on apples and other fruits, nuts, and their ornamental varieties. They may occasionally be found on elm, rose, mountain ash, and a variety of other ornamental plants. European red mite overwinter as eggs and hatch in early spring as new growth begins. Feeding activity and plant injury occur throughout spring into early summer.

Southern red mite (*Oligonychus illcis* [McGregor]). Adult females are 1/32" in length, blackish red, with backward curving spines. Adult males, nymphs, and eggs are light red. This species produces silk. They are common in the southeastern United States, New England, Ohio, and the Great Lakes states but are particularly damaging in the deep south. Southern red mite feed on broad-leaved evergreens, especially Japanese holly,Pyracantha, azalea, and Camellia, as well as other hollies, laurel, and Rhododendron. They overwinter as eggs on the foliage and twigs of their hosts.

A cool weather pest, Southern red mite develop damaging populations in early spring and late fall. These mites thought to aestivate in the egg stage during summer, with small populations becoming active during cool periods.

Spruce mite (*Oligonychus ununguis* [Jacobi]). Adults are 1/32" in length with spines on the back, dark green or reddish green to nearly black with tan legs. Eggs are reddish tan and nymphs greenish with tan legs. Spruce mites produce copious webbing between needles of host plants. They are widely distributed and may be found wherever suitable hosts occur. They attack only conifers; primarily hemlock, spruce, arborvitae, Chamaecyparis and juniper. Fir and pine are attacked to a lesser extent. This mite overwinters as eggs on the foliage and twigs of host plants.

They are most active in cool weather, so tend to increase in numbers and injury levels in early spring to early summer, and again in the fall, while they may go into aestivation to avoid hot, dry weather. Adults may be active in summer during cooler periods.

Twospotted mite (*Tetranychus urticae* ([Koch]). The common "spider mite." Adults are large (1/8"), and yellowish with two or more predominant dark spots on the back, which is sparsely covered with spines. These spots, which become more apparent as each instar matures, are caused by accumulated food material in the digestive tract. The eggs and nymphs are lemon yellow. They are found throughout the United States, especially indoors and in greenhouses.

There are over 250 known host plants including flowers, foliage plants, corn and other field crops, vegetables, brambles, and other herbaceous plants. They can be a serious pest of roses, flowering fruits, and shrubs, and are frequently brought outdoors on plants which were propagated or overwintered in the greenhouse. They overwinter as eggs on host plants and cause damage to host plants throughout the growing season. The warmer the temperature, the greater the rate of feeding and reproduction. The two-spotted mite becomes especially destructive during periods of hot, dry weather, but also feeds and reproduces during cooler periods.

The two-spotted mite can acquire several plant-infecting viruses during feeding on infected hosts, but has not been shown to transmit them to new host plants. Mites that enter houses can create a nuisance to home-owners and can cause stains if they are crushed.

Timing of Management Practices

Mite population cycles can be unpredictable, so timing of management practices must be based on observations of the pest. Timing of monitoring for mites is directly related to mite biology. For example, spruce mites may be active anytime temperatures are over 50° F, but once prolonged, hot, dry weather occurs in summer they enter a type of dormancy known as aestivation and generally do not become active again until fall. Aestivation occurs at about the end of June in the mid-Atlantic region, when daytime temperatures are consistently above 80° F.

Spruce mite aestivation corresponds to the time when the activity level and generation times of other mite species, such as the twospotted mite, the European red mite, and the southern red mite, are increasing. Consult the information presented for each species as well as the references for more detail on the population cycles of each mite species.

Mites are very small, so they must be knocked off the plants they are feeding on to be counted. This is done by holding a piece of white paper or a clipboard painted white under the plant and striking the branches with a rubber hose or ruler. Generally the plant is struck three to five times before the mites are counted. The number of times that this is done is not as important as doing it the same number every time.

Ten to fifteen seconds must pass before examining the clipboard for mites, since it takes this long for them to begin moving after being knocked off their host. Moving dots about the size of a period on this page should be examined with a hand lens to determine that they are indeed mites and to identify the species if possible. Population levels can be measured in a variety of ways, including a simple presence/absence, ranges (e.g., 1-10, 11-20, etc.), or actual population counts. In most cases, estimation of a population range will suffice. Eggs tend to remain attached to the plant, so individual branches must be examined to look for these. Again, estimating relative numbers is more important than an absolute count. The number of eggs relative to the number of adults will indicate if the population is increasing or decreasing.

Mite populations on plants that have cupped leaves, such as Japanese holly, also need to be determined by examination of the individual plant, since mites tend to remain in the cupped leaves when the plant is tapped.

Monitoring for Mites

It is a time-consuming process. If you are willing to tolerate some mite injury, the time required for monitoring can be reduced by focusing monitoring efforts on plants in hot, dry areas, plants which have been under heavy nitrogen fertilization, or plants which have had the most serious problems in the past. If low mite populations are seen on these plants, then monitoring of less susceptible plants can be skipped at that time. This is not recommended if the aesthetic threshold of the plants being monitored is very low (i.e. no injury can be tolerated).

Leaf discolouration and stippling caused by mite feeding can easily be confused with several other insect and disease injury symptoms. It is important not to assume that just because stippling is seen, mites are the cause. Mites, eggs, or shed skins on leaf undersides will facilitate a diagnosis. Stippling with tar-like frass on leaf undersides indicates lace bug; lack of frass or mite signs is a clue that the injury is from air pollution.

Mite Management Tactics

Once mite activity is detected, a decision must be made as to whether implementation of additional mite management tactics are warranted, and if so, which is most appropriate. While a few action levels for mites have been published, it is unclear how these apply in a generalized way. There is considerable evidence to show that host plant nutrient status and drought stress contribute to host plant suitability as a food source for mites. This means that action thresholds determined under one set of conditions may not be applicable in another system. Published thresholds should be used as a guide, but to modified as the need arises.

The resource manager must keep accurate records of mite population levels, plant injury symptoms, soil fertility, and rainfall at the individual park. Relate these to timing and type of management strategies used in the past to determine what works best at a particular site or on a certain plant species.

GOOD MITE MANAGEMENT

Good mite management combines regular monitoring to detect pest occurrence and timely implementation of the most appropriate management tactics. Monitoring is an essential part of a mite integrated pest management programme because injury cannot be seen until after feeding takes place and because mites may be active any time microhabitat temperatures rise above 50° F. This means that even though the ambient air temperatures are below 50° F, mites could be active on certain plants, such as those in sunny locations next to a building.

Cultural Control

As was mentioned earlier, there is a considerable amount of evidence to indicate that mite populations are higher on plants that have been under high nitrogen fertilization regimes. Thus, plants that have mites should not be heavily fertilized.

Physical Control

A strong, steady stream of water from a hose will wash mites from the surface of some plant leaves. Prolonged (several hours) periods of heavy rain have the same effect. This is only a temporary measure, most suited to an area where no pesticides can be applied. Adult mites will generally return to the plant within one day.

Biological Control Agents for Mites

A vast number of predators and pathogens have been examined for their potential to serve as biological control agents for mites. Some are currently being successfully used, others show potential, while the feasibility of others seems unlikely.

Mites in the family *Phytoseiidae* are important predators of plant-feeding mites and have been used in biological programmes for several pest species, particularly in greenhouses. Spiders, beetles, flies, thrips, true bugs, and lacewings have all been observed feeding on mites.

Species in the lady beetle genus Stethorus are voracious predators of mites and often eliminate infestations of European red mite and spruce mite. However, the control often occurs after the mite populations have peaked. Tetranychid mites are also susceptible to fungal and virus infections, but no pathogenic bacteria have been reported as occurring in mites. There are no known insect parasitoids of mites.

Predaceous mites have been used in greenhouses to control twospotted and other mite pests with good results. Predatory mites are available from commercial suppliers. Some commonly used predatory mites include the following:

Phytoseiulus persimilis is a predatory mite used primarily in Europe to control mite pests of greenhouse-grown tomatoes, cucumbers, and sweet peppers. It must be released periodically at carefully timed intervals for optimal control. It is used infrequently on greenhouse-grown ornamentals due to lower damage tolerance levels and lack of resistance to pesticides.

Insecticidal soap is toxic to the adult predatory mite at rates needed to obtain satisfactory phytophagous mite control. Insecticidal soap can be applied three days after predator release without significantly reducing control, apparently because it does not cause significant egg mortality.

A recent study of the effect of abamectin (a pesticide derived from a bacterial toxin) on this mite and the pest mite, *Tetranychus urticae*, demonstrated that abamectin will reduce the population of both, with a greater reduction in the population of the pest mite species than in the predatory mite. Thus, it could be used in an integrated pest management programme to reduce the predator/prey ratio and increase the effectiveness of Phytoseiulus persimilis as a predator.

Phytoseiulus macropilis, a related predatory mite, was found by Hamlen and Poole (1982) to give acceptable control on twospotted mite on greenhouse-grown Diffenbachia when applied at a ratio of 1:10 or lower and reintroduced every eight weeks. As with P. persimilis, predators must be introduced into low-density spider mite populations.

Mataseiulus (*Typholdromus*) occidentalis is a predatory mite that has been developed into several strains, one of which is resistant to most organophosphate insecticides and to carbaryl. Another strain does not go into dormancy under low light or short photoperiod conditions.

These strains are preferred in that they can prey upon twospotted-mites throughout the year in greenhouses. M. occidentalis is preferred for mite control for ornamentals and long-term crops such as roses grown for cut flowers because it gives long-term control from a single release. This predator is unlikely to bring about full control without leaf damage caused by the pest mite; therefore, application of selective acaricides are useful in an integrated programme. Researchers suggest that although this species does not give as good control of twospotted mite as does *P. persimilis*, it would be a better choice as a biological control agent in long-term crops on which pesticides will be used. They suggest that *P. persimilis* would be a better predator for twospotted mite on short-term crops that are grown with minimal pesticide inputs.

Chemical Control of Tetranychid Mites

Advances in the development of horticultural oils have made this the first pesticide to consider in the management of mites. New oil formulations do not have the problems of phytotoxicity that were so common among older formulations. Their effective control of mite populations with minimal impact on beneficials make them well-suited to an integrated pest management programme.

A drawback to the use of oils is the necessity of contacting the pest to be killed. Thus oils tend to give unsatisfactory control in dense plantings, on leaves that are cupped (e.g., *Ilex crenata* 'Convexa'), or on plants that are in hard-to-reach areas. In these instances, pesticides with some residual activity could be used. Consult your regional Integrated Pest Management coordinator concerning the best choice of pesticide for your situation.

Monitoring and Thresholds for Eriophyid Mites

Eriophyid mites are often overlooked because they are so difficult to see and because the injury they cause (especially necrosis and dieback) can be attributed to many other causes.

Thus, the first part of developing a management strategy for eriophyid mites is the education of plant monitors about this mite's biology and preferred hosts and the injury it causes.

Monitors should realize that they will most likely not see eriophyid mites without a microscope, and that they may need to submit a sample to the Cooperative Extension Service for identification.

It is difficult to outline a monitoring programme for these mites because the life cycles vary so much depending on the species. In general, monitors should be aware of the types of injury caused by eriophyid mites, and that the mites will be difficult to observe. In conifers, this is complicated by the fact that these mites often feed below the needle sheaths.

Identification and Biology of Eriophyid Mites

Eriophyid mites are a diverse family of arthropods, containing many species with a wide range of plant hosts and biologies. They can be divided into three categories based on the type of plant injury they cause: galls, twisted, distorted foliage and chlorotic, stunted growth. The gall makers are rarely detrimental to plant health, but are a concern among the public because they are so obvious.

In general, the mites that cause these galls overwinter as adults and begin feeding on expanding leaves in the spring. This induces formation of a gall which surrounds the mite as it feeds. Eggs are laid within the gall; nymphs mature within the gall and the emerging adults infest new foliage.

The eriophyid mites that injure foliage have varied life cycles. They are a more serious concern than the gall-makers because they can cause distortion and dieback of plant tissue.

Control of Eriophyid Mites

In the case of the gall-making eriophyid mites, no intervention is warranted. Three cases where intervention often is appropriate is on hemlock, privet, and white pine, where these mites can cause considerable injury. In these cases, an insecticide such as acephate is usually recommended, since they seem to give better control than oil or other miticides.

There have been many observations of predatory mites occurring in conjunction with eriophyids, but their role in population regulation is unknown.

A wide variety of insect and mite pests have been found in association with poinsettia production both in shade houses and in the greenhouse. These pests can feed on many parts of the poinsettia plant or be associated with the production areas. Pests of poinsettia, as well as natural enemies of these species, should be monitored using appropriate methods.

Direct observations of the undersides of a large sample of randomly selected leaves made on a regular weekly or semi-weekly schedule is the best method of early detection. Shaking or beating plant parts over an off-white cardboard sheet dislodges pests and can make small arthropods such as spider mites and thrips easier to detect. Yellow sticky traps (1 trap per 1,000 sq. ft. placed no closer that 150 ft. in the greenhouse) are useful for monitoring adult whiteflies, thrips, aphids, leafminers and fungus gnats. Pheromone traps and black light traps are also useful for monitoring populations of certain pests, particularly adult moths.

Natural enemies of insect/mite pests include insect pathogens like viruses, bacteria, fungi, parasites (those that develop on or inside their hosts) and predators. Every effort should be made to encourage populations of these beneficial organisms. Releases of certain natural enemies have proven to be effective in certain instances when other pests, such as aphids, requiring additional insecticide applications are not present.

Products containing Bacillus thuingiensis (Dipel, Thuricide) have been shown to control certain exposed caterpillar outbreaks. Use of broad spectrum insecticides/ miticides eliminates these natural controls. If insecticide/ miticide treatments are required, use of target-specific products that preserve populations of natural enemies is encouraged.

Preventive Treatment Programmes

Preventive treatment programmes for pests such as spider mites and whiteflies are often conducted using soil-applied systemic insecticides such as Oxamyl 10G (oxamyl) or Temik 10G (aldicarb, removed from the market), and/or foliar sprays. However, even after preventative treatments are rountinely applied, plants should be monitored for secondary pest outbreaks and pest resurgence. Management tactics work best when implemented when infestations are detected early.

When pesticides are used, select the materials least toxic to the user and to natural enemies of pests, if possible. Materials should be applied in strict accordance to instructions provided on the product's label.

Wear required protective clothing and heed all safety precautions and required reentry intervals specified on the label. Considerations for possible phytotoxic reactions (the ability for the pesticide to harm the plant) are very important in poinsettia production, particularly after the bracts show color. If the potential of phytotoxic reaction is not known, apply the material to a few plants and observe the plants for a few days before spraying the entire crops presents common symptoms.

Foliar applied insecticides/miticides can frequently be mixed with other pesticides (fungicides) and adjuvants (spreaders, stickers, buffers, etc.). When mixing materials together for the first time, do so in a clear container and observe any precipitation, settling or other reactions. Provided these materials go into solution, the mixtures may be phytotoxic or less active as a tank mixture. Again, a few plants should be sprayed and observed. Use of adjuvants is suggested only when warranted.

Managing Sweetpotato Whitefly

Bemesia tabaci (Gennadius), is a relatively new pest of greenhouse grown poinsettias in Texas. Although this species has occurred outdoors on other crops for some time, insecticide resistant/tolerant strains appeared in 1986 in Florida. In 1987, the first report of this stain was reported from greenhouses in Texas. Since then, it has spread to all greenhouse ornamental production areas of the state. This strain is difficult to control with "standard" materials used to control other species such as the greenhouse whitefly.

The sweetpotato whitefly can be identified by characteristics of the adult and the 'pupal' skin. The adult whitefly holds its wings 'roof-like' over its back, as compared to the greenhouse whitefly which holds its wings in one plane. The pupal skin, found on the undersides of older leaves is tear-drop shaped and is oval in cross section. On the small end of the tear drop are two prominent stiff hairs or setae. In contrast, the greenhouse whitefly pupal skin is oval, square in cross section and may or may not be spiny.

Management of the sweetpotato whitefly begins with good sanitation and cultural practices. Try to provide an interval in the greenhouse that is host free by removing and/or treating alternate hosts (they are known to attack over fifty plant species, including weeds!). Purchase cuttings or plants that are pest free and inspect plants carefully as they enter the production facility. Workers working in infested areas should avoid wearing yellow, which is attractive to the whiteflies, and thereby prevent movement into uninfested greenhouses.

Chemical control of the sweetpotato whitefly is difficult and may cause an explosion of the population after treatments are discontinued. Products that seem to be effective in one production area (presumably representing a select strain of sweetpotato whitefly) may not be effective in another area presumably representing another strain.

For poinsettias under more than minimal pressure, apply pesticides twice weekly for adult control and twice weekly for nymphal control through a period of one whitefly generation (about three weeks). Subsequent weekly applications of pesticides detrimental to adults and nymphs may be sufficient to maintain control.

Resistance management is the practice of utilizing selected control tactics, such as insecticide use, in such a manner to prolong the effectiveness of available materials. Use of one ingredient over many generations leads to the development of resistant/tolerant pest strains. Using tank mixtures over successive generations could lead to the development of "multiple resistance", pests that are resistant to a wide range of ingredients.

Growers are encouraged to rotate between classes of nerve active pesticides used, as much as practical between whitefly generations. Using the least toxic, most target specific material earlier in the production cycle amy delay the need for nerve active insecticides.

Application Methods

It should be scrutinized if control failures are detected. Use of any one method (smoke bombs, foggers, low or high volume sprays, soil-applied systemic) may prove to be inadequate to achieve thorough coverage of infested areas. Whole-house treatments, using several techniques may prove to be superior. Plants should be spaced to permit effective use of the proper pesticide application equipment. Under-the-leaf coverage is essential for successful sweetpotato whitefly control.

Mite Management in Coconut

Infested nuts turn brownish in colour with a characteristic pale triangular patch. Coconut mites (*Aceria guerreronis*) are microscopic and wind-borne. They infest the surface of tender nuts in typical patches, feeding on the whitish meristematic tissues covered by perianth bracts.

The third-fifth bunch nuts (post-fertilization) show peak populations that fluctuate unpredictably. The infested area turns brownish with a characteristic pale triangular patch progressing downwards externally. As the damaged nuts age, the discoloured tissues on the nut surface get tarnished at varying grades. The nut is smaller in size and inferior in quality. The external husk becomes very difficult to remove.

Immature Nuts

Immature nuts may also fall and the yield is 40 per cent less than normal. If the infested nuts are used as seeds, they are very slow to germinate with 10-25 per cent mortality in the nursery bed. The powdery white mites lay numerous eggs on the nut surface as well as on the inner side of the interior three bracts, which cover the nut surface.

The young ones and adults are minute, worm-like with only two pairs of legs anteriorly. The lifecycle is completed in a very short period. A three-year research on the ecology and management of the pest indicated that the following measures effectively combat the menace.

The coconut gardens with rich ground vegetation suffer much less damage than those gardens with only coconut palms devoid of cover crops. Spherical nuts with smaller perianth (less than 2 cm in radius) are much less susceptible to mite injury.

Those nuts with deeply clefted perianth are more susceptible to the mite than the nuts with less prominent perianth clefts as evident in Dwarf varieties that are comparatively much less than tall and hybrids, which possess bigger and deeply clefted perianth.

Insect/Mite Management in Annona

Within the Annonaceae, sugar apple and atemoya fruit have the greatest potential for utilization in Florida. The major constraints to high productivity of these include key pests and the lack of pollinating agents.

Pollinators and Pollination

The majority of Annonaceae are pollinated by beetles, although some are pollinated by thrips. The activities of beetles in the flowers, including feeding, mating, and quiescence, result in prolonged visits from several hours to a few days while the flowers advance from the female to the male phase.

In Florida, flowering of atemoyas begins in April, and sugar apples in May, and continues until early August. Atemoyas and sugar apples are most often pollinated by nitidulid beetles, which breed and feed in decaying fruits or sap flows. The beetles are attracted to the fruity, fermenting odor of Annona flowers, especially when they are hungry.

The number of beetles per flower affects the likelihood of fruit set, and also the quality of the fruit in some cases. All studies provide evidence for increased fruit set as numbers of visiting beetles increase.

In Florida, about nine species of native and exotic nitidulids (sap beetles) visit the flowers, but Carpophilus mutilatus is the most important pollinator in terms of efficacy and abundance in flowers, followed by *C. fumatus* and *Haptoncus uteolus*.

Pollinator Management

Trials to increase fruit set in atemoya orchards by augmenting sap beetle populations have yielded mixed results. Pollination by sap beetles can be improved by using chemical lures. The effect of nitidulid-pheromone bait stations on sugar apple and atemoya fruit set has been determined in south Florida.

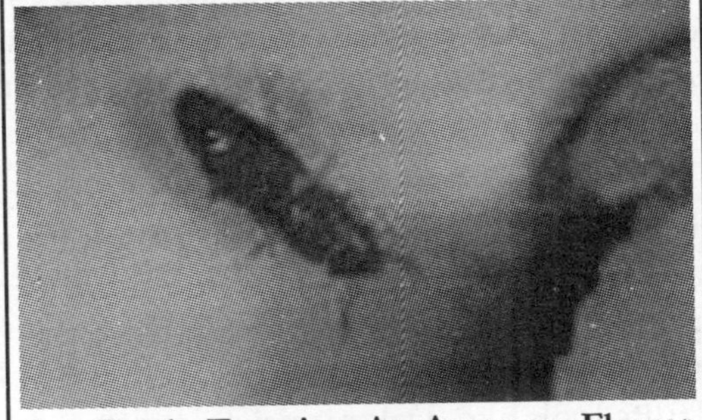

Sap Bettle Entering An Atemoya Flower

Maximum per cent fruit set fluctuates between 10-38 per cent during the first four weeks after treatment in plots with bait stations, and is significantly higher than in the control plots (5%).

Comman Species

Two hundred and ninety-six species of arthropods are associated with Annona spp. in the Neotropics.

The families most frequently observed are Coccidae (Homoptera), Noctuidae, Oecophoridae (Lepidoptera), and Eurytomidae (Hymenoptera). The most common species in Florida are *Bephratelloides cubensis*, (Hymenoptera: Eurytomidae), *Cocytius antaeus* (Lepidoptera: Sphingidae), and the papaya scale *Philephedra tiuberculosa*. Larvae of the moths, Gonodonta nutrix and *G. unica* feed on leaves, but they are heavily parasitized by braconid wasps.

The Annona Sead Borer, Bephratelloides Species

Bephratelloides spp. develop strictly in Annona seeds. Economic damage occurs when the adults chew their way out of the fruit, creating a 2 mm diam tunnel that provides entry for other insects and decay organisms. Bephratelloides cubensis is thelytokous, reproducing without males. It has approximately 4-5 generations per year. The egg stage lasts 12 to 14 days, the larval stage 6-8 weeks, the pupal stage 12-18 days, and the adult rarely lives beyond 15 days.

Adult of the Annona Seed Borer

Bephratelloides cubensis prefers to oviposit in fruits ranging from 1.5-5.5 cm in diameter, which corresponds to fruit ages from 3-7 weeks after bloom. Although fruits larger than 5.5 cm are probed, when *B. cubensis* populations are high, most of these attacks do not result in infestation.

Preferred fruit sizes presumably correspond with seeds that have not yet hardened and are easy to penetrate with the ovipositor, while the seeds of older fruits are probably too hard to penetrate. Larger fruits may be less preferred because the distance from the fruit surface to the seed may exceed the length of the ovipositor. The probes in young sugar apple and atemoya fruits look like dark pinpricks surrounded by a round whitish patch, and are visible for about two weeks; in older fruits the whitish patch does not appear, and the probe marks are permanent and often ooze sap.

Oviposition activity by *B. cubensis* begins at about 9:00 h and continues throughout the daylight hours with peaks in activity around 12:00-13:00 hour. The wasps spend the night on the underside of leaves on their host trees, and move to the upper surface at sunrise. Flying individuals can be observed soon afterwards and throughout the day.

Monitoring and Sampling

In Florida, *A. reticulata* sets fruit in September - November, and fruits remain on the trees as late as May. Atemoyas set fruit from April - August, and sugar apples from May- August. *Bephratelloides cubensis* populations in Florida overwinter mainly in A. reticulata and then move to atemoyas that begin to set fruit during April.

After a developmental time of nine weeks the adults emerge from the early atemoyas and infest younger atemoya and also sugar apple fruits. Second and third peaks of adult emergence and infestation occur in atemoya and sugar apples until young fruits are no longer available and the wasps switch to *A. reticulata* fruits in September. Wasp populations increase throughout the warm months because of the availability of large concentrations of atemoya trees, and are bottlenecked in winter because *A. reticulata* is grown only sporadically as a dooryard tree in Florida.

Low infestations in sugar apples may be due to low movement from atemoya to sugar apple orchards when plentiful fruits are available. No evidence of diapause has been found in mumified stemoya and sugar apple fruits that overwinter on trees or on the ground.

Control Tactics

Fenvalerate or permethrin provide significant adult mortality of the seed borer; however, sprays do not prevent fruit infestation. Fruit bagging is considered one of the best methods to prevent infestation by *B. cubensis* by several researchers. However, bagging encourages the growth of mealybugs on some fruits, probably because natural enemies are excluded. Although, the method is effective, a cost comparison must be made between bagging and other potential control methods to determine its economic feasibility.

Biological Control

No significant native parasitization or predation of *Bephratelloides spp.* has been reported. In Florida, the fungus *Beauveria bassiana* was applied to *B. cubensis* adults under laboratory conditions has provided 90 per cent adult mortality for eight days after treatment.

CHAPTER – 3

Acari and Acarology

Acari are also known as Acarina a taxon of arachnids that contains mites and ticks. The diversity of the Acari is extraordinary and its fossil history goes back to at least the early Devonian period. As a result, acarologists (the people who study mites and ticks) have proposed a complex set of taxonomic ranks to classify mites. In most modern treatments, the Acari is considered a subclass of Arachnida and is composed of two to three superorders or orders: Acariformes (or Actinotrichida), Parasitiformes (or Anactinotrichida), and Opilioacariformes; the latter is often considered a subgroup within the Parasitiformes. The monophyly of the Acari is open to debate, and the relationships of the acarines to other arachnids is not at all clea. In older treatments, the subgroups of the Acarina were placed at order rank, but as their own subdivisions have become better-understood, it is more usual to treat them at superorder rank.

What is Acarology?

Most acarines are minute to small (e.g. 0.08-1.00 millimetre or 0.0031–0.039 inch), but the largest Acari (some ticks and red velvet mites) may reach lengths of 10-20 millimetres (0.39-0.79 in). It is estimated that over 50,000 species have been described (as of 1999) and that a million or more species are currently living. The study of mites and ticks is called acarology and the leading scientific journals for acarology include Acarologia, Experimental and Applied Acarology and the *International Journal of Acarology.*

Diversity and Lifestyles

Acarines are extremely diverse. They live in practically every habitat, and include aquatic (freshwater and sea water) and terrestrial species. They outnumber other arthropods in the soil organic matter anddetritus. Many are parasitic, and they affect both vertebrates and invertebrates.

Most parasitic forms are external parasites, while the free living forms are generally predatory and may even be used to control undesirable arthropods. Others are detritivores that help to break down forest litter and dead organic matter such as skin cells. Others still are plant feeders and may damage crops.

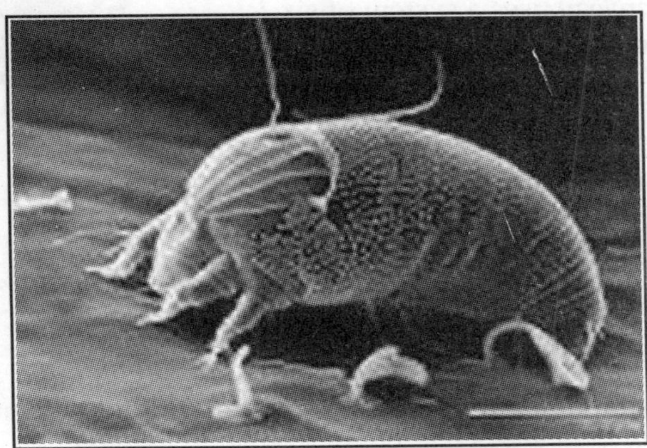

Rust Mite, Aceria Anthocoptes (Size: 50 Micrometres)

Economic Importance

Damage to crops is perhaps the most costly economic effect of mites, especially by the spider mitesand their relatives (*Tetranychoidea*), earth mites (*Penthaleidae*), thread-footed mites (*Tarsonemidae*) and the gall and rust mites (*Eriophyidae*).

Some parasitic forms affect humans and other mammals, causing damage by their feeding, and can even be vectors of diseases such as scrub typhus, rickettsialpox, Lyme disease, Q fever, Colorado tick fever, tularemia, tick-borne relapsing fever, babesiosis, ehrlichiosis and tick-borne meningoencephalitis. A well known effect of mites on humans is their role as an allergen and the stimulation of asthma in people affected by respiratory disease.

The use of predatory mites (e.g. Phytoseiidae) in pest control and herbivorous mites that infest weeds are also of importance. An unquantified, but major positive contribution of the Acari is their normal functioning in ecosystems, especially their roles in the decomposer subsystem.

Chemical agents used to control ticks and mites include dusting sulfur and ivermectin.

Taxonomy

Male Tick (Size: 2 mm)

The phylogeny of the Acari is still disputed and several taxonomic schemes have been proposed for their classification. The third edition of the standard textbook *A Manual of Acarology* uses a system of six orders, grouped into two superorders:

- Superorder Parasitiformes – ticks and a variety of mites.
- Opilioacarida – mites that superficially resemble- harvest-men (Opiliones, hence their name).
- Holothyrida
- Ixodida – hard and soft ticks
- Mesostigmata – bird mites, phytoseiid mites, Raubmilben.
- Sejoidea
- Trigynaspida
- Monogynaspida
- Superorder Acariformes – the most diverse group of mites.
- Trombidiformes – plant parasitic mites (spider mites, peacock mites, gall mites, red-legged earth mites, etc.), snout mites, chiggers, hair follicle mites, velvet mites, water mites, etc.
- Sphaerolichida
- Prostigmata
- Sarcoptiformes
- Endeostigmata – basal sarcoptiform lineages
- Oribatida – oribatid mites, beetle mites, armored mites (also cryptostigmata)
- Astigmata – stored product, fur, feather, dust and human itch mites, etc.

General Procedure for Submission of Specimen

Acarines (ticks and mites) which are suspected to be causative agents or vectors of humandiseases, may be submitted to the Acarology Unit of IDRC, for identification. Every specimen must be labelled clearly and accompanied by a pathological examination request form.

The form must be completed with the following information: brief case history of patient (for clinical specimens), description or identification of non-host(if any), description of habitat, locality where specimen is collected, date and time of collection, name and address of collector, and date specimen sent to the IMR.

The success of identification depends on the condition of the specimen sent. To ensure success and also to reduce exposure to hazards for the staff performing the identification, all specimens must be prepared carefully following the instructions below before despatching to the IMR.

Generally, all mites and ticks can be sent live or preserved in 70 per cent alcohol. It is preferred that specimens be sent in 70 per cent alcohol. If live specimens are sent, the container must be clearly labelled "Hazardous – Live Specimens". When live ticks, place the ticks inside a sealed container with a piece of damp filter paper inside to increase the humidity and prevent the specimen from dehydrating.

It is not advisable to send mounted mites. Mounting of mites is a precise process and experience is required. If not done properly, it may damage the specimen making identification difficult or impossible. Although, it is possible to remount specimens, some damage may occur too during remounting. The IMR will undertake the mounting of the specimens.

SPECIMEN COLLECTION AND PREPARATION

Acarines Specimens from Humans

Sarcoptes Scabiei (Scabies mite)

The mite can usually be found in the stratum corneum of the following areas: the clefts between the fingers and toes, flexor surface of the wrist, extensor surface of the elbow, theaxilla, penis, scrotum, and under the breast.

Skin scrapping is generally not suitable for the collection of scabies mites. The mites can be damaged by the procedure and the relatively large mass of skin cell debris makes it difficult to find the mites. Besides that, intact mites are required for accurate identification. If skin scrapings are submitted, the specimens must be sent in 70 per cent alcohol. Do not submit the skin scrappings in its original form as it may be hazardous to the person processing the specimen.

The recommended technique to collect scabies mites is first to locate the burrows made by the mites in the skin of the clefts between the fingers and the wrists of patients. Once located, a sharp sterile needle or lancet is used to slowly tease open the burrow until a small white object, which is the scabies mite, is observed. The mites can be picked up using the moistened sharpened end of an application stick and sent in 70 per cent alcohol.

Ticks in the Ear Canal

Ticks have been observed in the ear canal of patients. The ticks may cause facial paralysis unless removed. Ticks attached inside the ear canal can be removed by instilling warm water, mineral oil or 4 per cent lignocaine. The solutions shall induce the ticks to detach; these ticks can then be removed using forceps, placed in 70 per cent alcohol and sent to the IMR.

Other Ectoparasitic Acarines

This will require detailed examination of the whole body of the patient. A hand lens will assist in locating these acarines. Use fine forceps to grip larger mites as near to the skin as possible and pull gently away. Smaller mites should be teased from the skin using a sharp sterile needle or lancet.

Ectoparasitic ticks on humans are also removed by using sharp pointed forceps. Grip the tick on the gnathosome head) as close as possible to the skin of the patient. Pull away gently from the skin. Care must be taken not to separate the head of the tick from the rest of the body. The tick must be intact for accurate identification.

Other Endoparasitic Acarines

These are usually found in dissected or autopsy tissues. The tissues are examined under a dissecting microscope and the mites removed using needles and scissors. Specimens are put in 70 per cent alcohol and send to the IMR. If facilities and experience is not available for the removal of endoparasitic mites, then the tissues may be put in 70 per cent alcohol and send to the IMR.

Acarine Specimens from Animals

Ectoparasitic Acarines

Live animal hosts must be anaesthetised before extraction of ectoparasites. The following process is to be used for small animals such as rodents. Place each small animal in a cloth bag. Put the animal and cloth bag in a glass jar with a cotton wad soaked with chloroform. After five minutes, or longer for larger mammals, the cloth bag containing the animal is taken out off the glass jar.

The animal is next removed from the cloth bag. The cloth bag is turned inside out and shaken over a white enamel tray. The bag and tray is carefully examined for detached ectoparasitic acarines. These acarines can be picked up using the moistened sharpened end of an applicator stick. The acarines are put in 70 per cent alcohol and send to the IMR.

The animal is then placed on a white enamel tray and brushed with a fine-tooth comb. This will dislodge most mites and ticks. Check for these acarines in the enamel tray. The acarinescan be picked up with the moistened sharpened end of an applicator stick. The acarines are put in 70 per cent alcohol and send to the IMR.

Animals should be examined too for acarines which are not dislodged by combing. Where possible, examine the animal under a dissecting microscope. Use a pointed forceps to grip thegnathosome (head) of any tick present, as close as possible to the skin of the host. Pull away gently from the skin.

A sharp needle may be used to tease the skin around the attached ticks to assist in its removal. Care must be taken not to separate the head of the tick from the rest of the body. The tick must be intact for accurate identification. Place the acarines in 70% alcohol and sent to the IMR.

Endoparasitic Acarines

Internal organs and tissue of animals suspected to contain endoparasitic acarines should be removed and placed in 70% alcohol and sent to the IMR.

Specimens from the Environment

Ectoparasitic Acarines on Vegetation

Many unfed ectoparasitic acarines, especially ticks, climb onto surrounding vegetation such as tall grasses, leaves of small plants, shrubs, etc., to wait for a host to pass by. The vegetation and underside of leaves can be examined. Moisten the sharpened end of an applicator stick or a fine brush, to pick up any acarines found. Send the acarines in 70 per cent alcohol to the IMR.

A procedure known as 'flagging' is an effective way to collect acarines especially ticks from vegetation. A white flannel cloth is tied to a stout stick and used to brush/sweep the vegetation. Ectoparasitic acarines detach from the vegetation and attach to the moving cloth. The cloth is examined and any acarines found can be removed using the above stated procedure.

Black formica or plastic rectangular plates (usually 10 × 13 cm) can be placed beneath vegetation or inside ground burrows or holes to collect chiggers. After about 5 minutes, the plates are examined and any acarines found can be removed using the above stated procedure.

Leaf litter, animal nests or soil suspected to harbour acarines can be collected into plastic bags. A few pieces of damp filter paper or tissue paper are put in the bags to keep the contents moist. The bags are heat sealed and sent as soon as possible to the IMR.

Acarines in Houses

Occasionally acarines can be seen inside houses. Moisten the sharpened end of an applicator stick or a fine brush, to pick up any acarines found. Put the acarines in 70 per cent alcohol and send to the IMR.

Rodent and bird nests in houses (usually in the attic or roof) may harbour mites that can bite man. These nests can be collected into plastic bags. A few pieces of damp filter paper or tissue paper are put in the bags to keep the contents moist. The bags are heat sealed and sent as soon as possible to the IMR.

Dust that suspected to contain acarines is collected using a vacuum cleaner. Use a new vacuum bag for each sample. Place each vacuum bag in a plastic bag. Heat seal the plastic bag and send immediately to the IMR. Store the plastic bags in the lower compartment of a refrigerator if the bags could not be send to the IMR on the day the specimen is collected.

Mites (Acari or Acarina) are the most diverse and abundant of all arachnids, but because of their small size (usually less than a millimeter in length) we rarely see them. The ticks are an exception, in that they are usually big enough to see, especially when they are filled with blood. Red velvet mites are also among the giants of the Acari (to 10 mm), and can often be seen hunting on the ground or on tree trunks.

Water mites are rarely more than a few millimeters long, but their bright colours and rapid movement often bring them to our attention. At the smaller end of the mite size range are species like the human follicle mite or the honeybee tracheal mite - small enough to raise a family within a human hair follicle or within a bee's respiratory tube, and too small (ca. 0.1 mm) to see without a microscope.

Mites are also among the oldest of all terrestrial animals, with fossils known from the early Devonian, nearly 400 million years ago. Three major lineages are currently recognised: Opilioacariformes, Acariformesand Parasitiformes. About 45,000 species of mites have been described - a small fraction (perhaps 5%) of the number of species estimated to be alive today.

Mites are truly ubiquitous. They have successfully colonized nearly every known terrestrial, marine, and fresh water habitat including polar and alpine extremes, tropical lowlands and desert barrens, surface and mineral soils to depths of ten meters, cold and thermal surface springs and subterranean waters with temperatures as high as 50° C, all types of streams, ponds and lakes, and sea waters of continental shelves and deep sea trenches to depths of 5000 meters. Some idea of mite abundance and diversity can be gained from analysis of one square meter of mixed temperate hardwood or boreal coniferous litter, which may harbour upwards from one million mites representing 200 species in at least fifty families. Within this complex matrix of decomposing plant matter, mites help to regulate microbial processes directly by feeding on detritus and microbes, and indirectly by predation on other microfauna.

Many mites have complex symbiotic associations with the larger organisms on which they live. Plants, including crops and the canopies of tropical rainforests, are inhabited by myriads of mite species feeding on mosses, ferns, leaves, stems, flowers, fruit, lichens, microbes, other arthropods and each other. Many mites found on agricultural crops are major economic pests (e.g. spider mites) or useful biocontrol agents (e.g. phytoseiid mites) of those pests.

Mammals and birds are hosts to innumerable species of parasitic mites (e.g. scabies and mange mites), as are many reptiles and some amphibians. Insects, especially those that build nests, live in semipermanent habitats like decaying wood, or use more ephemeral habitats like bracket fungi and dung, are hosts to a cornucopia of mite commensals, parasites and mutualists. None of these mites exceed a centimeter in length, and the vast majority grow to less than a millimeter, yet they often have a major impact on their hosts.

Characteristics

The Acari can be defined by the following characteristics:

- Gnathosoma delimited by a circumcapitular suture.
- Loss of external evidence of opisthosomal segmentation, i.e. without tergites or sternites.
- Ingestion of particulate food (lost in many derived taxa).
- *Palpcoxal endites* fused medially forming a hypostome.
- *Hexapod prelarva* (lost in Parasitiformes and many derived Acariformes).
- Hexapod larval stage.
- Three octopod nymphal stages (variously abbreviated in derived taxa).
- Hypostome with rutella or corniculi (lost in many derived Acariformes).

Recognition of Major Lineages

Traditionally, the mites have been treated as a subclass of the Arachnida, and three major lineages have been recognised, though the names used to refer to these groups have varied considerably. Here, we generally follow the names used in Parker (1982), and consider that three superorders (sensu Evans 1992) of Acari exist. The Opilioacariformes consists of a single order and family (*Opilioacarida, Opilioacaridae*) with about 20 known species.

The Acariformes contains over 300 families and over 30, 000 described species. Two major lineages are recognised, the Sarcoptiformes (*Oribatida* and *Astigmata*) and Trombidiformes (*Prostigmata*). Additionally, eight families of very early derivative acariform mites are lumped into the *Endeostigmata*, usually considered a suborder of the Prostigmata, but clearly containing taxa that belong to both major acariform lineages. The Parasitiformes consists of three orders: Ixodida, Holothyrida and Mesostigmata. The Mesostigmata contains in excess of 65 families and 10,000 described species, the other two parasitiform orders each comprise three families. About 850 species of ticks are known, but only about thirty species of holothyrans have been recognised.

What then is a mite? Aside from being generally tiny chelicerate arthropods with hexapod larvae, a discrete gnathosoma, and a loss of primary segmentation, mites are difficult to characterise. Researcher pointed out that many of the characters used to define mites were present in other chelicerate orders, especially in the Ricinulei. He proposed eleven apomorphic characteristics for the Acari, but several of these character states are not present in the Parasitiformes and presumably have been secondarily lost. It seems that mites often are most easily recognised by what they are not - other arachnids, rather than by a discrete set of acarine characters.

Among acarologists, arguments about monophyly or diphyly of the Acari have yet to be resolved, although currently the monophyleticists seem to be dominant. The Parasitiformes and Opilioacariformes are thought to be sister groups, and in turn this taxon (the Anactinotrichida, so named because of the absence in their setae of optically active actinochitin) is considered the sister group of the Acariformes (also called the Actinotrichida). Outside of the acarological community, those interested in chelicerate phylogeny have tended to assume that the Acari were a monophyletic assemblage.

Recently, many acarologists have concluded that mites are closely related to the arachnid order Ricinulei. Scientists proposed a sister group relationship between the Ricinulei and the Acari in 1979, and named this taxon the Acarinomorpha. Scientists also supported this relationship, but like Weygoldt and Paulus, assumed that the Acari are monophyletic. They considered the Acari to be diphyletic, and the Acariformes and Parasitiformes at most distantly related.

According to van der Hammen, the Ricinulei and Anactinotrichida (Parasitiformes & Opilioacariformes) are sister groups and, within another lineage, the Actinotrichida (Acariformes) and the non-acarine Palpigradi also are sister groups. Lindquist (1984) presented four derived characters linking the Acari and Ricinulei and concluded that, within the Acari proper, the Opilioacariformes and Parasitiformes form a sister group to the Acariformes.

CHAPTER – 4

Crops, Insects and Mites

A crop is a non-animal species or variety that is grown to be harvested as food, livestock fodder,fuel or for any other economic purpose. Major world crops include maize (corn), wheat, rice, soybeans, hay, potatoes and cotton. While the term "crop" most commonly refers to plants, it can also include species from other biological kingdoms. For example, mushrooms likeshiitake, which are in the fungi kingdom, can be referred to as crops.

In addition, certain species of algae are also cultivated, although it is also harvested from the wild. In contrast, animal species that are raised by humans are called livestock, except those that are kept as pets. Microbial species, such as bacteria or viruses, are referred to as cultures. Microbes are not typically grown for food, but are rather used to alter food.

Many orchard pests are attacked by beneficial insects or mites and by various fungal, bacterial and viral agents. Often, these natural enemies provide good suppression of pest populations, especially indirect pests (e.g, aphids, mites, leafminers), defined as those that feed on or in leaves.

PREDATORS

Natural enemies of pests in orchards include both predators and parasitoids. Predators are generally as large or larger than the prey they feed on. They are quite capable of moving around to search for their food, and they usually consume many pest insects during their lifetime. Lady bird beetles, lacewings and syrphids are examples of insect predators.

Parasitoids

Parasitoids, or parasitic insects are smaller than their prey. One or more parasitoids grows and develops in or on a single host. The host is slowly destroyed as the parasitic larva(e) feed and mature. Most parasitic insects are wasps or flies. Adult parasitoids do not usually feed on insects, but are highly mobile, laying eggs in many hosts. Aphids, leafminers and leafrollers and other caterpillars are often attacked by parasitic insects.

Beneficial insects and mites can help prevent or delay the development of pesticide resistance in orchards by reducing the number of pesticides require to control a pest. They will also feed on the resistant pests that survive a pesticide application. Table 1 lists common beneficial insects and mites and their characteristics.

IPM programmes take advantage of the biological pest control provided by beneficial insects and mites by conserving or augmenting natural enemies in orchards. When chemical controls are necessary in an Integrated Pest Management (IPM) programme, pesticides recommended are those that have minimal impact on beneficial naturally occurring in the orchard. Predatory mites are now commercially available in Ontario for release into orchards. These mites have been selected for a high degree of resistance to commonly used insecticides.

The following are some common-sense methods of conserving beneficial insects and mites in your orchard:

- Learn to recognize beneficial and distinguish them from pests
- Avoid using broad-spectrum pesticides.
- Use insecticides and miticides compatible with IPM programmes.
- Maintain ground covers as a supply of alternate prey, pollen, nectar, and shelter for many predators and parasitoids.
- Monitor and record what levels of beneficials you observe in your orchard.

Table 4.1: Common Beneficial Insects and Mites Found in Orchards

1.	Predatory Mites
2.	Aphid Predators
3.	General Predators
4.	Parasitoids

Insects and Mites

Western Bean Cutworm

Scientific name: Striacosta albicosta (formerly *Richia albicosta* and *Loxigrotis albicosta*)

Order: Lepidoptera

Family: Noctuidae

Biological Description

- *Moths:* 1.5 inch wingspan; forewing has cream-colored stripe along leading edge; circle and crescent shapes outlined against black triangle on forewing
  (a) *Can be confused with:* Dingy cutworm, Spotted cutworm
- *Larvae*:
  (a) *Newly hatched:* Dull orange body; black head; black pronotum (plate immediately behind head); 8-10 black spots per body segment
  (b) *Mature larvae:* Tan or brown body with pale broad stripe down center of back; orange head; pronotum has two broad, dark brown stripes; no distinctive spots 1.5 inches long
- *Pupae:* Orange-brown colour
- *Eggs:* Round with small ridges from top to bottom; laid in clusters of 20 to 200; white when first laid then turn purple a day or two before hatching

Economic Importance

A mid- to late-season pest of field and sweet corn, larvae feed on corn ears damaging and consuming kernels. Unlike corn borers, they do not tunnel into stalks. Heavy infestations have caused yield losses of up to 40% in the western Corn Belt states. WBC damage to corn in Wisconsin has exceeded threshold (5% infestation for field corn, 4% infestation for processing sweet corn) in southern, northeastern and central Wisconsin fields since arrival in 2005.

- Susceptible crops:
  (a) Corn
  (b) Dry beans —larvae feed on leaves and blossoms, and chew holes in pod walls and developing seeds.
  (c) Not a pest of soybeans.

Life Cycle

- Western bean cutworm overwinters in Wisconsin as a full-grown larva within a soil chamber. Spring development begins when temperatures exceed 50°F.

- Larvae pupate in May.
- Moths begin to emerge from soil chambers in late June. Peak emergence in the Upper Midwest is typically between the second and third weeks in July.
- Adult females lay eggs just before corn tassels. Eggs are laid primarily on the upper surface of the flag leaf (top-most leaf on the plant).
- Eggs hatch in five to seven days. Larvae feed on pollen in the whorl until the tassels emerge, at which point larvae switch to eating green silks.
- By early September, mature larvae leave the ear and drop to the ground. They burrow into the soil and create a chamber for overwintering.
- Generations:
  - *(a)* One generation per year

Damage/Symptoms

- Western bean cutworm is a late-season pest. Damage becomes evident between early August and early September.
- Two types of damage:
  - *(a)* In pre-tassel corn: Larvae feed on pollen in the developing tassel.
  - *(b)* In tassel-stage corn: Larvae feed on shed pollen, leaf tissue, silks, and corn kernels.
- Ear feeding:
  - *(a)* Kernels at ear tip, middle, and near shank are fed upon.
  - *(b)* Some larvae enter via the silks, but other larvae enter through the corn husk. Multiple larvae can be found in a single ear.
- Secondary damage can caused by fungal pathogens.
- Larvae do not tunnel into stalks.
- Damage can be confused with:
  - *(a)* Corn earworm
  - *(b)* European corn borer

Scouting Procedure and Economic Threshold

- When to begin scouting (two methods):
  - *(a)* Degree-days (DD):

1. To calculate degree-days for a single day, take the average daily temperature (the high minus the low, and divide that number by two), then subtract the base temperature from that number
2. Starting May 1, add up daily DD using a base temperature of 50°F.
3. Begin scouting when 1,320 total DD have accumulated.

(b) Pheromone traps

1. Pheromone traps are easy to make. Click here for directions on how to construct one.
2. Traps should be set by mid-June and monitored weekly or more frequently until trap captures decline in August.
3. Begin scouting when the first moths are detected.

- Examine twenty consecutive corn plants at five locations in the field.
- Check the upper three or four leaves of each plant for egg masses and small larvae.
- Continue scouting for seven to ten days after peak flight.
- Thresholds:

(a) *Field corn:* foliar insecticide treatment should be considered when 5 per cent of 100 corn plants have egg masses and/or small larvae.

(b) *Sweet corn:* foliar insecticide treatment should be considered when 4 per cent of 100 corn plants have egg masses and/or small larvae.

- Corn in different stages need to be scouted separately.
- Remember to scout non-*Bt* refuges for western bean cutworm when the rest of the field is planted with a western bean cutworm-resistant *Bt* variety. Additionally, check Bt corn hybrid seed tag, remember not all *Bt* corn hybrids provide western bean cutworm control.

Integrated Control

Natural control: Heavy rains, cold weather, and high winds can cause extensive mortality of early instar larvae. Cold winter temperatures will kill western bean cutworm larvae overwintering near the soil surface.

Cultural control: Tillage has not been proven to be effective against western bean cutworm. Although plowing or disking soil may reduce survival of overwintering larvae in soil chambers, the effectiveness of tillage as a management tool requires further evaluation before it can be recommended as a cultural control.

Biological Control: Several predatory insects feed on western bean cutworm larvae including adult and larval lady beetles, as well as damsel bugs and spiders.

Chemical Control: Application timing is critical for foliar insecticides to be effective. Once larvae enter the ear, control is nearly impossible.

(*a*) If eggs have hatched and corn is tasseling: Apply insecticide after 95 per cent tassel emergence but before larvae enter ears.

(*b*) If eggs have not hatched and corn has already tasseled: Apply insecticide as close as possible to expected egg hatch (when egg masses have turned purple).

Some insecticides for western bean cutworm control can flare spider mites, if present. For current Wisconsin recommendations, consult University of Wisconsin-Extension Bulletin No. A3646, Pest Management in Wisconsin Field Crops for field corn and bulletin No. A3422 Commercial Vegetable Production in Wisconsin for sweet corn.

CORN ROOTWORM

Scientific name: *Diabrotica virgifera* (Western) and Diabrotica barberi (Northern)

Order: Coleoptera

Family: Chrysomelidae

Biological Description

- *Adults:* Beetles are about ¼ inch long. Northerns are tan when they first emerge but then turn pale green. Westerns are yellow with three black lines down the back. The lines on the male western blur together.
- *Larvae:* Fully grown larvae are approximately half inch long and the diameter of medium pencil led. Heads are brown to black and there is a dark plate on the dorsal side of the last abdominal segment.
- *Pupae:* White in color.
- *Eggs:* Eggs are oval, creamy, white, and measure about 0.1 by 0.02 inches (0.3 by 0.5 mm).

Economic Importance

- Corn rootworms are some of the most destructive insect pests of corn in the southern two-thirds of Wisconsin.
- Outbreaks:

(a) Late-planted corn is more susceptible to adult feeding injury on leaves and silks because beetles are attracted to fresh pollen and silk. Late-planted fields will attract beetles from surrounding, more advanced fields.

- Susceptible crops:

  (a) Corn (the only plant that larvae can feed upon).

  (b) Ornamental flowers (pollen feeding by adults).

  (c) Vegetables (pollen feeding by adults).

Life Cycle

- Northern and western corn rootworms overwinter in Wisconsin as eggs in the upper soil layers.
- In the late May and early June eggs complete development and larvae emerge. Larvae may be present throughout the summer, but commonly damage peaks mid-July.
- After three weeks larvae pupate. Pupation lasts about two weeks.
- Adults typically appear between July 16-24.
- Females begin laying eggs in corn about two weeks after emerging from pupation. In Wisconsin, this starts in early to mid-August and continues well into September. Females can lay up to 1,000 eggs, but 300-500 eggs is most common.
- Generations:

  There is one generation per year.

Damage/Symptoms

- Types of feeding:

  1. *Adults:* Feed on silks (reducing pollination, which can result in incomplete kernel fill), pollen and leaves.
  2. *Larvae:* tunnel into and feed upon roots, which can cause plants to lodge and gooseneck:

     (a) First instar larvae feed on smaller branching corn roots.

     (b) Larger larvae migrate toward roots at the base of the plant.

- Evidence of larval rootworm feeding consists of brown, elongated scars on the root surface, tunnels within the roots, and varying degrees of root pruning.
- Larval damage peaks mid-July.

- Lodging caused by root pruning is common after storms with heavy winds and rains. Slight to moderate lodging can result in reduced ear weight and a goose-necked stem.
- Adult beetles lay more eggs in moist soil than in dry soil.

Scouting Procedure and Economic Threshold

- Scouting is used to determine the potential damage to corn planted the following year.
- When to scout: Beginning late July through mid-September, scout three times in 7-10 day intervals.
- Examine ten random plants in five separate areas (total of 50 plants) for each variety and planting date.
  - *(a)* Move quietly through the field to not disturb the beetles.
  - *(b)* When approaching a plant, hold the ear tip tightly in your hand so beetles do not escape as you look for beetles on the rest of the plant first. When you are done with the rest of the plant open your hand slowly and count the number of beetles that come out of the silks as you strip the husk away from the ear tip.
  - *(c)* Pull leaves away from the stalk to adequately examine leaf axils.
- Record the number of northern and western corn rootworms per plant.
- Economic threshold: If an average of 0.75 beetles per plant is found during any of the three field samplings, a rootworm soil insecticide, crop rotation, or a Bt CRW hybrid is recommended for the following year.

Integrated Control

- Natural control: Low soil temperatures in the winter as a result of little snow cover may contribute to high egg mortality of the western corn rootworm.
- Cultural control:
  - *(a)* Crop rotation is an excellent way to control rootworm populations, though problems with extended diapause (northern) and egg laying in soybeans (western) have been noted in areas outside of Wisconsin. In 2005 and 2006 variant western corn rootworm was found in Wisconsin in high enough numbers to recommend treatment for particular first year corn fields.Larvae cannot survive if a crop other than corn is planted in an infested field.

(b) Planting early season corn will reduce the severity of injury caused by adult silk clipping because most of the corn will be finished pollinating by the time beetle emergence peaks.

(c) Late-planted corn usually avoids the worst root damage because roots are too small to feed the rootworm larvae. Corn planted after mid-June usually does not require a rootworm soil insecticide. Late-planted corn will, however, attract adults to the silks.

(d) Early harvest in August (e.g. for silage) can reduce the amount of eggs that are laid in that field.

(e) A semiochemical-based bait can be used to attract and kill adult corn rootworms. This type of bait pairs a small amount of insecticide with a natural feeding stimulant specific for rootworms. Used during oviposition, these baits can suppress adult population densities to below-threshold levels.

INSECTS PESTS OF CROPS

The unceasing struggle between man and his insect enemies started even before the dawn of civilization. In spite by the numerous advances made by man in evolving newer and deadlier weapons to fight the war against insects, he has not succeeded in eradicating even one of the thousands of serious pests which damages his food and other agricultural products, destroys his possessions and even attack himself and injure his domestic animals.

There generally exists an uneasy truce between the insects pests and man , and this is termed as 'balance in nature'. This balance is the result of two opposing phenomena, the 'biotic potential', i.e., the tremendous capacity of insects to reproduce and multiply and the environment resistance which keeps their numbers under check. The environment resistance results in the death of adults before oviposition, in the mortality of eggs, larvae or pupae of the insects because of desiccation, starvation, parasites, predators, diseases and other adverse environmental conditions. Even any slight slakening of any of the processes of 'environment resistance' results in a population explosion of an insect species and the consequent epidemic.

The change in 'environment resistance' may take place owing to a number of causes, either natural of operated by different agencies. Man is perhaps the single most important agent, who has, from time to time, disturbed the 'balance of nature' and this has caused numerous pest problems and pest epidemics.

The nature too, plays an important role in causing pest epidemics. Favourable conditions which reduce the natural mortality and bring down the rapid development of the insect coupled with the conditions unfavourable to the natural enemies of that insect, often result in the rapid increase of its population leading to a sudden pest outbreak.

PRINCIPLES OF INSECT-PEST CONTROL

The first princlple undelying the control of an insect is its correct identification. When it is correctly identified, we can refer to the available information on the biology and the habits of the insect and determine its most vulnerable stage, the appropriate time and the most suitable method or methods to control it. Once it is established that an insect is causing economic losses, it becomes necessary to control it.

Ecoligical Factors

The knowledge and understanding of the ecological factors, both biotic and abiotic, affecting the population of the insect pest is necessary for planning the proper strategy for controlling it. A lot of attention is paid to this aspect now and elaborate procedures and 'models' have been evolved to pinpoint the 'key factors', dominantly affecting the development and multiplication of a particular pest.

The choice of the proper method or methods of control becomes easier, when the above mentioned information becomes available in respect of a particular pest. Some of the important methods for control of insect pests are discussed below:

Physical and Mechanical Control

This is one of the oldest methods, and has been in use since time immemorial. It includes measures like, collection of egg masses and other inactive stages, the removal of infested parts or wholeplants, the beating of drums or tins or trenching. This method can prove to be effective during the initial stage of the pest incidence and when practised as a concerted effort by a large number of farmers in a particular area.

Cultural Control

This is a preventive method which is inexpensive and may prove more efffective and efficient, if employed after acquiring a through knowledge of the life history and habits of a pest. Deep ploughing after harvesting the crop (to expose the hiding and resting insects), the removing and destroying of the suitable and other trash, adjusting the time of sowing (to avoid the peak incidence period), clean cultivation, the removal of alternative wild hosts, catch crops and suitable rotations are some of the important measures included under this method of control.

Host Plant Resitance

Host plant resistance has generally been considered one of the components of cultural method, but because of its importance, it desrves an independent status as a major method of protecting cropsagainst insect damage.

The method involves the utilisation of the inherent property of certain strains or varities of crops, of being less infected or less dameged than other strains or varities of same crop. Enormous economic benefits have been achieved by using this method in the case of crops, e.g. wheat,maize, cotton and alfalfa.

Very little attention has so far been paid in India to the exploitation of this method. However under the various co-ordinated projects on the improvemnet of any crop, special attention is being given to the evolvement of varities resistant to major insect pests. It is realised that the success of this method requires the close co-operation of entomologists, geneticists and plant-breeders.

Biological Control

Practically every crops pest has its natural enemies in the form of parasites, predators and disese causing organisms. The biological control involves a large scale multiplication of and liberation of such agents, or creating conditions under which the naturally occuring agents can act effectively. This type of control cannot be undertaken by individual farmers and has necessarilt to be carried out by specialised agencies.

Some very outstanding successes have been achieved by using this method, but the method suffered a set-back owing to the large-scale and indiscriminate use of insecticides. The approach at present is to evolve methods by which the biological and chemical methods can be intergrated, so that the harmful effects of insecticides do not interfere with the activities of the natural enemies.

Legislative or Regulatory Method

Legislative or regulatory method is a method mainly employed to prevent the introduction of pests from other countries or to prevent the spread of a pest from one area to another. The method is operated through specific regulations known as palnt-quarantine laws. In India some states have special pest acts, by which it becomes obligatory on the part of the cultivators and govermental authorities to take appropriate steps to control a particular pest when it appears in an epidemic form.

Chemical Control

After the discovery of the insectisides properties of DDT in 1939 by Paul Muller, the chemical control of insects has become most popular. As a matter of fact, the method has become so popular that most of the cultivators and extension workers speak only about insecticides, whenever the question of insect control is raised. The main reason for its popularity is the spectacular and immediate results obtained by the ude of such chemicals.

Hundereds of insecticides are noe available to control diffrent insect pests. These are mainly used as dusts, sprays or granules on the crops; dust and granules can also be incorporated into the soil for the control of soil inhabiting insects. In recent years, the soil application of some of the systemic insecticides has proved to be effective in controlling insect attacking crops in the early stages of their growth.

Some of the serious limitations of the insecticides have been highlighted in recent years. Out of these, the problems of insecticides residues on crops and other products used as food and fodder and on pollution of environment have been agitating the minds of people in developed and developing countries of the world. This realisation has resulted in certain extremist quarters demanding the banning the use of the most of the insecticides.

However the sensible approach suggested and generally accepted is for a judicious and restricted use of insecticides. It is strongly felt that in the near future, there is no possibility of replacing the chemical method of controlling insects entirely by any other method.

SOME OTHER METHODS OF INSECT CONTROL

In addition to the major methods of controlling insects described above, there are number of other methods, which have either been employed successfully for controlling certain specific pests, or are still in the experimental and developmental stages. Increased attention is being paid now to the incorporation of such methods in the programmes of insect control.

Some of these methods are: the use of attractants, repellants and anti-feeding compounds, radiations for sterilization (the well known example of eradicating the screw-worm by using sterile-male technique), chemosterilants, juvenile and sex hormones. These methods can in future replace or supplement the use of insecticides.

CHOICE OF PROPER METHODS

The guiding principles for selecting an appropriate method or methods of control should be that the method chosen must be economical, free from creating any other problem, immediately or in future, it should not harm the natural enemies of the pest and should be easy to operate and be readily available to an ordinary cultivator.

The choice of the proper method (or methods) of control becomes easier when the biology and the habits of the pests are known and its most vulnerable stage has been determined. However so far the general tendency among those who are responsible for carrying out the control operations is to employ an easy method, giving quick results and disregarding other unfavourable consequences which may follow the completion of the operations.

Keeping in view the guiding princlples in the selection of pest-control methods, it is generally realized that any single approach to the problem of insect control is not feasible. Each method has its own advantages as well as its disadvantages and also has limitations under a particular set of conditions.

The current thinking all over the world is to suitably synthesize the use of as many methods as possible to control the insect pests effectively, economically and without any adverse after-effect. This approach is now popurlarly known as 'Integrated Pest Control'.

Despite a number of serious limitations from which insecticides suffer, it is felt that the use of these chemicals in the control of insect pests will continue for a long time to come and in the strategy for 'Integrated Pest Control', this method will occupy an important place as a curative methods for reducing losses because to pests.

CONCEPT OF USING CHEMICALS

The concept of using chemicals for controlling insect pests is not new; however, its importance and popularity increased only after the discovery of the insecticidal properties of DDT. Originally, these chemicals were classified on the basis of their mode of entry in the bodies of insects,viz. stomach poisons, contact poisons and fumigants.

However, this classification has become outdated, because most of the synthetic organic insecticides act both as stomach and contact poisons and some have also the added fumigant action. At present, the generally acceptable classification is based on the chemical nature of the insecticides.

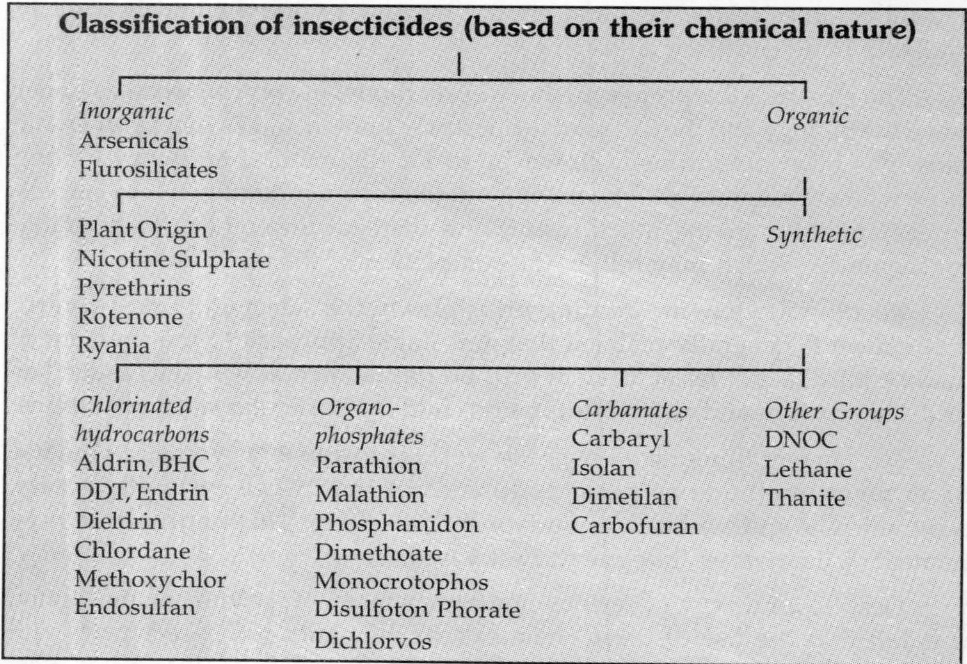

The inorganic insecticides were widly used before the synthetic organic insecticides were developed and marketed. At present, hardly any of these insecticides are being used in India. There is a feeling in some quarters that we can perhaps advantageously use arsenicals against the leaf-feeding insects, especially where some parasities or predators are known to be active against them.

Insecticides of plant origin have also been regulated to the background by the synthetics and at present relatively very little quantities of insecticides, like Pyrethins and Nicotine sulphate, are used to control insect pests of agricultural importance. The problems of residues on insecticides on food and fodder crops has emphasized the necessity of using insecticides which are less toxic to mammals or breakdown into non-toxic components in a resonable short time. Thus the insecticides of plant origin can be usefully employed to control a number of insect pests, especially where the products are to be consumed within a short time after treatment (vegetable and fruits).

The use of synthetic organic insecticides has increased with leaps and bounds throughout the world. In India, only about 10,120 hectares of crops were treated with pesticides in 1946-47; this area increased to about 17.4 million hectares by 1965-66 and the target for 1973-74 was 80 million hectares. The various insecticides required for controlling insects during this period is estimated to be 40,850 tonnes.

Starting with the manufacture of BHC in 1958, India today produces technical grades of 39 pesticides (insecticides, fungicides, rodenticides, molluscicides, nematocides and herbicides), including the following insecticides used for controlling crop pests:

BHC, DDT, Malathion, Parathion (Methyl), Toxaphene, Pyrethrum extract, Nicotine sulphate, Fenitrothion, Methyl-demeton, Phosphamidon and Dimethoate.

TOXICITY OF INSECTICIDES

Practically all insecticides are toxic to man and other animals;however they differ in their degree of toxicity. Thus the hazards to man and his domestic animals depend on the values and nature of toxicity (oral or dermal).

The United States Environmental Protection Agency,Washington, has recognized three categories, viz. danger-poison, warning and caution on the basis of these values.

Available data on some of the common insecticides are presented in Table 4.2.

Table 4.2: Acute Oral LD_{50} Values of Some Common Insecticides for White Rats

	Insecticides	Oral LD_{50} (mg/kg)		Remarks*
		Males	Females	
1	2	3	4	5
(A)	*Chlorinated hydrocarbone*			
	Aldrin	39	60	Toxic
	Benzene hexachloride(BHC)	1250	–	Less toxic, sex not mentioned
	Chlordane	335	430	Toxic
	DDT	113	118	Less Toxic
	Dieldrin	46	46	Toxic
	Endosulfan	43	18	Toxic
	Endrin	17.8	7.5	Highly Toxic
	Heptachlor	100	162	Toxic
	Lindane (gamma BHC)	88	91	Toxic
	Toxaphene	90	80	Toxic
(B)	*Organo phosphates*			
	Aldicarh	.93	–	Highly Toxic, sex not mentioned
	Diaxinon	108	76	Toxic

(Contd...)

1	2	3	4	5
	Dichlorvos	80	56	Toxic
	Dimethoate	215	–	Toxic
	Disulfoton	6.8	2.3	Highly Toxic
	Fenitrothiop	740	–	Less Toxic, sex not mentioned
	Malathion	1375	1000	Less Toxic
	Methyl parathion	14	24	Highly Toxic
	Mevinphos	6.1	3.7	Highly Toxic
	Monocrotophos	17.5	20	Highly Toxic
	Parathion	13	3.6	Highly Toxic
	Phorate	2.3	1.1	Highly Toxic
	Phosphamidon	23.5	23.5	Highly Toxic
(C)	***Carbamates***			
	Carbofuran	11	–	Highly Toxic, sex not mentioned

PRECAUTIONS IN THE USE OF INSECTICIDES

The improper, excessive and careless use of insecticides may prove injurious to man and his domesticated animals. Proper safeguards are, therefore, necessary to protect the persons handling the insecticides. The crops to which they are applied, the consumers who have to use produce of the treated crops, and the domesticated animals which feed on such produce, the pollinating insects, the parasites and predators of insects, likely to be affected by coming into direct or indirect contact with the insecticides applied. Also, the pollution of air, soil and water is to be avoided as far as possible.

Some of the basic precautions to be taken while handling, using and storing insecticides are as follows:

Keep the insecticides in closed, properly labelled containers in a dry and cool place, away from food and fodder, and in places where children and animals cannot reach them.

Use the insecticides according to the instructions given on the cointainers, and adhere to the dosages recommended.

Persons handling insecticides should avoid the contact of the insecticides with their skin (specially that of the insecticides listed as toxic and highly toxic) and the inhalation of dusts, vapours or mists. The minimum precautions of wearing rubber gloves and covering the eyes and nose should be taken. The operators must not smoke, eat or drink anything while applying insecticides. After finishing their work, they should take bath, wash their hands and face with soap throughly and change their clothes. The clothes worn by them during the operations should be washed properly.

INSECTICIDES — APPLICATION EQUIPMENT

The proper choice of equipments to apply insecticides depends on number of factors, the first of which is the formulation to be used. Insecticides can be applied as dusts, sprays(as high-volume and low-volume sprays, aerosols, mists or fog), or as granules, and the spplication machinery has to be chosen accordingly. The next important factor to be considered is the size of the area to be treated. For small holdings, hand-operated applicators may be suitable, whereas for large holdings power operated machines will be needed. Similarly, due consideration is to be given to the crop to be treated and the pest to be controlled.

Different kinds of dusters and sprayers available in the market are listed below.

Dusters

Manually-operated dusters for small holdings: These are plunger-type bellows duster, knapsack duster, and crank or rotary duster (very commonly used in India).

Power dusters: These dusters are used to cover large areas and for quick coverage. These are engine and traction-operated.

Manually-operated dusters for small holdings: These are plunger-type bellows duster, knapsack duster, and crank or rotary duster (very commonly used in India).

To obtain good results and for proper coverage, a duster should produce a continuous and uniform cloud of the insecticide. The dust should be dry and fine enough not to clog the hopper or lump inside it. The duster should be light and portable and should be easily repaired even by the village blacksmith.

Sprayers

Manually-operated sprayers: These are hand sprayers or atomiser (for treating a few plants only), stirr up pump or sprayers, slide-pump sprayer (pneumatic or battery-operated), compressed-air sprayer, rocker sprayer, foot or pedal sprayer and wheelbarrow sprayer. Pneumatic knapsack and foot or pedal-pump sprayers are commonly used by the Indian farmers with small holdings.

The power-operated sprayers include the equipment operated with gasoline engines, such as stretcher sprayers, wheelbarrow sprayers, boom sprayers and self-propelled high clearance sprayers. Power-sprayers are generally available with village panchayats or zilla parishads, from which the farmers can obtain them on hire, whenever necessary.

In addition, there are special types of machines for producing mists, fogs and aerosols which have limited use. Recently, granule applicators have been marketed for applying granular insecticides.

The proper care of application equipment is of utmost importance. The machines should be kept in good working order even when not required immediately. They should be cleaned thoroughly, oiled and greased before storing after use. In the case of sprayers, insecticides should be completely removed from the tank and the delivery tube be properly tied; their nozzles should be cleaned and any leaks should be immediately repaired.

Dosages of Insecticides: For controlling the insect pests of crops, the usual practice is to indicate the dosage, ie., the quantity of the active ingredient to be applied per unit area (acre or hectare). However, the dosage may have to be varied, depending on the type and stage of the crop. Another method is to indicate the concentration and the quantity of an insecticide to be dustered or sprayed. Here also the quantity of the dust or of the spray liquid has to be adjusted according to the type and growth stage of the crop and according to the application equipment available. In the following pages, concentrations of insecticides have been recommended, keeping in view the general use of high volume sprayers, by which plants may be throughly covered up to the run-off stage. The quantity of the spray may, therefore, have to be adjusted accordingly.

IMPORTANT CROPS AND THEIR MAJOR PESTS

The crops grown in India are attacked by a large number of different pests, some of which are specific to a particular crop or feed or related species of a particular family, or to crops grown in particular season. However, their are other insects, such as termites, armyworms, cutworms, grasshoppers and locusts which attack a large variety of crops in different seasons. Out of them, Locusts occupy a unique position because of their swarming habit and migrations to distant areas irrespective of international boundaries. An account of these group of insects, specially the desert locust, which is regarded as 'Farmer's enemy No.1', is given seperatly.

LOCUSTS

India has been subjected, from time immemorial, to locust invasions which cause immense damage to crops and trees, and sometimes resulting in severe fodder faminies and considerable loss of livestock.

General Characteristics

Locusts are closely allied to short-horned grasshoppers from which they differ markedly in certain respects. Both are anatomically very similar, feed on vegetations, lay eggs in the soil and pass through several instars before they become adults. Whereas grasshoppers feed on specific cropsonly, locusts devour almost all plants and vegetation, and even feed upon dead and dying locusts, i.e. they are omnivourous. Unlike grasshoppers, locusts exists in two phases: *(i)* the solitary phase; and *(ii)* the gregarious phase. In solitary phase, they are very active, live and breed as scattered individuals, and are relatively harmless. In the gregarious phase, they are very active, acquire the habit of congregation and forming bands, breed rapidly, and in adult stage fly long distance during migration even overseas. Climate, weather, soil, vegetation and their mass destruction organised by man cause the transformation of the gregarious phase into the solitary phase.

KINDS OF LOCUSTS

There are eleven main species of locust, of which three, viz. the Bombay locust, the migratory locust and the desert locust, are found in India. The first two species live and breed in the country and are found scattered all over western India from Rajasthan in the North to Karnataka and Tamil Nadu in the south. They rarely form swarms. They mainly feed on plants of the grass family and occasionally when they become gregarious, do considerable damage to jowar, bajra and other millets.

DESERT LOCUST

Distribution

The desert locust in the most destructive intenational pest, its distribution extending from India in the east to Africa in the west, passing through pakistan, Afganistan, Iran, Iraq, southern USSR, Arabia and in the north, east and west of Africa. In this vast region, the locust lives and breeds endemically, forming swarms and undertaking long flights to distant places. The locust invasions occur in cycles, the duaration of a cycle as well as of the period between two cycles being variable.

Phases

In the solitary phase, the locust is more or less harmless, whereas in the gregarious phase, when its hoppers congregate and march in bands, destroying all the vegetation in their path and give rise to swarms, it is very destructive. The hoppers of the solitary phase are green throughout their life, but the hoppers of the gregarious phase are black in the first two phases of development and their dark color turns greenish yellow and orange in the later stages. The adult locust of the solitary phase remains grey, but the adult is pink at first, but turns grey and yellow as it matures.

Breeding

There are generally two breeding seasons in a year:

1. winter-spring; and
2. summer-monsoon.

In regions where the rainfall is received in winter and early spring, e.g. in sout-east Arabia, southern Iran and Baluchistan, the locust breeds in spring. In India and other countries where the rainfall is received during the summer months, breeding takes place at that time of the year. The swarms produced during winter and spring in the middle east and Baluchistan usually fly eastwards into pakistan and India, in summer. With the advent of monsoon in this area, they lay eggs from June to September. The swarms resulting from this breeding return during autumn to the areas of winter rainfall when conditions in the summer rainfall area become dry and unsuitable for breeding. A number of swarms developed in the country fly also to the north, south and east, and thus invade all parts of India and damage the kharif crops.

Sometimes, breeding takes place in winter, specially in Punjab and Haryana when they damage the rabi crops as well.

Life History

The female of the gregarious phase lays eggs in clusters of 40-120 in a hole in moist soil to a depth of 75 to 150 mm and covers them with a liquid material that soon hardens to form a protective covering. Young hoppers hatch from the eggs in two or three weeks in summer, and in three to four weeks in autumn and spring. There are five stages in the development of hoppers. At each stage they cast off their skin every sixth or seventh day as they progressively become bigger. As long as they are hoppers, they have only rudimentary wings. After the fifth moulting, they develop wings from the wing-pads present the later hopper stages. During summer and monsoon, the hoppers complete their development in four to five weeks;and during autumn and spring in six to eight weeks. As the hoppers moult, they undergo a changer in color and size. In early stages, they are almost wholly black, and in the later stages, they are black, with orange and yellow patterns. When they acquire wings, they are pink and ultimately turn yellow, when fully mature.

Both hoppers and adults feed on all types of vegetation, though there are some plants which they would not touch, or eat only with reluctance.

BIOTIC THEORY OF PERIODICITY OF LOCUST CYCLES

The theory has been recently propounded to explain the causes of periodic locust ourbreaks. Accoding to this theory, the actually adverse climatic conditions of the desert are, in fact, favourable to the locust, as they adversely affect its enemies (specially cold-blooded reptiles), which are responsible for not allowing the locust to breed outside the desert, where the conditions are otherwise very favourable. The desert environment becomes more inhospitable to the enemies of the locust during the minima of the sun-spot cycle (periods of drier and more intense heat), leading to a reduction in the population of the locust enemies which consequently results to an increase in locust population and swarm formation. During the maxima of the sun-spot cycle (period of less dry and less intense heat) on the other hand, the desert environment becomes favourable to the enemies of the locusts which migrate to the interior of the desert from the periphery and bring down the locust population, thus breaking the locust cycle.

This biotic theory has made it possible to visualize the possibilities of checking the start of the locust cycle in the early stages by creating suitable ecological niches in the locust-breeding areas, so that their enemies can migrate and survive the adverse conditions in such areas and continue to keep down the locust population.

Control Measures

There are two main methods of locust control, viz. (i) the use of poison baits; and (ii) dusting and spraying with insecticides. Poison baiting, though cheap, is not very practicable, dusting and spraying have been found to be very effective. In the egg stage ploughing or flooding the land has been practised in the past. This method is not much effective in as much as it destroys only about 30 percent of the eggs and renders subsequent control measures with insecticides difficult. Spraying the egg-infected, uncultivated land with Aldrin is very effective, as it leaves a poisonous film on the surface with which emerging hoppers come into contact and die. Once the hoppers have emerged, they can be effectively controlled by dusting or spraying or both, as the hopper stage is the most vulnerable. For dusting, BHC is the most effective insecticide. For young hoppers, 3 to 5 per cent dust is sufficient to kill them; for advanced stage 5 to 7 per cent dust is necessary; and adults need 10 per cent BHC. Dusting or spraying may be done on the hoppers directly or it may be done on strips of ground, two to three metres wide, in the path of the advancing hoppers. Another method is to dig trenches 45 to 75 cm deep and 30 to 60 cm wide depending on the size of the hoppers, in front of the moving hoppers to which they may be driven and buried alive. The duating and burning of bushes in which hoppers rest can also be resorted to.

Adult locusts, flying in swarms, are most difficult to control. If the alight in any field or in a piece or ground try to kill as many of them as possible, by beating or cruching, specially in the morning when they are lazy. Burning them by setting fire to dry bushes or wastelands, or by flame throwers, if they are settled on green bushes, hedges or trees, if useful. This method works well if the locusts have settled for resting, mating or egg-laying. Poison baitspread at the rate of 20 to 50 kg per hectare are useful if locusts have settled to feed in cropped feeds. If the swarm consists of pink locusts, dust them with 10 per cent BHC. Aerial spraying of the flying swarms and ground hoppers has to be resorted to with Aldrin solution in oil in the case of very serious infestation. However, this cannot be done when the swarms and hoppers are in the populated areas.

Despite the discovery of a large number of potent insecticides, which can be used against locust, both from the ground and air, the farmer has been finding himself to be only a helpless onlooker once the locust swarm settles in his field. Though part of the swarm may be killed, he invariably loses hiscrop.

Situation has materially changed recently after the discovery of the anti-feeding property of the neem kernels. It has been found that 0.1 per cent spension of neem kernels, sprayed on the crop affords protection against locust feeding for about 14 days. The cultivator can locally collect and preserve the neem seeds till required. By spraying his crops with neem kernel suspension, when the invasion of his fields, by hopper bands or swarms is immenent a cultivator can now ensure the safety of his crops. Simultaneously, the control operations can be carried out by adopting suitable methods.

CHAPTER – 5

Acarines for Weed and Nematode Control

Alternative practices for weed management, such as integrated weed management (IWM) may allow the persistence of weed populations below a given economie threshold. Increased species diversity of weeds also may resuit. If diversity increases, and the number of ecological interactions also increases, weed species should be viewed as an interactive community, rather than an unrelated set of targets for control. In this chapter we will study how diversity is evaluated in unmanaged systems, examine how integrated weed management techniques may alter the diversity of weed species and suggest how strategies can be developed for managing weed diversity under integrated weed management. Methods used to evaluate diversity in natural systems may be used to evaluate weed diversity in alternative systems of weed management.

We made preliminary calculations of diversity for reduced tillage, modified herbicide use, crop rotation, critical period of weed control, techniques to improve crop competitiveness, and alternative control methods. Many of these integrated weed management techniques potentially may resuit in changes in weed species diversity.

We examined potential effects of these changes in weed diversity wi thin six primary elements of community ecology: colonization, disturbance, the physical environment, interactions with other communities, community interactions and community dynamics. Opportunities to evelop strategies of community management exist wi thin each of these elements. If diversity could be managed while maintaining acceptable crop yields, some previously unrealized benefits of the presence of weeds could be seen, as predicted by relationships among plants of unmanaged communities.

Moreover, the goal of producing a more sustainable system that incorporâtes the diversity of the weed community would be complemented by trends in policy towards encouraging biodiversity in agroecosystems.

MANAGEMENT APPROACH

Currently there are strong environmental and economie incentives for adopting alternative practices for weed management, such a integrated weed management (IWM). Integrated weed management may provide a more sustainable approach to crop production, reducing the reliance on external inputs that characterizes conventional agriculture.

One goal of integrated weed management is to maintain weed populations below an economie threshold level. Manage ment to achieve this goal reduces emphasis on strategies of eradication or prophylaxis and promûtes a strategy of containment. Thus, IWM must incorporate a containment strategy for potential increases in weed diversity, because of increased survival of existing species or colonization by new species.

Ecologists hâve studied the subject of diversity extensively in unmanaged Systems. It would be valuable to link ecological theory of community diversity wi th potential changes in weed diversity under IWM and to develop a management approach that would view weeds as a communi ty rather than as individual species. Weeds of intensively managed crops hâve been studied mostly at the species level, and thus there is relatively little information available on the impact of weed diversity on weed management.

EVALUATING DIVERSITY IN NATURAL SYSTEMS

There are a number of key terms used in the discussion of diversity in ecology. Species diversity, in terms of species richness, is measured as the number of species in a community. Diversity could also be measured within species {e.g. different weed biotypes) but this paper primarily deals with diversity among species.

Two communities with an identical number of species can differ in terms of evenness, and hence it is also useful to know the proportional or relative abundance of species with in the community. If a community is dominated by one or two species, it can be said to be less diverse than a communi ty wi th an equal number of species wi th a more equitable distribut ion of population sizes.

Indices hâve been developed to combine species richness wi th proportional abundance wi thin a single value. Examples include the Shannon index, the Simpson index etc. As yet, no one index has been adopted as the most appropriate or practical index, and the choice may depend on the data set. In particular, it is important to account for the biases towards species richness, evenness or dominance. These biases reflect the difficulty inherent in combining species richness and relative abundance into a single parameter.

Weed research has also employed synthetic importance values that attempt to account for the patchiness of weed abundance and sampling error. This may be useful when ordering specie by abundance in studies of weed diversity. For example, scientists computed relative abundance by combining frequency, density and uniformity into a single abundance value, with uniformity calculated from the number of quadrats containing a given species expressed as a percentage of the total number of surveyed quadrats.

The advantage of synthetic importance values is to provide a single parameter that provides a comprehensive measure of abundance by including considerations of scale and sampling. However, such values lose some of the information contained in the data used to derive them.

Theory

Simply measuring the diversity of a community is not directly meaningful; for theories to be developed and tested, diversity must be related to ecosystem processes and properties. Investigations of species diversity wi thin theoretical ecology primarily hâve involved relationships between diversity and area, relative abundance patterns, and relationships between diversity and stability. Knowledge of diversity-area relationships is useful in accounting for the spatial scale at which diversity is evaluated. Attempts hâve been made to relate mathematical distributions of relative abundance patterns to niche differentiation or habitat patchiness.

Regardless of the mathematical distribution, relative abundance curves (i.e. cumulative relative abundance plotted against species) are useful indicators of dominance-diversity relationships.

Relationships between diversity and stability hâve received attention from both theoretical and applied biologists. Although the idea of higher species diversity leading to higher stability has intuitive appeal, there are other aspects to consider. One important aspect frequently considered is the complexity of the community, which consists of the number of ecological connections among organisms in the community. Conceptually, the interaction strength of these connections may be difficult to apply to plant communities where ail species are at the same trophic level. Comprtmentalizaton is also important; a simple ecosystem may consist of a single food web involving ail organisms present, whereas more c omplex ecosystems may consist of numerous compartments, with a high degree of connectivity within, but not between compartments.

When agronomie practices undergo long-term changes, fundamental changes in weed communities may occur. Surveys hâve linked agronomie practices to differences in weed diversity. Characteristics of weeds, such as short life cycles, seed dormancy, plasticity, colonization ability and high reproductive rate, facilitate rapid turnover of communities. At present, many alternative management practices are under consideration, which, if adopted on a large scale, may alter the structure and diversity and perhaps even the stability of weed communities. A better understanding of these potential changes is necessary to facilitate a reasonably efficient transition from conventional to alternative management approaches such as IWM.

Preliminary comparisons of diversity under alternative management practices with diversity under conventional. These comparisons are selected cases where there was a large difference in density between alternative and conventional treatments. When control measures are integrated under IWM, the composition of the resulting weed communi ty results from the trade-offs among various management practices. Nevertheless, it is useful to look at the potential impacts of each practice on weed diversity.

Crop yields in the United States are reduced by the impact of a variety of pests. Weeds are potentially the most damaging, followed by approximately 8000 species of insects and at a longer lever by plant pathogens and nematodes. Control of pest insects has been achieved through chemical, cultural, and biorational controls, but biological control has unique advantages over the other tactics.

Biological control has been defined as the "actions of parasites, predators, and pathogens in maintaining another organism's density at a longer average than would occur in their absence". Some scientists would include host plant resistance, autocidal control, and pheromones under the category of biological control, but, while these biorational approaches to pest control have a biological basis, many investigators do not consider them to be biological control. Generally, biological control has been achieved by the use of one of three approaches—classical, augmentation, or conservation.

Classical Biological Control

"Classical" biological control is based on the importation of exotic naturel enemies (parasites, predators, or pathogens) and their long-term establishment in the new environment, a strategy which may then provide long-term control of the target exotic pest arthropod or weed. This approach to biological control has been rewarding; hundreds of successful projects have reduced damage caused by a wide array of exotic pest arthropods and weeds. In addition, once a successful programme is achieved in one location, the same naturel enemies are frequently used to control the same pests elsewhere in other climatically similar locations.

Around the world, about 170 successes were achieved between 1964 and 1976 by introducing naturel enemies into a second site after they had been proven effective in the original geographic site of introduction. Natural enemy importation thus remains an important and effective tactic in pest management, particularly in the management of those arthropod and weed pests that are exotic. This approach to biological control, unfortunately, has received less support than it deserves.

Preventing Exotic Pests

While many scientists are worried about the extinction of animal and plant species in ecosystems, agricultural pest management specialists are concerned about additions to the fauna and flora of agroecosystems. In 1971, the U.S. Department of Agriculture established a task force to review the effectiveness of plant quarantines in preventing the entry of exotic pests and to quantify the risks associated with the entry of such pests and diseases. A list of immigrant insects and related arthropods in the United States was compiled that categorized the immigrants as pests, beneficial species, and those of no known economic importance.

The list continues to grow as additional species are found. At the conclusion of the 1971-1972 study, 1115 species were recognized to be of foreign origin and this number had increased to 1385 by 1977. Sixteen insect orders, mites (Acarina), and spiders (Araneae) are represented among the exotic arthropod species.

Foreign insect and mite species are considered to be responsible for a major part of all crop losses; one estimate is that they are responsible for 50 percent of such losses in California. When viewed nationally, foreign species comprise 39 per cent (235) of approximately 600 important arthropod pest species. Another 630 foreign species are on the list as pests of lesser importance, and an additional 420, or almost 25 per cent of the immigrant fauna, are species of no known importance, while the remaining 398 are in some degree beneficial.

Exotic invaders include such pests as the Japanese beetle, European corn borer, Florida red scale, Rhodesgrass scale, spotted alfalfa aphid, gypsy moth, cottony cushion scale, California red scale, olive parlatoria scale, European red mite, imported southern red fire ant, Russian wheat aphid, and boll weevil.

Arthropods probably will continue to be added to the fauna of the United States at the rate of about eleven species per year, despite the efficacy of the national quarantine system. Of the eleven, seven are likely to be pests of some importance, and about every third year a pest of major significance will be discovered. Assuming that many of these pests are not or cannot be eradicated, classical biological control will remain of crucial importance in controlling new exotic pests in forests, range lands, and agroecosystems.

Classical biological control has been actively practised for about 100 years in the United States. Worldwide, approximately 2300 introductions directed against insect pests have provided complete biological control in about 100 cases. Substantial control was provided in an additional 140 cases. Estimates of project outcomes that are successful range from 16 to 34 per cent.

Many factors affect success in classical biological control programs, including climate, natural enemies, habitat type, genetics, host compatibility, host phenology, and operational procedures. Thus, while classical biological control is effective and has yielded complete and lasting control in many important situations, there are several aspects of this pest management tactic that require additional research. Many attempts have been only casual or have involved use of a particular natural enemy against unsuitable species or in unsuitable environments. The possibilities for controlling the notorious codling moth in this way, or the Mexican bean beetle, or the cotton boll weevil, for example, have only been explored superficially.

There are many views as to what the research priorities in classical biological control should be. There is little disagreement about the fact that this control has been under-exploited and underfunded. In one sense, it has been oversold; the dramatic cases in which complete biological control has been achieved through a small investment in research funds has, in my opinion, resulted in unrealistic expectations as to the resources needed to properly conduct classical biological control programs. This could be labeled the "cottony cushion syndrome."

Augmentation

Augmentation involves efforts to increase populations or beneficial effects of natural enemies of both native and exotic pests. Augmentation involves various techniques, including periodic releases and environmental manipulation. Periodic releases may be labeled inundative or inoculative, depending upon the numbers of natural enemies released and the interval during which they are expect' to provide control.

Environmental manipulation may include provision of alternative, factitious hosts or prey, use of semiochemicals to improve natural enemy performance, provision of environmental requisites such as food or nesting sites, and modification of cropping practices to favor natural enemies. Augmentation has been particularly successful glasshouse crops.

Inundative releases are designed to control a pest by the actions of the released natural enemies, not by the actions of their progeny, and thus can be considered "biotic insecticides." Inundative releases are currently hampered by our limited ability to produce high quality, inexpensive, mass-reared natural enemies. Thus, advances in current research on synthetic diets, artificial hosts, quality control, and genetic manipulation could result in increased of this tactic.

Another emerging technology is the use of semiochemicals to improve the efficacy of natural enemies in augmentation schemes. Parasitic insects use various chemical cues to locate their hosts. Recent reports, indicate that learning can modify the responses of parasites to these chemicals. The complexity of host seeking behaviour exhibited by arthropod natural enemies is only beginning to be understood and could lead to the more sophisticated use of natural enemy augmentation.

Conservation

Conservation involves protecting and maintaining natural enemy population Conservation is crucial if both native and exotic natural enemies are to be maintained in agricultural ecosystems. Most commonly, conservation involves modifying pesticide application practices so that they occur only when the pest population exceeds specified levers.

In some cases, conservation of naturel enemies can be achieved by changing the active ingredient, rates, formulations, timing, and location of pesticide applications. Or, existing populations of naturel enemies can be protected by maintaining refuges. According to Tauber et al (1985). It is probable that the most dramatic increase in the utilization of biological control in agricultural IPM systems could come through the judicious use of selective pesticides in conjunction with effective naturel enemies in specific cropping systems, in specific geographic regions. While we have some knowledge of pesticide selectivity, it is woefully inadequate to generally allow such precise usage.

As long as key pests cannot be controlled biologically, culturally, or through host plant resistance, agricultural chemicals will be needed. Learning how to conserve naturel enemies in the agroecosystem is an effective way to increase the use of biological control in agriculture.

Emerging Technologies

Genetic manipulation of naturel enemies of arthropods offers promise of enhancing their efficacy in agricultural cropping systems. Genetic manipulation of other beneficial arthropods, such as silkworms and honey bees, has been conducted for hundreds of years. Such manipulation of biological control agents seems to be a logical extension of the domestication of crop plants and animals that has been part of agriculture for thousands of years, since many agricultural systems are artificial.

As in crop breeding, three potential genetic manipulation tactics exist, i.e., artificial selection, hybridization (use of heterosis), and recombinant DNA (rDNA) techniques. To date, only artificial selection of arthropod naturel enemies has been successfully employed, and the potential role of heterosis or rDNA technologies remains to be documented.

What are some of the constraints to initiating a genetic improvement project of arthropod naturel enemies? First, the factors limiting the efficacy of the natural enemy must be identified. This means that a great deal must be known about the biology, ecology, and behaviour of the naturel enemy. This first step is extremely crucial, since improper identification of the trait needing improvement could lead to an expensive and time-consuming project of little practical value. Second, genetic variability must be available upon which one can select if using artificial selection.

If such variability does not occur in naturel populations, it must be provided for through mutagenesis or, perhaps, through recombinant DNA methods. Third, the "improved" naturel enemy must be documented to be effective in the field. Finally, one must assume that the cost of the project will be justified by the benefits achieved.

Benefits and Coasts

Scientists recently reviewed the benefits and costs of an integrated mite management programme in California almond orchards that involves the use of a genetically manipulated predatory mite. Metaseialus occidentalis (Nesbitt) is an effective predator of spider mites in deciduous orchards and vineyards in western North America.

It acquired resistance to organophosphorus insecticides (OPs) through natural selection in apple orchards in Washington and this resistance allowed the predator to survive in orchards even though an OP insecticide (azinphosmethyl or Guthion) was applied to control codling moth. In 1977, a genetic improvement project with M. occidentalis was initiated, with the goal of developing additional pesticide resistance in this predator in order to increase its usefulness in orchard and vineyard pest management programs.

Selection for resistance to carbaryl and permethrin was successful, and multi-resistant strains of M. occidentalis were obtained through laboratory crosses and additional selections. The laboratory-selected strains were then tested in small plot trials for two years, to determine whether they could become established in orchards or vineyards, survive the relevant pesticide applications in the field, spread, multiply, overwinter, and control the spider mites. The small plot trials were then followed by three years of research to learn how to implement the predators in an integrated mite management program in almonds. Implementation involved developing mass rearing methods, monitoring methods, and learning how to use reduced rates and numbers of applications of insecticides and acaricides selective to this predator.

The economic analysis suggested that almond growers who adopted the programme would save $60 to $110/hectare. The programatic benefit/ cost analysis suggested that the return on the research investment will range from 280 to 370 percent per year, depending upon the level of adoption by almond growers on the 158,000 hectares of almonds grown in California.

This high rate of return on research investment was attributed, in part, to the fact that more than half of the research resources were allocated to field testing and implementation research. Thus, genetic improvement with M occidentalis has been shown to be efficacious and cost effective.

Economic Analysis

Genetic improvement projects with several phytoseiid species have included selection for enhanced fecundity, temperature tolerance, and non-diapause as well as pesticide resistance. Selection projects are currently being conducted in the U.S.A., China, New Zealand, and France and field trials are being conducted with some of the selected strains. The successful implementation and economic analyses of costs and benefits of these genetically manipulated predatory mites will provide impetus to this tactic in biological control.

Genetic improvement projects with natural enemies of insects have been conducted for improved climatic tolerances, improved host finding ability, changes in host preference, improved synchronization with the host, insecticide resistance, non-diapause, and induction of thelytokous reproduction, but to date none of these genetically manipulated natural enemies has been used in the field. Several current projects also are in progress and planned field trials will determine whether use of genetically manipulated insect natural enemies can be implemented in agricultural ecosystems. Aphytis melinus. a parasite of the California red scale, has been selected for resistance to carbaryl and the resistance level achieved appears to be sufficiently high that field trials are justified to evaluate this strain's efficacy in California citrus orchards. The walnut aphid parasite Trioxys pallidus, has been selected for resistance to azinphosmethyl, and this strain was tested in California walnut orchards during the 1988 growing season. If *A. melinus* and *T. pallidus* are able to establish, survive, parasitize their hosts, and successfully overwinter, then genetic improvement may be documented to be effective with insect parasitoids as well as with predatory mites.

Among the organisms associated with termites, the most numerous and least studied are the mites (Acari). Mites are commonly seen in termite colonies. Some mites are only incidentally found in termite nests, while others are obligate associates.

Generally, most mites associated with termites were considered saprophagous or phoretic. These mites do not have any signiûcant effect on the health of their termite hosts in nature. Few mites feed on termites. Some, such as Acotyledon formosani Phillipsen and Coppel, a species that should be assigned to the genus Australhypopus, are abundant in weak termite colonies and cause death.

The phoretic instar or deutonymph of A. formosani appeared to negatively affect a large laboratory colony of Coptotermes formosanus Shiraki by fastening primarily to termite heads and mouthparts, thereby impeding normal feeding. Conversely, termite-associated mites may beneût the termites by scavenging on other arthropods or fungi. Despite the abundant and diverse mite fauna existing with termites, little is known for their diversity, biology, ecology, and the nature of their associations.

Termites have been recorded as being parasitized by various species of nematodes. Some of these nematodes caused mortality to termite hosts in laboratory observations. Mermis sp. and Neosteinernema longicurvicauda Nguyen and Smart may kill their termite hosts upon emergence. However, their rate of parasitism apparently is very low and has been recorded only by the above authors. There is little information on the abundance of species of nematodes associated with termites.

MATERIALS AND METHODS

Collection and Maintenance of Termites

Reticulitermes flavipes and *R. virginicus* were collected in mixed forests in Washington county, and in loblolly pine (*Pinus taeda L.*) forests in Pearl River and Harrison counties in Mississippi.

They were kept in cylindrical plastic containers (15.5 cm diameter, 4 cm deep) with 1-2 cm deep vermiculite and sand (1:1 by volume). Corrugated cardboard and/or pine wood blocks were added as food. One hundred to 2,000 individuals were collected from each termite colony. At least 15 colonies of each species were collected from each of the three counties during the period of October, 1998-August, 2000.

Samples from ten *C. formosanus* colonies were collected from pine wood bait buried near trees in a university campus in the city of Guangzhou, China, in August 1999. One sample of *C. formosanus* colony was collected from a pine stump in the city of Cenxi, Guangxi, China. Two *C. formosanus* samples were collected from the cardboard bait buried in a city park in New Orleans, Louisiana on 15 June 1999 and 17 August 1999, respectively. Each *C. formosanus* sample had over 2,000 individuals. The termite colonies were kept for a maximum period of 120 day from field collection date at room temperature (21-25°C) in the laboratory.

Termites (number varied depending on purpose of the observation) from each colony were checked for mites and nematodes under a dissecting microscope (70-400×). To examine the density of Laelaptonyssus n.sp. (Laelaptonyssidae), 300 termites (workers and soldiers) were examined from each of the three colonies sampled from Washington County (total n = 900). The Termites were kept in the laboratory up to 30 d before examination. We assumed that the mites and nematodes associated with termites remained on/inside the termite body after the termites were transferred to the laboratory. General collections of mites were made by putting termites in 70 per cent ethanol and immediately examining the location and number of mites.

The mites dislodged slowly from termite body once submerged in 70 per cent ethanol. To check for nematodes, termites were dissectedwith two No. 3 insect pins and the specimens washed with a drop of water so the nematodes could be seen in suspension. White traps were used to extract adult nematodes from termites. Ten white traps were made.

Temporal Changes

Each trap consisted a 90 × 15 cm petri dish and a 5 cm diameter moist ûlter paper disk resting on a platform. The temporal changes in abundance of mites and nematodes were examined from one laboratory reared R. ûavipes colony. The colony (about 5,000 individuals) was collected in a forest in Washington Co., Mississippi and maintained in a plastic box (31 × 24 × 11 cm) with 5 cm deep sand and pieces of corrugated cardboard. Twenty to 120 workers were examined weekly. We also checked weekly for presence of adult nematodes in the rearing medium and around dead termites using a dissecting microscope.

To examine the relationship between the abundance of mites and nematodes, the same individuals of R. ûavipes and *R. virginicus* were examined for both mites and nematodes. They were first checked using a dissecting microscope formite densities, then they were put on a glass slide and dissected to check for presence of nematodes.

Nematodes and mites from *C. formosanus* were examined from different individuals. Termites had been kept in the laboratory for 60-80 day at examination date since collection.

Effect of *Australhypopus* sp. on *R. flavipes*

The most abundant mite in Reticulitermes colonies was an undescribed species in the genus Australhypopus (Acaridae). The only species currently placed in this genus is the type-species, *A. flagellifer.* Scientists described from deutonymphs collected from feces of a numbat, *Myrmecobius fasciatus* Waterhouse, a termitophagous marsupial, in Western Australia.

Examination of type material it indicates that three other termitophilous acarid species should also be placed in this genus: *Acotyledon formosani Phillipsen* and Coppel, A. lishimei Samsinák, and *Tyroglyphus viduus* Berlese and Leonardi.

In our laboratory colonies of both species of Reticulitermes, when dead termites were present there were enormous numbers of *Australhypopus* sp. This mite was propagated by mixing dead termites (killed by freezing) with healthy termites.

The termites were then placed in cylindrical plastic containers (15.5 cm diameter, 4 cm deep) with 1 cm deep vermiculite and sand as rearing medium and corrugated cardboard as food. Termites were kept at room temperature (21-25°C). Large numbers of adults and nymphs of *Australhypopus* sp. were present 15 day later and were harvested by brushing them from the inside surface of the container into a small round plastic container (5.0 cm diameter, 3.5 cm deep) filled with 0.01 per cent Triton X-100 (wetting agent) (Sigma-Aldrich, Inc.) fluid.

Mite density was determined. Mites (in feeding stages) were then transferred to 100 × 15 mm petri dishes with 40 healthy termite workers per dish and a corrugated cardboard disk at rate of five and ten mites per worker (200 and 400 mites per dish, respectively) using a 5 ml pipet.

A total of 5 ml solution was added to each dish. The mites evenly dispersed soon after being transferred to the dishes. The experiment was a completely random design with each treatment rate was replicated three times. The control dishes received only 0.01 per cent Triton X-100 solution. All of the replicates were from the same termite colony. Dishes were kept at 26°C, 85 per cent RH in a dark chamber. Observations for termite mortality were made every seven day for five week.

CHAPTER – 6

Acarines As Biocontrol Agents

ACARINA FOR BIOLOGICAL CONTROL OF PHYTOPHAGOUS MITES

Ixodidae

Dermacentor variabilis (Say), American dog tick.— This species is widely distributed in the U.S. east of the Rocky Mountains, but is also found in California, Mexico and Canada. It causes irritation to dogs and sometimes to livestock. Its greatest importance is as a vector of Rocky Mountain spotted fever in the Central and Eastern U.S., and is occasionally known to *vector tularemia.*

The life cycle may vary from one to three years. There is little activity during winter or in the warmest part of summer.

Adults are most active in the spring and may live more than two yrs without food. This is the only stage known to infest humans, dogs and domestic animals. Small mammals, especially mice and rabbits, are considered to be the main hosts. Mating occurs on the host. After becoming engorged, they drop from the host, and the females deposit their eggs in protected places in masses of 4,00-6,500 eggs after which the females die.

Eggs hatch into six-legged larvae, which attach to a passing host. After feeding for several days, they become engorged, drop to the ground and molt to the nymphal stage. When the nymph is ready to feed, it similarly seeks a host on which to attach. When the nymph has become engorged, it also drops to the ground where it molts to the adult stage. Both larvae and nymphs were observed to live over a year if food was not available.

In the U.S. a culture of the encyrtid parasitoid *Hunterellus ookeri* Howard (formerly *Ixodiphagus caucutei* du Buysson) was introduced from France where it was propagated and released on Naushon Island, Mass. Small numbers of nymphs of *D. variabilis* parasitized by the French strain of *H. hookeri* were released on Capers Island, SC. in 1931. A larger effort was made on Martha's Vineyard Island, Mass, where an estimated 90,000 females of *H. hookeri* were released in two locations on the island during 1937-39. The strain of parasitoid used originated in Texas.

In the season following the releases of *H. hookeri* on Naushon Island, immature parasitoids were found in a single nymph of the American dog tick and a single nymph of another tick species. In both a few *H. hookeri* were found, but none was recovered from the American dog tick. Both this species and Ixodes scapularis Say were still observed in abundance; therefore, there was no evidence that any success was achieved on the island.

Scientists reported recovery of the parasitoid from a single nymph of D. variabilis on Capers Island two yrs after release were made. In an assessment of results of releases of *H. hookeri* in Martha's Vineyard in 1937-39. No parasitoids from ticks in the release areas and observed no reduction in tick abundance that could be attributed to the parasitoid. A later report by scientists also indicates that the attempt was unsuccessful.

Natural Enemy Biology

Hunterellus hookeri is an internal parasitoid of wide distribution, having been recorded not only from North America but from Europe, Africa and South America. It was reared from several species of Dermacentor, Ixodes, Haemaphysalis, Thripece-phalus and Hyalomma.

The parasitoid oviposits in the body cavity of fed larvae and fed or unfed nymphs of the ticks. Oviposition may occur when the ticks are attached to the host animals. Apparently the parasitoids do not develop in the larvae or the unfed nymph, development proceeding after the nymph has become engorged.

Overwintering may thus occur in the unfed nymph, with the parasitoids emerging the following spring after the nymph ticks have engorged with blood. The nymphs show no signs of parasitism until sometime after feeding on the host animals is completed.

The period of development appears to be rather long. Scientists found that at 22°C. the average time from dropping of engorged nymphs from the host animal to emergence of adult parasitoids was two and half months.

A number of eggs is laid in a single host, and it was observed that more than one parasitoid may lay eggs in the same host. The parasitoid larvae seem to consume all of the contents of the body cavity of the host for successful transformation to the adult stage.

Therefore, the size of the adult is inversely proportional to the number in a single host. An average of ca. 20 parasitoids emerges from a single nymph of *Dermacentor andersoni* Stiles or *D. variabilis*, and the highest number observed by scientist was 73.

Dermacentor Andersoni Stiles, Rocky Mountain Wood Tick

This tick is a vector of Rocky Mountain spotted fever, a rickettsial disease that can be fatal to humans, but is primarily a disease of wild animals. It can also harbor tularemia, another disease primarily of wild animals but also infectious to humans. This tick is also responsible for tick paralysis, which affects the motor nerves starting in the legs and gradually spreading to the rest of the body. It results usually if the tick feeds at the back of the neck or the base of the skull, and removal of the tick usually results in recovery. The species occurs in the western U.S., primarily in the Rocky Mountains and also in Canada. Spotted fever occurs in other areas also, but its chief vector there is the American dog tick, *D. variabilis*.

Eggs of *D. andersoni* are deposited on the ground. They hatch in springtime or early summer into six-legged larvae and climb onto grass or other vegetation where they wait attachment to passing animals, usually small rodents. When fully fed in a few days, the larvae drop to the ground to molt to the nymphal stage, which usually does not feed until the following spring, when they attach to small animals, become engorged and drop to the ground to transform to the adult stage.

Although some adults may attach to hosts the same season, they seemingly pass the rest of the summer and winter in hiding and find a host the following spring. Mating takes place on the host, and when fully fed the female drops to the ground to deposit her eggs. Only the adult stage is known to attack humans and large animals.

Natural Enemies Sought

In the U.S. a culture of the encyrtid parasitoid H. hookeri Howard, originating in France was started in Montana for colonization against the Rocky Mountain wood tick. More than four million parasitoids were liberated during 1927-32, mostly in Montana but also in Colorado, Idaho and Oregon. Various methods were used, including release of adult parasitoids, scattering parasitized nymphs in grass and low vegetation, and liberating squirrels which had been infested with parasitized nymphs. The method of mass rearing the parasitoid on *D. andersoni* was described by Morton.

Only one instance of recovery occurred in 1929, when a few parasitoids emerged from *D. andersoni nymphs* taken from squirrels captured in the Bitter

Root Valley of Montana. No reduction in the tick population was observed and no evidence had been obtained that the parasitoids were established in nature.

ASSEMBLAGE OF SMALL ARTHROPODS

Mites and ticks (Acari) include a vast assemblage of small arthropods which rivals the Insecta in diversity of living habitats. They can be readily distinguished from insects by a reduction in segmentation, presence of four pairs of legs in adults, and the absence of compound eyes, antennae and wings. The Acari are separated into several subgroups, generally recognized at ordinal or subordinal rank. Three of these, the Astigmata, Mesostigmata and Prostigmata, include species that prey on or parasitize armored scale insects.

These species included within ten families may be divided into two functional groups: those for which biological data or claims for control are available and those which seem to be of lesser importance. These taxa are discussed separately, with families containing obligate or potentially important diaspidid parasites or predators considered first. Secondly, taxa occasionally associated with diaspidids and polyphagous predators will be mentioned. Finally, some mites which are often found in association with scale insects, but which do not appear to have any potential for control, will be noted.

Hemisarcoptidae

The Hemisarcoptidae (Astigmata) is a group of small, soft-bodied mites associated with arboreal habitats such as polypore fungi, vertebrate nests, and subcortical habitats. The family may be recognized in the female by the position of the ovipore between or behind coxal fields IV, in the male by the presence of a median sucker anterior to the genital region and in all feeding stages by the sucker-like pretarsi which lack empodial claws. Deutonymphs are characterized by the loss of pretarsi from legs IV, the reduction to a maximum of four setae of tarsi III-IV, and the presence of a single large pigment spot under the propodosomal ocelli.

The genus *Hemisarcoptes lignieres* is the only genus in this family associated with armored scale insects, but all known species of this genus are obligate parasites or predators of diaspidid scales.

Species of Hemisarcoptes have been known as important generalized predators of diaspidids for more than 100 yrs and are found on many genera of host scale insects. Hemisarcoptes alus (Shimer) was not only one of the first mites described from North America, but was also the first mite utilized in a biological control programme for insect pests. It is quite evident that the oyster-shell scale [*Lepidosaphes ulmi* (L.)] is in many places kept in check by mites. Of these mites, the most efficient was Hemisarcoptes malus. Similar claims regarding the same pest in Canada were made Hemisarcoptes were the most efficient predators of the date palm scale, *Parlatoria blanchardi* (*Targioni Tozzetti*) in the Sahel region of Niger, West Africa. Claims of relatively high rates of predation affecting other economically important diaspidids were summarized by scientists. A literature survey on the worldwide distribution of these mites shows non-specificity of diaspidid host preference. A surprising feature is that no records appear for one of the five major divisions of the Diaspididae, namely, the Odonaspidini. Regardless of the enthusiastic reports concerning Hemisarcoptes, very little data are available on their biology and potential for biological control. Problems include taxonomic uncertainties, scattered information on distribution and bionomics, apparent uneven predation performance in the field, and lack of publications on mass production techniques.

Taxonomic Ambiguities

Problems of misidentification and incomplete description are found in the literature on Hemisarcoptes. Scientist described the adults of the first species which he named "Acarus" malus, from Illinois. This species was apparently first noted in 1873 by the scientists, but mistook another mite for malus, and acrid mite of the genus Thyreophagus. This confusion most likely arose because these mites occur in association with many species of diaspidid scale insects, both are very small, and the general body forms are similar enough to be confused considering the optics of the era.

This misrepresentation of malus led to propose a new genus, Hemisarcoptes, for a species he described as H. coccisugus from France, while he regarded a species of what is now recognized as Thyreophagusas being identical with malus. The confusion of the genera Hemisarcoptes and Thyreophagus was recognized by the scientists who correctly aligned the European species of Lignieres (*H. coccisugus*) with its American cogener (*H. malus*).

All researchers after Michael have regarded the European *H. coccisugus* as synonymous with the American *H. malus* despite the lack of detailed study. Contemporary workers have also had to rely on erroneous illustrations to distinguish species of Hemisarcoptes. The species *H. coccophagus* Meyer, described from South Africa, and *H. dzhashii* Dzhibladze, described from Soviet Georgia, were distinguished from *H. malus* only on the basis of very schematic figures of *H. malus*. None of these species is recognizable on the basis of the original descriptions.

More confusion regarding Hemisarcoptes concerns the dimorphic life cycle of these and other free-living astigmatid mites. The deutonmyph (second nymphal instar, or hypopus) of these species is highly modified morphologically and disperses by phoretic association with other animals. These deutonymphs are so morphologically divergent from the other lifecycle stages that association between stages is only possible through rearing or collection of moulting deutonymphs. Deutonymphs of Hemisarcoptes were first positively identified by by the scientists in phoretic association with the coccinellid beetle, Chilocorus stigma (Say), in laboratory cultures in California.

The specific identity of these mites in uncertain. Deutonymphs of *H. coccophagus* from laboratory cultures and natural populations in Israel. These deutonymphs were associated with the coccinellid, *Chilocorus bipustulatus* (L.). A deutonymph collected from *Chilocorus cacti* (L.) in Texas, as *Vidia cooremani*. This species in the genus Hemisarcoptes. The adults of *H. cooremani* (Thomas) remain undescribed. The species-level systematics of Hemisarcoptes on a worldwide basis is currently under study.

Bionomics

Hemisarcoptes coccophagus is most abundant in the field in Israel during summer, although winter activity also occurs. Worldwide, Hemisarcoptes species seem to be quite resistant to extreme climatic conditions. In Canada *H. malus* is the major natural control agent of the oyster-shell scale during cold periods, as the mites may survive even when temperatures decrease to -34°C. The other major natural enemy in these areas, the aphelinid wasp, *Aphytis mytilaspidis* (LeBaron) is killed at -25°C. Observations on H.malus in New York by Houck & O'Connor indicate that egg production continues throughout the winter. In the other extreme, *Hemisarcoptes coccophagus* acted as "a most efficient predator" of date palm scale in the hot, dry climate of the Sahel region of Niger, while Chilocorus bipustulatus, which was introduced to control the pest, was rendered ineffective by the unusually harsh environment.

Freshly laid *H. coccophagus* eggs hatch within four to seven days at 21°C in the laboratory, and within 2-5 days at 28°C. Emerging larvae wander around the host scale avoiding strongly lighted sites, and settle down to feed. These usually progress through thee moults (to protonuymph, tritonymph and adult), feeding during each active stage. The adults mate and females produce an average of sixteen eggs. A complete life cycle uninterrupted by a deutonymphal stage, requires ca. 26-28 days at 21°C, and 15-17 days at 28°C. The sex ratio is ca. 2 females/male. Individual H. coccophaguswhich subsisted on insufficient food (i.e., moribund scales) as larvae or protonymphs went through a deutonymphal (hypopodial) stage in their development which was consequently quite prolonged.

The deutonymphs, which also serve to disperse the species, survived for two to three weeks in the laboratory at 22°C under saturation conditions. In cultures of *H. malus* grown by scientists, deutonymphs have never been produced in one year and six months of continuous culture even though the scale hosts were allowed to completely desiccate. Since deutonymphs of *H. malus* do occur in field populations, they may be rare, or their appearance may require chemical or mechanical stimulation by the scale-piercing behaviour of the Chilocorus beetles upon which the deutonymphs are phoretic.

The deutonymph of *H. coccophagus* may be seen wandering among scale insect colonies, but it is most commonly encountered on *Chilocorus bipustulatus* in israel. Occurrence on the beetles followed a seasonal trend, peaking in late summer. By that time most beetles examined carried some deutonymphs, with an average of over 30 per beetle (max. 202). The deutonymphs lack mouthparts and do not harm the beetles, although heavily-laden Chilocorus appeared somewhat sluggish. Deutonymphs were evenly distributed on male and female beetles, indicating a similar attraction. This was later confirmed by choice-chamber experiments, which also demonstrated strong vector attraction for the deutonymphs, as 84.7 per cent of all mites moved towards the Chilocorus containing cells. Species of Chilocorus are also predators of diaspidids, with the various beetle species attacking a wide range of scale insect taxa.

The potential for defining the full geographic range for Hemisarcoptes can be evaluated in terms of the known ranges of the phoretic partner as indicated above. The affinity of emisarcoptes deutonymphs for Chilocorus beetles has been demonstrated by examination of museum collections of these and related beetle species. Scientists have examined specimens of 29 of the known species of Chilocorus in American museums, with 12 of these species yielding collections of Hemisarcoptes. Examination of their scale-feeding beetles has yielded only one non-Chilocorus host for these mites, the related chilocorine species Axion tripustulatum. The only other reported host for these deutonymphs is the coccinellid *Zagloba ornata* Casey, and this record is from laboratory cultures.

Distribution

Hemisarcoptes species distribution may be estimated from the literature and records of mite deutonymphs obtained from museum collections. Knowledge of actual species distributions is encumbered by problems of identification. On the basis of specimens examined by scientists, *Hemisarcoptes malus* is regarded as widely distributed in North America, probably corresponding to the range of its phoretic host, *Chilocorus stigma*. *Hemisarcoptes cooremani* is probably parapatric with *H. malus*, with a known range extending from southern Texas and California south through Honduras in association with Chilocorus cacti. In the old world, the only recognizable species is *H. coccophagus*. This species has been verified from southern Europe (Spain), North Africa and the Middle East in association with Chilocorus bipustulatus and from eastern and southern Africa associated with *C. distigma* (Klug).

Collections of Hemisarcoptes deutonymphs from other areas in western North America, Africa, India, Indonesia and the Philippines represent undescribed species. The specific identity of central European Hemisarcoptes remains questionable pending the examination of specimens. No deutonymphs have as yet been recovered from Chilocorus bipustulatus nor *C. renipustulatus* (Scriba) from this area.

Also, the identity of Hemisarcoptes reported from South America must be reexamined. There are no species of Chilocorus native to this region, although *Ç. bipustulatus* has been introduced, probably from Europe, and is now widespread. There is a possibility that South American and European populations may be conspecific. Hemisarcoptes species are not yet reported from Japan or China, despite the diversity of species of Chilocorus in these areas. A large series of Japanese Chilocorus were examined without obtaining any Hemisarcoptes, although future collecting in these areas may reveal their presence. However, the absence of Hemisarcoptes from the Australian region may be predicted on the basis of the absence of Chilocorus species from that area.

Field Investigations

There have been no controlled experimental studies published concerning the field potential for biological control of scale insects using Hemisarcoptes. The uneven field performance of these mites has been noted by several authors. Researchers reported them to attack from 1-100 per cent of the white peach scale, *Pseudaulacaspis pentagona* (Targioni Tozzetti), in Bermuda. More than 70 per cent of one population of the California red scale, *Aonidiella aurantii* (Maskell) were attacked by *H. coccophagus* in Israel, but that this rate dropped to ca. 20 per cent later. Mite parasitism rates of 42-66 per cent on the San Jose scale, *Quadraspidiotus perniciosus* (Comstock), in California during certain months, but scarcity or absence during others. Some of this variance in predation might be due to variable occurrence of mite predators (e.g., *Cheletomimus berlesei* Oudemans), slow dispersal rate of mobile stages, undetermined responses to chemical sprays, and seasonal shifts in temperature and moisture conditions.

When living under optimal physical conditions and without chemical assault, as in laboratory populations of diaspidids, Hemisarcoptes mites may reduce population growth and actually endanger these scale cultures.

Hemisarcoptes species usually occur in the field on or under ovipositing scale insects which may still continue to produce progeny. Both female scale insects and their eggs are fed upon, although crawlers, second instar nymphs and prepupal male scale insects may also be less frequently parasitized. Feeding mites (usually more than one per scale) tend to take up the body color of their hosts. For example, Hemisarcoptes malus is bright purple on *Lepidosaphes beckii* (Newmann), red on *Epidiaspis leperii* (Signoret), and yellow on *Quadraspidiotus juglansregiae* (Comstock). This coloration often makes them difficult to locate.

Regarding control potential, the effect of Hemisarcoptes species on their host scale insects appears to be cumulative; i.e., parasitized scale insects continue to deposit at least some eggs. The following general rule to female scale insects parasitized by *H. coccophagus* when fewer than five mites developed on a single host, its fecundity would be reduced. A scale insect attacked by five to 10 mites would fail to produce any progeny, while the feeding of more than 10 mites usually causes the death of the host. Scale insect species, size, age and sex, as well as mite species, may modify this generalization.

The efficacy of Hemisarcoptes as biological control agents of scales was verified by two introduction projects. The apparent absence of these mites from western Canada suggested that they could be used there to control the oystershell scale. Introductions of *H. malus* from eastern Canada began in 1917, and 23 years later the mite was widely distributed and at times important in British Columbia.

This a successful biological control attempt. The other project took place in Bermuda, follow·ıg an outbreak of *Lepidosaphes newsteadi* on cedar trees. Several natural enemies were introduced against this pest, including *Hemisarcoptes malus*. The mites were introduced as deutonymphs on the bodies of 235 coccinellid beetles, mostly *Chilocorus* spp. and were subsequently found to attack the purple scale, *Lepidosaphes beckii* on citrus.

Hemisarcoptes mites are susceptible to many common pesticides. Sulfur and winter oil were quite detrimental to the mite, but DDT, lead arsenate, nicotine sulfate or summer oils had little effect under field conditions in Canada. Researchers who had to eliminate Hemisarcoptes from their laboratory cultures of diaspidids, used the acaricide Neotran with success.

Mass Production

Mass and individual mite rearing methods were described by large numbers of *H. coccophagus* were produced by growing diaspidids on potato tubers at 80 per cent RH and colonizing them with deutonymphs obtained from elytra of *Chilocorus bipustulatus*. Observations on individual mites were made possible by substituting the scale insects' shields with artificial covers. These consisted of a small amount of collodion dissolved in isoamyl-acetate.

A few drops of the resultant solution were placed on a smooth surface, and upon drying were used to cover young female scale insects whose original shields had been removed. Only a small aperture was left open, through which mites or their eggs were introduced. Use of the artificial shield made direct observations on these mites possible.

Under certain conditions, especially when they are the only active natural enemies, Hemisarcoptes species may be important control factors of armored scale insects. However, this implies that they are not very efficient in the presence of other predators and parasites. The diversity of species of Hemisarcoptes, their close association with Chilocorus beetles, and their restriction to diaspidid hosts imply a relatively long evolutionary association among members of this community. Therefore, it is not surprising that the mites appear to be better adapted for coexisting with their diaspidid hosts than for killing them directly, since such long associations often tend toward reduced pathogenicity of the parasite.

This evolutionary trend might also explain why scales parasitized by Hemisarcoptes normally produce at least some progeny, ensuring hosts for the progeny of the mites. However, deductions based on the natural biology of the mite Chilocorus community may not be valid in managed agroecosystems. Unpredictable performance, as has been reported for Hemisarcoptes, upsets control schedules and introduces unknown factors, detracting from the mites' potential for biological control. Future studies should strive to better understand Hemisarcoptes control performance in such managed systems. A sound systematic base is an obvious prerequisite; some of the unpredictability in prior studies may have resulted from the interaction or succession of more than one species.

Camerobiidae

The Camerobiidae (Prostigmata) are a small family of mites with long, "stilted" legs, a ventrally directed gnathostoma, weak palpi and looped peritremes. Species in one genus, Neophyllobius, have been reported to feed on diaspidid crawlers.

The crawlers subsequently relax and allow their body juices to be sucked out. These observations, reporting that nymphs and adults of *N. ambulans* Meyer fed on crawlers of the California red scale, Aonidiella aurantii, but not on settled scale insects.

The predator appeared to be rather scarce on South African citrus trees, and therefore Meyer noted that it was probably of no economic importance in natural control of red scale. A different opinion was by scientist who believed that a species of Neophyllobius was the principal predator of *Quadraspidiotus ostreaeformis* (Curtis) in New Zealand.

The mites were very common wherever the scale insect was abundant, but no crawlers were actually observed consumed. In the laboratory the predatory mites were seen with their mouthparts inserted in adult scales, sucking them dry. The mites appeared to be injecting some relaxing chemical into prey, as the latter did not struggle.

Cheyletidae

The majority of the prostigmatid family Cheyletidae are free-living predators, while others are ectoparasites of birds, mammals or rarely insects. Free-living cheyletids are slow-moving, yellow or orange and usually ambush prey. The morphological characteristic best defining the Cheyletidae is the prominent palpal thumb-claw complex, with the palptarsus bearing strong sickle and/or comb-like setae. These mites often occur on plants, and several species have been observed to feed on diaspidid crawlers. *Cheletogenes ornatus* was observed feeding on crawlers in many parts of the world. The role of this predator in citrus groves in Israel. The mite was reared in plaster-of-Paris cells and fed crawlers of the chaff scale, *Parlatoria pergandii* Comstock. Females deposited a dozen eggs throughout their lives under these conditions. Egg development took ca. ten days, the larva and two nymphal instars another 47 days, and each molt required 2.5 days, total immature development taking 64 days. Oviposition started after another 25 days, indicating the total egg to egg cycle was about three months at 28°C. During this study, female mites consumed an average of 90 crawlers during their adult lives, which lasted an average of 43 days.

Cheletogenes ornatus was reared on eggs of the olive scale, *Parlatoria oleae* (Colvee). It was reported that the predator's complete development took about 25 days at 29°C. Mites in that study produced an average of 16.8 eggs per female, and each female consumed ca. 170 scale insect eggs (males 125) and lived for 16.6 days.

Such differences in life cycle parameters obtained in the two laboratory studies of this mite have also been reported for other species. Female survival is dependent on the ambient RH, and at 28ºC, mites kept at 0 per cent RH lived only three days, with the survival time at 21, 50 and 80 per cent RH being 12.5, 14.5 and 26 days, respectively. Starved females (at high RH and 28ºC) survived an average of 16 days (range 1-33).

Exposure of *C. ornatus* females to citrus leaves dipped in several pesticides showed that the fungicide zineb had little effect on mite survival. The acaricide chlorobenzilate, however, was very toxic, causing almost total mortality 24 h post-treatment. Field studies indicated that this predator was much more common on citrus bark (where diaspidids flourish) than on leaves or fruit. Mite numbers were usually low during winter, rising in summer and peaking during autumn. These observations, along with the laboratory data noted above, indicate that *C. ornatus* has two summer generations on citrus in Israel. Reproduction ceases during winter, probably in connection with female diapause.

Available information indicates that *C. ornatus* has a low rate of increase, a pronounced winter ebb and is difficult to rear in the laboratory. But it is a hardy species capable of survival under adverse conditions, and it is also the dominant acarine predator of armored scale insects on citrus.

Eutogenes africanus Wafa & Soliman consumed an average of 186 and 156 eggs of *Parlatoria oleae*, respectively. The life cycle at 29°C required ca. 31 days, and each female deposited an average of sixteen eggs. Other cheyletids observed feeding on armored scale insect crawlers in the field include *Hemicheyletia bakeri* (Ehara) which feeds on the yellow scale, *Aonidiellacitrina* (Coquillett) in Florida and *Cheletominum berlesei* (Oudemans) on the latania scale, *Hemiberlesialataniae* (Signoret) in California and on *Parlatoria* spp in Israel. *Cheletominus berlesei* has also been observed feeding on Hemisarcoptes mites associated with *Lepidosaphes beckii* in California, with numbers of Hemisarcoptes negatively correlated with Cheletominum density. Additional cheyletid species, some as yet undescribed were observed to feed on various diaspidids on fruit trees in New Zealand and the Cook Islands.

Eupalopsellidae

This family of prostigmatid mites is characterized by very long palpi and chelicerae, a rather reduced palpal thumb-claw complex and the modification of the pretarsal empodia into two pairs of capitate raylets. Species in two genera are known to feed on diaspidids.

Saniosulus nudus Summers is an active predator of crawlers of *Parlatoria* spp. on citrus in Israel. The prey is held by the mite's anterior legs as the predator inserts its cheliceral stylets into the crawler's body. Feeding may proceed for 30-40 min until the dried prey remains are pushed off the chelicerae. All active stages of this species feed on diaspidid eggs and crawlers. Second-stage nymphs and adults are also attacked but do not appear to be seriously affected.

Observations once a month in a citrus grove indicated that populations of *S. nudus* on bark peaked during late summer and then declined. These mites have been subsequently observed feeding on various other species of diaspidids in Israel. The species was experimentally cultured on Florida red scale, *Chrysompha lusaonidum* (L.), reared on green lemon fruits.

The generation time of *S. nudus* was ca. three weeks at 24°C and two weeks at 28°C, the latter being less than half the time required for diaspidid generations. Each female produced 40-50 eggs, regardless of prior mating. Copulation itself is rather prolonged, with the female dragging the male around behind her. if introduced into laboratory cultures of armored scale insects, *S. nudus* may affect them to the extent that control measures must be implemented.

Eupalopsis maseriensis (Canestrini & Fanzago) has also been collected from citrus bark in Israel. It is a rare predator, whose feeding habits are similar to those of *S. nudus*.

Phytoseiidae

This family among free-living mesostigmatid mites is characterized by having 20 or fewer pairs of dorsal setae. Some species are efficient predators of phytophagous mites and have been intensively studied. Several species of Phytoseiidae were collected near armored scale insects but their role in such communities is uncertain.

Typhlodromus baccetti Lombardini was a constant associate of juniper scales, *Carulaspis* spp., in Tuscany, Italy. Mites gain access under the scales' shields, where they feed on the eggs. The predator overwinters as an egg, matures in May and undergoes two summer generations.

It was considered a scale-insect predator of some importance. Other phytoseiid species have been observed to feed, oviposit and complete their lifecycles when offered diaspidid crawlers as food in the laboratory. Whether such diets are also used in the field, and to what extent, remains unknown.

Two of the main areas in which parasitic fungi are beneficial to man are in the use of fungi to control pests and in the prevention of herbivory in plants.

Biocontrol of Pests

Biocontrol is the reduction of the amount of inoculum or disease producing activity of a pathogen accomplished by or through one or more organisms other than man. Biocontrol uses natural or modified organisms, genes or gene products to reduce the effects of undesirable pests and to favor desirable organisms such as crops, trees, animals and beneficial insects and microorganisms. The prime tactics used in biocontrol involve:

(a) modifying cultural practices to favor antagonistic plant pathogens;

(b) introducing antagonists of plant pathogens into the environment or onto the plant; and

(c) inoculate the plant with incompatible or hypovirulent organisms.

Fungi to Control Plant Diseases

Two yeasts have been pinpointed that produce killer toxins that block the growth of other yeasts. The yeast, *Pichia inositovora* and *P. acaciae*, have been shown to produce antifungal cytotoxic proteins that will inhibit the growth of a number of other yeasts. This phenomenon has been put to work where toxins of Kluyveromyces lactis fights against unwanted yeasts that may contaminate fermenting "sake" or rice wine.

Species of Trichoderma are used to control root diseases of many crops, stem blight of peanuts, dry bubble on mushrooms, and silverleaf of plums,Verticillium to control cotton wilt, Sphaerellopsis to control rust diseases on a number of plants, and several others. These belong to an array of mycofungicides. Prime examples of some are given below:

Chestnut blight, caused by the perithecial fungus *Cryphonectria parasitica*, entered the U.S. on European chestnut timber brought into lumber mills in New England. The fungus was extremely virulent to North American chestnuts that had never been exposed to the fungus.

Chestnuts were then the dominant hardwood lumber tree in this country. The pathogen spread first into New York, being first detected on chestnuts at the New York Botanical Garden in 1904. It soon spread throughout the range of the American chestnut into the southern Smoky Mountains where by 1935 essentially all trees had been killed

Biocontrol of Insects

The knowledge of entomogenous fungi dates back for several centuries. Numerous groups of entomogenous fungi were described during the 19th century. Pasteur, however, was one of the first to suggest that microorganisms could be used to control insect pests. Extensive research on the use of Beauvaria to controlchinch bugs in Kansas had mixed success. One of the earliest successes in biocontrol was the use of Aschersonia aleyrodes to control citrus white flies in Florida. More than three decades ago, Rachael Carson's Silent Springs pointed out the dangerous effects of a number of our most effective pesticides. This eventually led to the prohibition of the use of chlorinated hydrocarbons as insecticides. Her book sparked considerable interest in finding alternative ways of controlling insects.

By the 1960s there were a number of attempts for the commercial production of fungi for biological control. Close to 750 species of entomogenous fungi had been identified by the 1980s. Almost all of the major groups of fungi have entomogenous species, many of them have been used as mycoinsecticides.

Quite a number of insects can be controlled with fungi; these include the cabbage loopers (Fig. 6.1) in which the body cavity becomes overwhelmed with spores (Fig. 6.2).

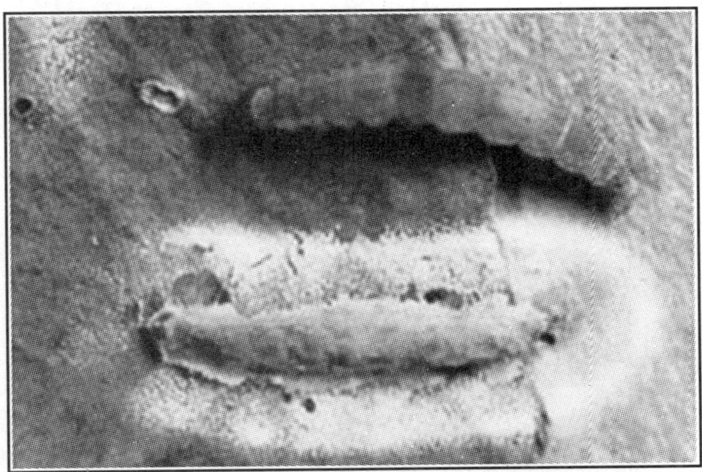

Fig. 6.1: **The Control of Cabbage Loopers with the Fungus *Noumorea rileyi***

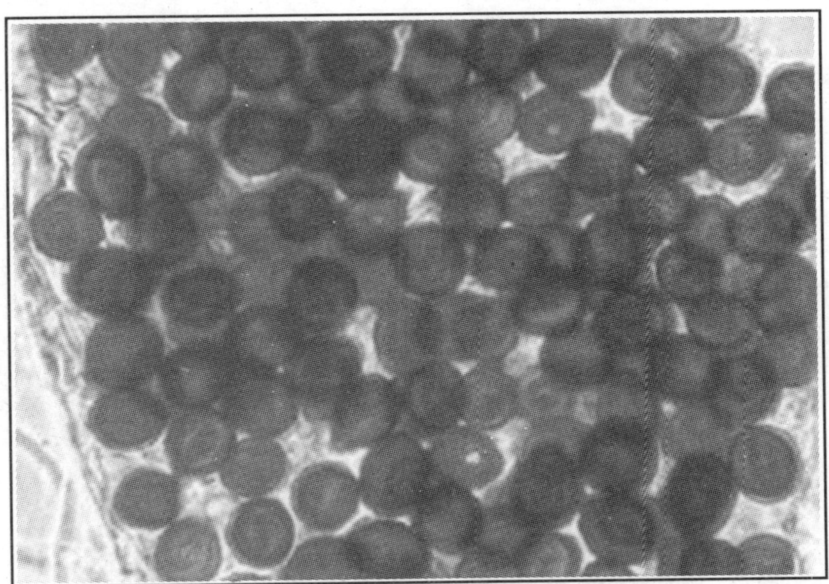

Fig. 6.2: **Insect Cavity Filled with Fungal Spores**

Species of Cordyceps that infects the larvae of many beetles and moths (Fig. 6.3), even those deeply embedded in the soil (Fig. 6.4).

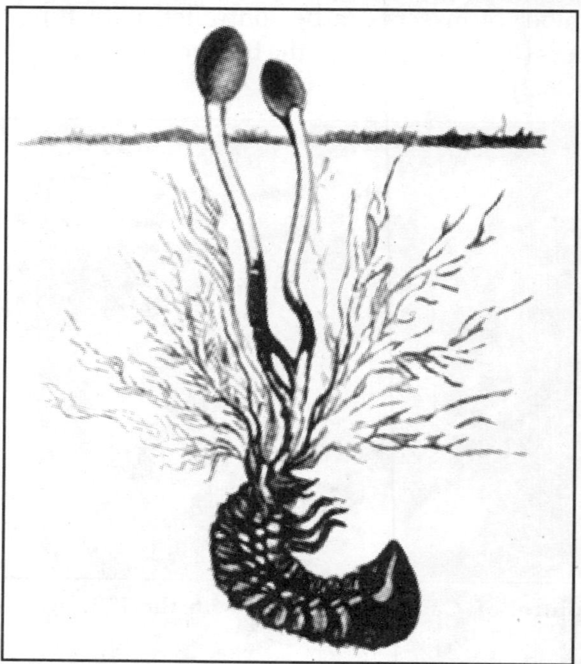

Fig. 6.3: **An Insect Larva Infected with Aspecies of Cordyceps**

Fig. 6.4: **Insect Larvae with Several Perithecialstroma**

Species of Zoophora on flies; Stilbella on weevils (Fig. 6.5).

Fig. 6.5: **A Weevil Highly Infected with Stilbella**

Hirsutella on the larva of a citrus mite,Paecilomyces on beetle larvae (Fig. 6.6), and species of Beauvaria (Fig. 6.7) that will infect a large number of insects.

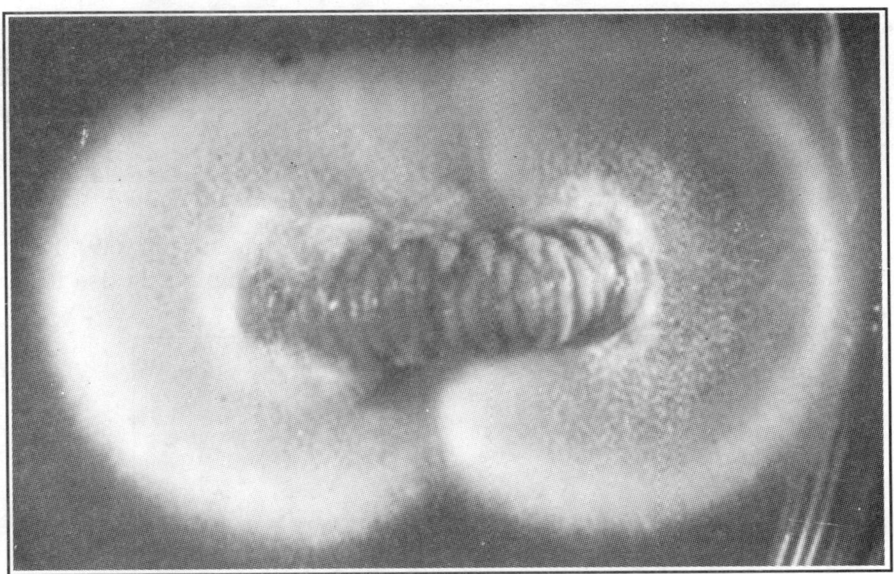

Fig. 6.6: **Colonies of Paecilomyces Variotiigrowing out of a Beetle Larva**

Fig. 6.7: **Beauvaria Bassiana Infecting a Weevils**

In Florida, species of Aschersonia commonly infects citrus white flies and Noumorea on soybean looper (Fig. 6.8).

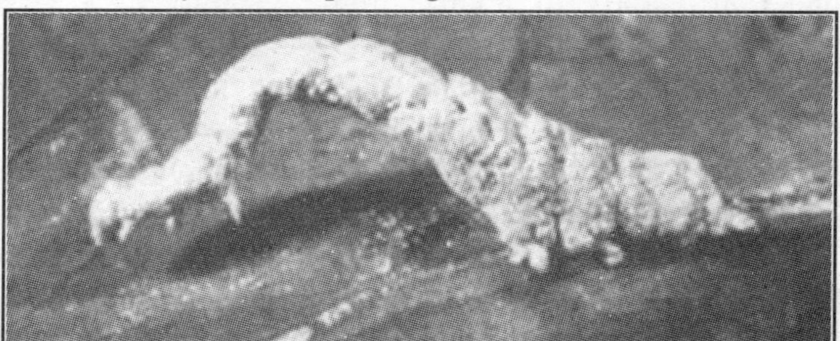

Fig. 6.8: **Noumorea Rileyi Infecting a Soybean Looper**

Species of Metarrhizium infects a number of insects (Fig. 6.9), forming long chains of spores (Fig. 6.10); a feature that has enabled its use in novel roach traps using the fungus rather than chemicals.

Fig. 6.9: **A Beetle Larva Infected with a Species of Metarrhizium**

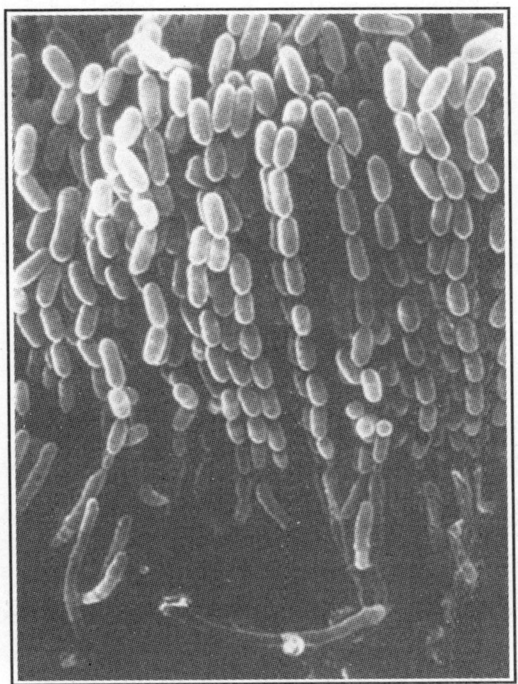

Fig. 6.10: **Chains of Conidia Characteristic of Metarrhizium**

The use of a fungus in roach traps is superior to chemical use because chemicals will kill only the insects that enter the chamber; whereas, insects that become infected with Metarrhizium will carry the fungus to their hiding places and infect their neighbors. Isn't that neat?

One of the most puzzling problems in insect control has been the control of mosquitoes. Mosquitoes have long been of concern to people because their bites are painful and they transmit some of our most important diseases. Dr. John Couch and his students and colleagues at the University of North Carolina spent several years on studies of species of the aquatic fungus Coelomomyces that infects mosquitoes. After exhaustive research projects, they were never able to reinfect healthy mosquitoes with zoospores released from infected ones. It was not until the studies of Dr. Howard Whisler at the University of Washington that the answer came. Whisler found that Coelomomyces washeteroecious, i.e. a species that requires two hosts on which to complete its life cycle. The primary hostof this fungus was mosquitoes and the alternate hostwas a small copepod. Zoospores released from the copepod fused to form a flagellated zygote that was capable of infecting mosquitoes (Fig. 6.11).

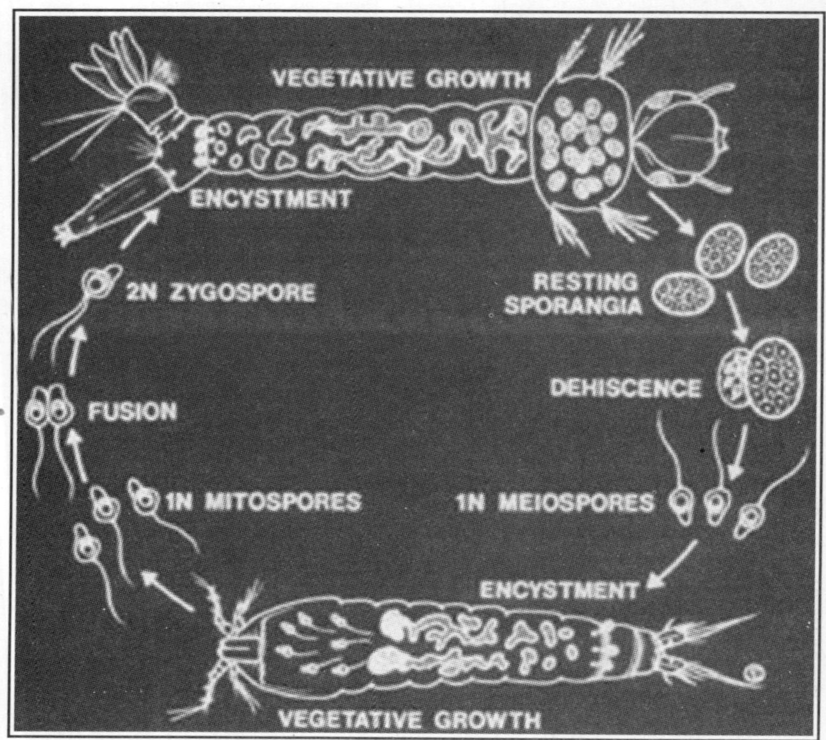

Fig. 6.11: **The Life Cycle of Coelomomyces Psorophora in Mosquitoes (top) and copepods (below).**

CONTROL OF TWO-SPOTTED SPIDER MITE

Spider Mite, Tetranychus Urticae Koch

The two-spotted spider mite (TSM), Tetranychus urticae (Koch), belongs to the family Tetranychidae. It is perhaps this species, which is the most economically important pest of the family affecting many field and greenhouse crops. The increase in the pest status of this mite can be linked to to the rise in large-scale use of chemical insecticides against insect pests which reduced natural enemies, there by causing a decline in predation pressure, which allowed the TSM numbers to increase.

Chemical pesticides have mostly been relied upon to control TSM populations; however, their continuous use has also resulted in pesticide resistance among TSM populations. The factors contributing to this are its great egg-laying potential, very short life cycle allowing numerous generations in a growing season, a high mutation rate. Besides the problem of pest resistance, there is also concern about the high residues and toxicity of common miticides to humans.

Agrochemical Control Measures

Concerns about the use of agrochemical control measures have led to search for alternative control measures to suppress TSM populations, including the use of biological control, particularly by applying predatory phytoseiid mites.

Nonetheless, the control provided by predatory mites is often insufficient and supplementary sprays with selective chemical acaricides have been required. The use of microbial control agents as part of an integrated pest management (IPM) strategy is likely to reduce the reliance on these chemical acaricides. Fungi of the genera *Neozygites* (Zygomycetes: Entomophthorales) are specific pathogens of TSM under natural conditions. However, artificial production of this fungus is reported to be difficult and therefore its application as an inundative biological pesticide is so far impracticable.

Members of the mitosporic (Hyphomycetes) entomo-pathogens are also promising microbial control agents against acari. These fungi invade the host by growing through the external cuticle, which is important for pests with sucking moutnparts such as TSM, which are less likely to acquire pathogens per os; they can be mass produced using low input technology; they can be formulated as myco-pesticides suitable for spraying using conventional chemical spraying equipment; and are less harmful to non-target arthropods and mammals and are therefore ideal for integrated pest management (IPM) programme strategies.

Unfortunately, there are very few research reports on successful utilization of these fungi against TSM, most having been developed and registered for use against insect pests.

Dry and Hot Environment

The most difficult problem facing TSM control with entomopathogenic fungi is that this mite generally occurs in dry and hot environments, which are unfavourable for the development of the entomopathogenic fungi. A second problem is that entomopathogenic fungi take some time to kill their hosts. Because of the short generation time of TSM and its high fecundity rate, this time delay in mycosis development may impede the short term efficacy of the entomopathogenic fungi.

Hence for their successful utilisation as myco-pesticides, other strategies such as high virulence and speed in killing, survival under a challenging environment, and compatibility with other control agents, are required.

Taking these strategies into account, the present thesis reports the work devoted to investigating the use of the Hyphomycetes *Beauveria bassiana* (Bb)

(Balsamo) Vuillemin as a biological control agent (BCA) against TSM. Several strains were screened in laboratory and greenhouse experiments for their virulence against the pest. Oil enhancers are known to protect fungal biocontrol agents from harmful environmental conditions and to enhance their activity at the target site.

CHAPTER – 7

Method of Bioassay

Bioassay or biological standardization is a type of scientific experiment. It is commonly used shorthand for biological assay, Bioassays are typically conducted to measure the effects of a substance on a living organism and are essential in the development of new drugs and in monitoring environmentalpollutants. Both are procedures by which the potency or the nature of a substance is estimated by studying its effects on living matter.

DEFINITION

"The determination of the relative strength of a substance (as a drug) by comparing its effect on a test organism with that of a standard preparation."

Purpose

- Measurement of the pharmacological activity of new or chemically undefined substances
- Investigation of the function of endogenous mediators
- Determination of the side-effect profile, including the degree of drug toxicity
- Measurement of the concentration of known substances (alternatives to the use of whole animals have made this use obsolete)
- Assessing the amount of pollutants being released by a particular source, such as wastewateror urban runoff.

Use

Bioassays are procedures that can determine the concentration of purity or biological activity of a substance such as vitamin, hormone and plant growth factor. While measuring the effect on an organism, tissue cells, enzymes or the receptor is preparing to be compared to a standard preparation. Bioassays may be qualitative or quantitative and Quantitative bioassays are typically analyzed using the methods of biostatistics.are used for assessing the physical effects of a substance that may not be quantified, such as abnormal development ordeformity.

An example of a qualitative bioassay includes Arnold Adolph Berthold's famous experiment on castrated chickens. This analysis found that by removing the testes of a chicken, it would not develop into a rooster because the endocrine signals necessary for this process were not available. Quantitative bioassays involve estimation of the concentration or potency of a substance by measurement of the biological response that it produces.

Types

Bioassays are of two types:

Quantal

A quantal assay involves an "all or none response". For example: Insulin induced hypoglycemic convulsive reaction or the cardiac arrest caused by digitalis. The response is either +ve or -ve , there is no intermediate response e.g. either convulsion occurs or doesn't occur; similarly is with cardiac arrest.

In case of toxicity studies, the animal receiving a dose of drug either dies or does not die. Also, no intermediate response is possible. This is also known as the "all or none" response assay. The quantal method though not accurate is employed for bioassay of substance in the following ways:

(a) Comparison of threshold response, or

(b) Comparison of effective dose (ED_{50}) or median lethal dose (LD_{50}).

Graded

Graded assays are based on the observation that there is a proportionate increase in the observed response following an increase in the concentration or dose.

The parameters employed in such bioassays are based on the nature of the effect the substance is expected to produce. *For example:* contraction of smooth muscle preparation for assaying histamine or the study of blood pressure response in case of adrenaline.

A graded bioassay can be performed by employing any of the below-mentioned techniques. The choice of procedure depends on:

1. the precision of the assay required.

2. the quantity of the sample substance available.
3. the availability of the experimental animals.

Techniques

1. Matching Bioassay
2. Interpolation Method
3. Bracketing Method
4. Multiple Point Bioassay (i.e., Three-point, Four-point and Six Point Bioassay)

Matching Bioassay

It is the most simple type of the bioassay. In this type of bioassay, response of the test substance taken first and the observed response is tried to match with the standard response. Several responses of the standard drug are recorded till a close matching point to that of the test substance is observed. A corresponding concentration is thus calculated. This assay is applied when the sample size is too small.

Since the assay does not involve the recording of concentration response curve, the sensitivity of the preparation is not taken into consideration. Therefore, precision and reliability is not very good.

Interpolation Bioassay

Bioassays are conducted by determining the amount of preparation of unknown potency required to produce a definite effect on suitable test animals or organs or tissue under standard conditions. This effect is compared with that of a standard. Thus the amount of the test substance required to produce the same biological effect as a given quantity the unit of a standard preparation is compared and the potency of the unknown is expressed as a % of that of the standard by employing a simple formula.

Many times, a reliable result cannot be obtained using this calculation. Therefore it may be necessary to adopt more precise methods of calculating potency based upon observations of relative, but not necessarily equal effects, likewise, statistical methods may also be employed. The data obtained from either of assay techniques used on which bioassay are based may be classified as quantal or graded response. Both these depend ultimately on plotting or making assumption concerning the from of DRC.

Environmental Bioassays

Those are generally a broad-range survey of toxicity. A toxicity identification evaluation is conducted to determine what the relevant toxicants are. Although bioassays are beneficial in determining the biological activity within an organism, they can often be time-consuming and laborious. Organism-specific factors may result in data that is not applicable to others in that species. For these reasons, other biological techniques are often employed.

Water pollution control requirements in the United States require some industrial dischargers and municipal sewage treatment plants to conduct bioassays. These procedures, called whole effluent toxicity tests, include acute toxicity tests as well as chronic test methods. The methods involve exposing living aquatic organisms to samples of wastewater.

Activated sludge is a biomass produced in raw or settled wastewater (primary effluent) by the growth of organisms in aeration tanks in the presence of dissolved oxygen. The term "activated" comes from the fact that the particles are teeming with bacteria, and protozoa. Activated sludge is different from primary sludge in that the sludge contains many living organisms which can feed on the incoming wastewater.

Activated Sludge Process

The activated sludge process is a wastewater treatment method in which the carbonaceous organic matter of wastewater provides an energy source for the production of new cells for a mixed population of micro-organisms in an aquatic aerobic environment. The microbes convert carbon into cell tissue and oxidized end products that include carbon dioxide and water. In addition, a limited number of microorganisms may exist in activated sludge that obtain energy by oxidizing ammonia nitrogen to nitrate nitrogen in the process known as nitrification.

The activated-sludge process is a biological method of wastewater treatment that is performed by a variable and mixed community of microorganisms in an aerobic aquatic environment. These microorganisms derive energy from carbonaceous organic matter in aerated wastewater for the production of new cells in a process known as synthesis, while simultaneously releasing energy through the conversion of this organic matter into compounds that contain lower energy, such as carbon dioxide and water, in a process called respiration. As well, a variable number of microorganisms in the system obtain energy by converting ammonia nitrogen to nitrate nitrogen in a process termed nitrification. This consortium of microorganisms, the biological component of the process, is known collectively as activated sludge.

Bacteria constitute the majority of microorganisms present in activated sludge. Bacteria that require organic compounds for their supply of carbon and energy (heterotrophic bacteria) predominate, whereas bacteria that use inorganic compounds for cell growth (autotrophic bacteria) occur in proportion to concentrations of carbon and nitrogen. Both aerobic and anaerobic bacteria may exist in the activated sludge, but the preponderance of species are facultative, able to live in either the presence of or lack of dissolved oxygen.

Fungi, rotifers, and protozoans are also residents of activated sludge. The latter microorganisms are represented largely by ciliated species, but flagellated protozoans and amoebae may also be present. Protozoans serve as indicators of the activated sluge condition, and ciliated species are instrumental in removing *Escherichia coli* from sewage. Additionally, viruses of human origin may be found in raw sewage influent, but a large percentage appear to be removed by the activated-sludge process.

The success of the activated-sludge process is dependent upon establishing a mixed community of microorganisms that will remove and consume organic waste material, that will aggregate and adhere in a process known as bioflocculation, and that will settle in such a manner as to produce a concentrated sludge (return activated sludge, or RAS) for recycling. Any of several types of activated sludge solids separations problems indicate an imbalance in the biological component of this process.

In the ideal "healthy" system, filamentous organisms grow within a floc (a large aggregate of adherent, or floc-forming, microorganisms, such as bacteria) and give it strength, with few filaments protruding out into the surrounding bulk solution. In such a system, there is no interference with the compaction and settling rates of the activated sludge prior to its recycling.

Main Goal

The overall goal of the activated-sludge process is to remove substances that have a demand for oxygen from the system. This is accomplished by the metabolic reactions (synthesis-respiration and nitrificaction) of the microorganisms, the separation and settling of activated-sludge solids to create an acceptable quality of secondary wastewater effluent, and the collection and recycling of microorganisms back into the system or removal of excess microorganisms from the system.

Aactivated-sludge process contains five essential interrelated equipment components. The first is an aeration tank or tanks in which air or oxygen is introduced into the system to create an aerobic environment that meets the needs of the biological community and that keeps the activated sludge properly mixed. At least, seven modifications in the shape and number of tanks exist to produce variations in the pattern of flow.

An aeration source is required to ensure that adequate oxygen is fed into the tank(s) and that the appropriate mixing takes place. This source may be provided by pure oxygen, compressed air or mechanical aeration. Just as there are modifications in the shape and number of aeration tanks that can be used in the activated-sludge process, different equipment systems exist to deliver air or oxygen into aeration tanks.

In the activated-sludge process, aeration tanks are followed by secondary clarifiers. In secondary clarifiers, activated-sludge solids separate from the surrounding waste water by the process of flocculation (the formation of large particle aggregates, or flocs, by the adherence of floc-forming organisms to filamentous organisms) and gravity sedimentation, in which flocs settle toward the bottom of the clarifier in a quiescent environment.

This separation leads ideally to the formation of a secondary effluent (wastewater having a low level of activated-sludge solids in suspension) in the upper portion of the clarifier and a thickened sludge comprised of flocs, termed return activated sludge, or (RAS), in the bottom portion of the clarifier.

Return activated sludge must be collected from the secondary clarifiers and pumped back to the aeration tank(s) before dissolved oxygen is depleted. In this way, the biological community needed to metabolize influent organic or inorganic matter in the wastewater stream is replenished.

Activated sludge containing an overabundance of microorganisms must be removed, or wasted [waste activated sludge, or WAS], from the system. This is accomplished with the use of pumps and is done in part to control the food-to-microorganism ratio in the aeration tank(s).

Biological Component of Sludge System

The biological component of the activated sludge system is comprised of microorganisms. The composition of these microorganisms is 70 to 90 per cent organic matter and 10 to 30 per cent organic matter. Cell makeup depends on both the chemical composition of the wastewater and the specific characteristics of the organisms in the biological community.

Bacteria, fungi, protozoa, and rotifers constitute the biological component, or biological mass, of activated sludge. In addition, some metazoa, such as nematode worms, may be present. However, the constant agitation in the aeration tanks and sludge recirculation are deterrents to the growth of higher organisms.

The species of micro-organism that dominates a system depends on environmental conditions, process design, the mode of plant operation, and the characteristics of the secondary influent wastewater. The microorganisms that are of greatest numerical importance in activated sludge are bacteria, which occur as microscopic individuals from one micron in size to visible aggregations or colonies of individuals.

Some bacteria are strict aerobes (they can only live in the presence of oxygen), whereas others are anaerobes (they are active only in the absence of oxygen). The preponderance of bacteria living in activated sludge are facultative—able to live in either the presence or absence of oxygen, an important factor in the survival of activated sludge when dissolved oxygen concentrations are low or perhaps approaching depletion.

STUDY OF BIOASSAY METHODS

The testing conditions of beneficial organisms (honeybee, silkworm and fishes) safety evaluation on pesticides were studied. The results of the various testes are listed:Honeybee: The methods of Pro-treatment, sugar concentration, experimentation utensil, filling substance, the methods of bioassay and surface-active agents, these testing conditions had were proved that effects were remarked. The other way round, fodders, the time of illumination and the place of dropping had hardly effects of the testing results.Though optimizing the testing result, bioassay methods of beneficial organisms evaluation safety on pesticides had come into being.

The concrete operation of this bioassay method: The collection honeybee is the best test insect. Four groups of 20~30 honeybees subjects each. Better pre-treatment method is low temperature or no-treatment. Fifty per cent cane sugar syrup or honey feed honeybee and feed toxicity. The culture utensil (d=12cm) or the gauze cage (d=9cm) serves as testing vessel. The testing filling is gauze. The temperature of recovery room must be controlled at 25°c and the illumination keep glimmering. The mortality will be registered after 96 hours. The topical application is dropping 1.75HL pesticides on the tergum of fro-thorax or abdomen.

Silkworm

Four pesticides had done the testes time after time. These testes included silkworm stadiums, the ages in days of two stadia and three stadia, the quantity of mulberry leafages that had were dipped pesticide, how long being the leafages of mulberry dipped pesticide, whether or not feeding silkworm before the test, the quantity of pesticide in culture utensil, the temperature of recovery room, bioassay methods, spring or harvest silkworm and the bioassay methods of osculatory toxicity.

All of this has remarkably affected the testing results.Though all testing data were assayed, we had the ascertained a suit of the rational bioassay methods of silkworm evaluation safety on pesticides. The operations of the bioassay method are as follows.The test insect is half-blooded silkworm; the sensitive period of silkworm on pesticide is the second age in day of the third stadium or the second age in day of the second stadium. The time of mulberry leafage ought control in three minutes. The quantity of poisonous mulberry leafage need attain 20-30 per cent avoirdupois of silkworm. The temperature of the recovery room keep at 25°c . Before testing, the silkworm mustn't feed about 10-12 hours. The culture utensil (d=9cm) adds 0.8mL pesticide when drug film is done. Each group includes ten silkworms and repeats 3 groups. Other the test result must be made out what spring silkworm or harvest silkworm is used in test.

The harvest silkworm is more sensitive than spring silkworm, but have some exception.Fishes: The leading fishes bioassay method evaluation safety on pesticides is half static feed in poisonous water. Though the testing results were found that the variation of fishes, aeration status, and the temperature of water had obviously affected the LC_{50}. The status of feeding and illumination hadn't effect for the LC_{50}.

CHAPTER – 8

Role of Entomologist

An entomologist is a zoologist who focuses specifically on the study of insects. Given that the insect world is vast and incredibly diverse, most entomologists focus on a specific order or family of insects. Careers in entomology are incredibly varied, ranging from forensic entomology to agricultural entomology. Numerous colleges and universities around the world offer training in entomology to people who are interested in this field of study.

Entomology is probably a very old science. Humans have had an interest in the insect world for centuries, thanks to agricultural pests and home invaders of the insect variety. Early entomologists probably learned to identify potential crop pests and to treat infestations of unwanted insects, and entomology was even involved in forensics at a fairly early state in human history. Many prominent scientists including Charles Darwin and E.O. Wilson were also entomologists.

There are a number of branches within entomology. Entomologists may look at insect behaviour, morphology, nutrition, and ecology. They can also study the ways in which insects interact with other animals and agricultural sites; such an entomologist might look at insect vectors of disease in humans, for example, or the impact of locusts on crops in the Middle East. Entomologists are also active in fields like paleontology, learning about the evolution of insects, and in forensics, using insects as tools to learn more about victims of crimes.

Entomology (from Greek *entomos*, "that which is cut in pieces or engraved/segmented", hence "insect"; and logia) is the scientific study of insects, a branch of arthropodology. At some 1.3 million described species, insects account for more than two-thirds of all known organisms, date back some 400 million years, and have many kinds of interactions with humans and other forms of life on earth.

It is a specialty within the field of biology. Though technically incorrect, the definition is sometimes widened to include the study of terrestrial animals in otherarthropod groups or other phyla, such as arachnids, myriapods, earthworms, land snails, and slugs.

Like several of the other fields that are categorized with inzoology, entomology is a taxon-based category; any form of scientific study in which there is a focus on insect related inquiries is, by definition, entomology. Entomology therefore includes a cross-section of topics as diverse as molecular genetics, behaviour, biomechanics, biochemistry, systematics, physiology, developmental biology, ecology, morphology, paleontology, anthropology, robotics, agriculture, nutrition, forensic science and more.

ENTOMOLOGY IN ART AND CULTURE

Gil Grissom on the CSI: Crime Scene Investigation (CSI) TV show is an entomologist, who is played by actor William Petersen. Similarly, entomologist Jack Hodgins of Bones, portrayed by TJ Thyne, helps his team by analyzing insects such as Hydrotaea and "particulates" near to or attached to decomposed victims, often identifying the precise location a murder originally occurred; he is also an expert in botany and mineralogy.

In Arthur Conan Doyle's story, *The Hound of the Baskervilles,* the villain is a naturalist who collects butterflies, making him an "evil" entomologist.

The Aubrey–Maturin sea novels of Patrick O'Brian have frequent appearances by Sir Joseph Blaine, a Royal Navy intelligence official who is also an avid entomologist. He recruits Dr. Stephen Maturin, one of the principal characters, as a spy. Their conferences on espionage activities invariably make room for their shared interest in naturalist studies.

There are numerous science fiction books which have plots based on humans becoming smaller and having to deal with insects at their level. Some examples are *The Insect Warriors* by Rex Dean Levie, *Atta* by Francis Rufus Bellamy, *Bug Park* by James P. Hogan, *The Micronauts series* by Gordon Williams, and The Forgotten Planet by Murray Leinster. *The Forgotten* Planets plot is twisted in that the insects are the size of men (or larger) on a planet "seeded" to prepare it for human habitation. Robert Asprin wrote *The Bug Wars,* a novel about war between reptiles and insects on an interplanetary scale.

There are quite a few films about insects, or at least prominently featuring them. Widespread attitudes of revulsion and fear toward insects are often exploited by Horror and Science Fiction films through insect/insect-like monsters (Them! is a famous early example), or by showing humans transformed into (The Fly) or attacked by insects. Another more positive type of insect film is animation withanthropomorphized insects as characters.

Study of Entomology

The study of entomology can provide interesting clues into the history of life on Earth, and it can also be used to make projections about the future. Entomologists can participate in a wide range of projects, ranging from genetically engineering insects which attack crop pests to looking at the role that insects play in the life cycles of many plants.

An entomologist who focuses on butterflies is known as lepidopterist, while one who studies bees is called an apiologist. A coleopterist studies beetles, while myrmecologists look at ants. There are several other broad fields like these within the study of entomology, and an entomologist may choose to focus on a specific subset of a field, like honeybees or dung beetles.

If you are interested in a career as an entomologist, you should start by getting a strong grounding in the sciences. If there is a particular subfield of entomology which interests you, try to get training in this field. Some entomologists accept interns, for example, while schools which offer entomology tend to have several programmes with specific focuses available.

Typically, entomologists attend both undergraduate and graduate institutions, and many of them pursue post-doctoral work as well. This field is incredibly vast and interesting, and you are unlikely to be bored as an entomologist.

FORENSIC ENTOMOLOGIST

Data Collection

Forensic entomologists are required to take copious amounts of data at the scene. An intense amount of time and energy go into to data collection because everything they collect and observe must hold up in the court of law. The first portions of information gathered include the climate of the area, both during the time of initial contact to within three to five days afterward. One to two weeks afterward may be required to estimate a rough post mortem interval.

Climate approximation is imperative for determining the specific life cycle of insects found at the scene. Good or harsh conditions will either speed up or slow down insect development which gives important information regarding how long the victim may have been decaying. In addition to climate, ambient air, soil (around and below the body), and maggot mass, temperatures are needed since they are essential to determining the speed of growth of the insects collected during the investigation. All documentation must be concise to avoid confusion. A death scene form is one of the most important tools a forensic entomologist has.

He or she can make note of many key observations quickly such as placement of the maggot mass on the body, temperatures, and stage of decay. The evidence must be able to pass through the "chain of evidence" (the process of using evidence legally in the judicial system) without fear of contamination, tampering, or any other outside variable that could affect its legitimacy during trial in a court of law.

Ten Basic Rules for Collection

Conditions vary when it comes to arthropod collection and sometimes local procedural regulations apply. However, Mark Benecke developed the following basic guidelines which are used by federal agents of the Federal Bureau of Investigation (FBI), the Bundeskriminalamt in Germany, and rookie forensic entomologists:

1. Take good close-up photos of all locations from which arthropods are collected. The state of decomposition can change greatly within hours due to insect activity and weather conditions. Also mite bites should be noted.
2. Since maggots tend to become invisible and "flash out" when photographed, do not use flash photography, especially on digital photos.
3. Always use a metric and an inch scale on every picture taken to determine the length of the larvae. The use of international scales is important due to different units of measurement in different countries.
4. Gather one spoon full of insects from at least three different areas of the crime scene and the body and place into three clearly labeled jars.
5. Do not put insects in isopropyl or formalin. Instead use 98 per cent ethanol for half of the insects collected.
6. Kill the insects with hot water before placing in ethanol.
7. Place half of the specimens in a cool, refrigerated place if available.
8. Label everything excessively with dates, initials, exact times and locations.
9. Ask an experienced forensic entomologist any questions that arise.
10. Identification must be performed by an experienced entomologist. Keys that are applicable to the local fauna may be used.

ENTOMOLOGISTS TOOLS

Tools

Forensic entomologists use a variety of tools to determine post-mortem interval:

- Net
- Sticky Traps
- Vials/Kill Jars
- Preservation Chemicals: Ethyl Alcohol and Acetone
- Latex Gloves
- Forceps
- Live Specimen Containers
- Shovel
- Thermometers
- Labels (both adhesive and non-adhesive)
- Small Paint Brushes
- Foil
- Vermiculite and Food
- Graphite Pencil
- Hand Towel
- Camera
- Ruler
- Paper Towels
- Sifting Screens
- Death Scene Form

COLLECTION OF INSECTS

Insect Collection

Collecting Insects at a Mock Crime Scene

Collection of adult insects in the area, including flies and beetles, follows as they may become disturbed enough to leave due to the high amount of law enforcement personnel in the vicinity. The most common method is sweep netting, although sticky traps placed near the corpse are utilized as well. Collection of insect adults provides a basis as to what species may be on the corpse in larval form. Collection of larvae is the next step as it is the main route of PMI determinance. Flies prefer to deposit their eggs in any available orifice on the body such as the eyes, ears, nose, anus and mouth. They will also utilize any open wounds to give the developing offspring easier access to necrotized (dead) flesh to feed upon.

Different species of larvae have different migration patterns. This refers to the stage of life where they are preparing to pupate, so they migrate away from their original food source to a safer region less vulnerable to prey. It is up to the forensic entomologist on scene to not only collect from around the body itself, but also directly under it. Some larvae burrow up to three feet (0.91 m) in the ground as well so some digging is required. If the corpse is in an advanced state of decomposition, samples of the morgue chamber climate and insects present from the body bag and during autopsy must be taken as well.

Overall, two types of collections are taken: one for immediate observation (preserved using boiling water and "kill jars" or ethyl acetate) and one for insect rearing for larval or pupal identification. Both methods help provide a positive identification for the insect genus and species. One of the most important facets of the forensic entomologist's job is documentation.

Collection During an Autopsy

It is essential that an experienced and knowledgeable forensic entomologist is present at the crime scene to ensure thorough use of entomological evidence. Sometimes, if an investigation is not carried out to its full potential, the entomologist will attend the autopsy and work alongside a forensic pathologist.

The corpse will most likely arrive at the morgue in a "body bag", especially if the corpse is in an advanced state of decay. Sometimes, the outer and inner surfaces of the bag can be infested with insects which should be collected and labeled accordingly. Insects that are found on the inside of the body bag may have crawled from the body due to temperature changes. If the remains have been refrigerated prior to the autopsy, the forensic entomologist must record the following: temperature of the chamber, the total time the body was cooling, temperature changes dealing with the transfer of the body to the morgue, and the temperature of the maggot mass when the body is removed from the cooler. Clothing should also be carefully examined for insects. Moist areas on clothing are good places to look for fly eggs.

Areas of the body where there is concentrated insect activity should be photographed in order to keep a record of the insect composition and infested area. Collection should also take place at greatly infested areas. On a fresh corpse, the face is the most likely area to have insect colonization.

Also, genital and rectal areas should be checked as they attract ovipositing flies. The hair line must be examined for the presence of lice eggs as well as fleas, ticks, and mites. Eyelashes and eyebrows should also be examined as they can be homes for follicle mites.

ROLE OF THE AMATEUR

Amateur entomologists usually engage with insects in one of the following ways:

Biological Recording and Conservation

Entomologists who record insect species perform an important function. By monitoring and getting to know their local species, they are in an excellent position to spot any unusual population changes that can reflect environmental changes.

Amateur recorders often get involved in surveying nature reserves or sites due for development, and in this way they can contribute substantially to conservation and protecting biodiversity.

For example, amateurs currently run a network of 85 moth traps across the UK, recording common species. The network is coordinated by professional entomologists at Rothamsted Experimental Station, and this 'joint venture' between amateurs and professionals has shown long-standing traps have shown that the numbers of moths in the South East of England have fallen by 30 per cent over the past 35 years. Elsewhere in the UK, moth numbers have actually risen during this period.

Expert Amateurs

Just as 'birders' and serious ornithologists study bird behaviour and biology rather than just merely record them, there are entomologists who study insects in great depth. Some of these—such as the Late Dame Miriam Rothschild—have made substantial contributions to insect science. Professional entomologists often consult with amateur specialists who have expert knowledge about particular insect groups.

It is worth mentioning that many knowledgeable amateurs who have embarked on the study of insects late in life have ended up becoming experts in specific insect orders, contributing their own unique skills and experience to insect science, and sometimes authoring widely-regarded reference books on their chosen entomological speciality.

Keeping and Rearing Insects

Whatever your age, you can rear and keep insects in captivity. Stick insects are a good example of pets that children learn to rear and look after, while learning about nature at the same time.

The AES has published caresheets describing how you can look after some commonly kept insects. Native insects, such as caterpillars you find in the garden that later become butterflies, are also a source of fascination for the young entomologist.

Collecting

Many people like to learn about insects and record them in their gardens or in the countryside, rather like 'twitchers' record birds and birdsong. Indeed, many bird spotters turn to entomology once they have exhausted the species of birds they can log.

People in this category usually specialise in particular orders of insects. Unlike birds, which number a few thousand species, there are over a million described species of insects in the world (and many more waiting to be described)!

Many people start withbutterflies (57 varieties in the UK) before 'graduating' to moths (some 900 species of larger British moths, and another 1500 'micros') and then to other orders.

Traditionally, collectors have amassed reference collections of dead insects, stored in cork-lined drawers in cabinets. While a reference collection of insects can be useful, the widespread availability of affordable digital cameras is gradually making the physical collection of specimens less necessary.

Why Study Insects?

Insects make up about 80 per cent of all known animals present on the earth, which makes them the most important for the survival of most animal and plant species on our planet. Without insects, human beings as a species would face certain extinction within a very short period of time.

Insects play an important role and are essential to maintaining the balance of nature. Predators and parasites help to control populations of other organisms. Scavengers and decomposers help to clean up the environment and recycle nutrients for plants. Pollinators are responsible for ensuring the renewal of vegetation and let's not forget, insects themselves are a primary food source for most animals and other insects.

Insects are an integral component of the ecological web. Throughout the world, habitat alteration has caused the extinction of many organisms, including insects. By identifying endangered species and studying their habitats, entomologists help describe and restore threatened ecosystems.

Entomological Research

Entomological research has helped the United States to become a model for all industrialized countries in solving pubiic health problems. A century ago, malaria was a major problem in North America. It is now of minor importance because of entomologists and their research. Despite this success story, much work remains to be done. Few problems present greater challenges to medical and veterinary entomologists than the widespread distribution of insect-borne disease agents.

ANALYSIS OF THE BODY

Clothing

Different types of insects are found on carrion depending on the location. Entomologists give a detailed examination of clothing if found on the carrion. Examination of the clothing is important due to the different types of insects and stages of insects that may be present such as eggs, larvae, pupae, or even adults.

Entomologists examine the clothing carefully, such as looking through the folding of shirts, pants, socks, etc. Fly eggs are often found in moist areas such as nostrils, eyes, and mouths. This is due to the attraction of moisture and shelter, which is also used for deposition on these specific body parts.

Buried Corpse

Remains that are buried carry different types of insects as mentioned above. Due to lower, constant temperatures at different depths of the soil, the decomposition process is slower for burials as to a corpse being found out on a hot summer day. Blowflies, for example, are usually the first insects to reach a dead corpse. They often fly from their birth place to the corpse to feed. Entomologists might find flesh flies and muscidae larvae on the corpse. Coffin flies or Scuttle flies can also be found in this type of setting.

Study in Paramo, Colombia

In Paramo, Colombia it is said that the minimum post mortem interval could be estimated by the knowledge of the pattern of insect succession on a corpse. This is due to the different types of insects that develop in different types of regions due to weather. Different types of insects assist in determining the five stages of decomposition.

Calliphora nigribasis was found at the fresh stage and Compsomylops verena was usually found at the bloated stage. Compsomylops boliviana can be found at the active decaying stage and Stearibia nigriceps and Hydrotaea sp. can be seen during the advanced decay. Finally, Leptocera species usually arrive for the dry remains of the body.

Success Parameter of Entomologist

Interpreting the recorded weather data is an important feature to a forensic entomologist's success. Weather samples include temperature and conditions for that particular day and two weeks prior. All weather data must come from a credited national weather service. Any faults in their report can negate a court case.

A forensic entomologist must record ambient air temperature, ground temperature (if a body was buried), and maximum/minimum air temperature for three to five days after the crime/event and approximately two weeks before the incident. This information allows for calculation of Accumulated Degree Days (ADD). Accumulated degree days are based on weather temperature, these recordings can help predict when a developmental stage will be reached based on heat requirement. Accumulated Degree Day Formula: (Average Temperature-Minimum threshold) x [unit of time])

'Weather Technology'

Conditions such as rainfall or any extreme weather condition come into play. All these factors can prove or disprove how long the body was there according to the insects found. Many insects live in certain habitats, these play a vital role in an entomologist's job. These investigators must know:

1. what insects lived in or around the area?
2. what insects on the body are not local to the area?

The entomologist needs to understand weather and weather patterns in order to give a professional and accurate report. New technology in meteorology has allowed for vast improvements in forensics. HailTrax gives an accurate estimation of where hail has fallen and also determines hail size within an area. This information can prove to be helpful for a forensic entomologist when hail was possibly a factor in the case.

Entomologists usually specialize in a particular field of study, such as applied agriculture and forest entomology, apiculture (bee culture), classification and evolution, insect ecology, insect physiology or insecticide toxicology. They often work with other scientists on joint projects such as developing crops resistant to insects, or containing animal and plant diseases caused by insects transmitting infectious organisms. Some also work with parasitologists and other microbiologists to help develop vaccines and medicine to combat insects that spread disease, such as the malaria-carrying anopheles mosquito.

Entomologists work in jobs that include teaching about insects, raising bees or other insect farms, enforcing quarantines and regulations, doing insect survey work, consulting on integrated pest management topics, selling insecticides, controlling pests, and conducting research on insect classification, taxonomy, biology, ecology, behaviour, or control.

Those working mainly in research will study the anatomy, habits, life histories, physiology, and classification of insects and investigate various types of chemical and biological controls.

Personal Characteristics

Entomologists need the following characteristics:

- a keen interest in invertebrate biology
- the intellect, curiosity, creativity, patience and perseverance required to pursue answers to complex research questions.
- the ability to work well independently and as part of a team.
- the ability to communicate effectively with their colleagues and the general public.

They should enjoy synthesizing information, conducting research, preparing reports, performing tasks requiring precision and supervising research projects.

Career Prospects Entomology

Entomology careers in research involve studying and understanding the anatomy, habits, life histories, physiology and classification of insects and investigating various types of chemical and biological controls. Increasingly, basic information is required to supply answers to complex questions and problems involving insects.

Many entomologists are involved with research in integrated pest management. IPM uses all suitable pest control techniques to keep pests below economically injurious levels. Each pest control technique must be designed carefully so it is environmentally sound and is compatible with producer and user objectives. But IPM is more than chemical pesticide management — it also includes biological, cultural and sanitary control practices. Once sound, reliable information on insect control is gathered from research, the results are given to farmers and other people who deal with insect pests.

There are many teaching opportunities for entomologists at colleges and nonprofit educational institutions and organizations. For example, the Cooperative Extension Service in each state plays an important role in providing information on insects and pest control to homeowners, farmers and others.

Entomologists at CES work closely with individuals and businesses to help solve their insect problems. Another important extension job is the survey entomologist, who reviews all important crops in a given state or area for possible insect outbreaks and alerts farmers and growers before a major problem arises.

Many entomologists work for government agencies. For example, U.S. regulatory entomologists help prevent the entrance of harmful, destructive pests from foreign countries. Both federal and state governments have set up plant and animal quarantine agencies. All plants, fruits, vegetables, artifacts, baggage and animals are examined at international ports of entry, and these inspections are performed under the supervision of trained entomologists and other scientists.

Entomologists also impose strict quarantines in areas where introduced insects have established a foothold. In some cases, roadblocks and inspection stations are erected to prevent the spread of pests. Most states have laws and regulations requiring the inspection of nursery stock, many types of agricultural produce, logs and bee hives. Many states also have laws regulating the activities of pest control operators (exterminators) and pesticide applicators. Entomologists help enforce those important laws and provide technical information and counsel for those in this type of insect control work.

Medical and public health entomologists work for federal, state and local public health departments and deal with pest control problems. Entomologists engaged in public health work in different areas of research and in the control of house flies, mosquitoes, cockroaches, lice, fleas, ticks and many other pests that pose a health hazard or nuisance problem.

Military entomologists work for various branches of the armed forces and supervise pest control operations at a large number of military bases in the United States and abroad. Research work and the protection of military personnel against insect-borne diseases and parasites are important aspects of entomology in the military service.

Forensic entomology is a new field of study. Entomologists in this specialty area use their knowledge of insect life cycles and behaviour to help police solve crimes.

Role of Agricultural Entomologists

Agricultural entomologists work to protect valuable crops from insect pests. Annual losses to agricultural insect pests are enormous and in some areas can result in up to a 25 per cent loss in yield. Agricultural entomologists, pest management consultants and pest scouts all are involved in research and control of crop pests.

The rapid growth of the forest products industry has set the stage for forest entomology. The United States uses an enormous amount of lumber, pulp and paper products annually, yet yearly losses from forest insects also are substantial. Forest entomologists work to protect these valuable resources from insect pests.

Commercial entomologists work for industry rather than public agencies. These jobs can involve field-service work, research, insect-control services and insecticide sales. Selling insecticides is part of the large agribusiness industry that supplies farmers and growers with goods and services.

Some entomologists work to control pests affecting shade trees, lawns, ornamental plants, homes, warehouses, stores, hotels and restaurants. Other work includes spraying farm crops and orchards as well as urban areas for flies and mosquitoes.

Commercial entomologists also can work as private consultants to the pesticide industry, pest control operators and agribusiness (pest management services, for example). Entomologists in this field can establish their own company, can work for a small business or can work for a large commercial company.

EDUCATION AND TRAINING

Individuals interested in a career in entomology should prepare themselves by taking classes in math and science (biology, zoology, botany, ecology and chemistry), by becoming familiar with the steps of the scientific method and by practicing keeping records and presenting information, data and conclusions. They should conduct investigations of the insect world; visit libraries and stores to find interesting educational books, videos and software about insects; look for summer jobs with companies, universities, state experiment stations or government agencies that deal with insects; or simply spend the day with a museum curator, beekeeper, pest control operator or other professional entomologist to help provide insight into entomological careers and the decision to enter a career in entomology.

Training is also available through youth groups such as scouts, 4-H, science and bug clubs and the Young Entomologists' Society. Through organizations such as the Young Entomologists' Society, young insect enthusiasts can interact with others interested in insect study, trade insect specimens and information, publish interesting information on insects and read about the latest discoveries in insect study.

Entomologists are employed by municipal, provincial and federal governments, post-secondary institutions and museums. For example, entomologists employed by the Canadian Food Inspection Agency work to prevent the spread of invasive invertebrates. Pharmaceutical and chemical manufacturing companies and large pest control companies also hire entomologists to conduct research and demonstrate new products for people in the agriculture, forestry and medical communities. A few entomologists are independent consultants who provide insect identification services, advise clients on insect control or conduct environmental impact assessments.

Graduates of bachelor's degree programmes may be hired for technical positions in research programmes, entry level government jobs such as forest health survey coordinator, customer service positions in pest control companies, or junior positions in environmental consulting companies. A Ph.D is generally required for independent research, administrative work or teaching at the post-secondary level.

Entomologists are part of the larger National Occupational Classification 2121: Biologists and Related Scientists. In Alberta, 80 per cent of biologists and related scientists work in the following industries:

- Professional, Scientific and Technical Services
- Public Administration
- Health Care and Social Assistance.

The employment outlook in this occupation will be influenced by a wide variety of factors including:

- Time of year (for seasonal jobs).
- Trends and events affecting overall employment (especially in the industries listed above).
- Location in Alberta.
- Employment turnover (work opportunities generated by people leaving existing positions).
- Occupational growth (work opportunities resulting from the creation of new positions that never existed before).
- Size of the occupation.

Employment turnover is expected to increase as members of the baby boom generation retire over the next ten years.

Forest health and the maintenance of ecosystems are important issues facing public land managers. Insects play a significant role on ecosystem functions and habitat succession, both of which influence our land management activities. Forest Service entomologists work with foresters, botanists, ecologists, plant pathologists, silviculturists, other forest management and natural resource specialists to provide for healthy forests and rangelands. In addition, they work in partnership with state officials, pest and weed control boards, and numerous other groups and individuals on critical entomological issues. Entomologists with the Forest Service are often involved in:

- Using insects and other naturally occurring biological agents to combat other insects, noxious weeds and forest diseases
- Monitoring the extent of defoliation and mortality caused by insects
- Participating in periodic reviews and revisions of forest plans, providing qualitative and quantitative estimates of insect impacts and prognosis modeling
- Providing recommendations and training on timber harvesting and other land management activities
- Developing forest and rangeland management prescriptions that employ a variety of techniques to contend with harmful insects
- Providing technical assistance in all aspects of pest management to State and private groups and to individuals who manage the non-federal forested land throughout the country.

Entomologists are hired at many different grade levels. College graduates may be hired at the GS-5 or GS-7 grade level. They spend their first year or two in training and development, and then may be promoted to the GS-9 grade level. Entomologists with advanced degrees and experience may be hired at higher grade levels, especially to meet research programme needs. To start a career as an entomologist in the Forest Service, you must meet one of the following requirements:

- Have a degree in entomology or a related discipline of the biological or physical sciences that includes at least 16 semester hours in entomology, or
- A combination of education and experience equivalent to a major that includes course work as shown above, plus appropriate experience or additional education.

Applicants with major fields of study in biology, zoology, or invertebrate zoology may fully meet the basic education requirements if their academic preparation included substantive instruction including appropriate laboratory and field work in basic general entomology, taxonomy, physiology, ecology, general and organic chemistry, general physics, and mathematics or statistics that provided some training in the analysis of variables.

FORENSIC ENTOMOLOGISTS IN THE U.S.A.

There are several different occupations for forensic entomologists since the field itself is still so very young. Many state universities employ a number of entomologists to teach. Dr. Jeffery Tomberlin (former president of the North American Forensic Entomology Association) is an assistant professor for Texas A&M University's entomology department. His responsibilities as an instructor include teaching, maintaining a research programme, advising and working with students who have an interest in working in the field of forensics. Dr. Tomberlin says that, in his spare time, he works with law enforcement agencies and conducts workshops to teach detectives, crime scene investigators, and others on the use of insects in crime scene investigation (CSI).

He serves as a consultant in forensic investigations and can even be called upon at times to investigate the presence of insect evidence at crime scenes to determine PMI as discussed earlier. Dr. Tomberlin is most proud of his work with Dr. John Wallace (of Millersville University) in initiating the first conference on forensic entomology to be held in North America. First held in Las Vegas, Nevada, about 50 people registered for the conference which is now in its sixth year and has paved the way for the development of the North American Forensic Entomology Association. The conference has since gone from an annual meeting to the formation of an official society for those interested in the field of forensics. He had the luxury to serve as the NAFEA's first president and was later succeeded by Dr. Wallace.

Although he's been working in the field for a number of years and has experienced the surge of new developments and advances within forensic entomology, Dr. Tomberlin believes that there is still a great deal more progress to be made in the near future. The urban and stored product entomology arenas are the areas, in his opinion, with the most potential for growth since they both impact the majority of the country in a way much closer to home. He also hopes for more recognition of these two areas and their contribution to the field of entomology. The wide variety of experiences and opportunities for employment help to make forensic entomology among the most diverse careers to have developed among the scientific professions and it looks as though at this rate it will continue to be for a number of years.

A fellow educator and member of the NAFEA, Dr. M. Eric Benbow, currently Assistant Professor of Entomology at Michigan State University, provided his own perspective on his career as well. Dr. Benbow's own line of work involves his giving seminars and lectures that have to do with forensic entomology, routinely doing research involving both case and laboratory experiments, and serving on graduate student committees.

Previously, he has done research that has involved understanding life history characteristics, larval growth rates, and the environmental factors that influence both. When asked if there was anything in his career of which he was especially proud, Dr. Benbow's response was rather sentimental. The first accomplishment he shared was his writing of a $2 million grant to study the ecology of an infectious disease and his role as an expert witness for a contested case hearing for surface water issues in the Hawaiian Islands. Second on his list of accomplishments was his writing of numerous letters of support and recommendation for students that have gone on to graduate, medical, and law school. Dr. Benbow's pride in his ability to impact the lives of his students becomes obvious when he later stated that being able to interact with students and having the freedom to pursue research that interests him is the most enjoyable part of his job.

Forensic entomologists' roles in academic settings provides them with opportunities to exploit their passions for teaching, discovery, and invention. Many spend their careers making great contributions to their field, colleagues, and a number of students fortunate to have such dedicated instructors. It is this commitment to continuing the education of their students that not only proves rewarding for these teachers, but also ensures that there will be others to take over their line of work in the still developing future of forensic entomology.

FAMOUS ENTOMOLOGICAL CASES

First Recorded Entomological Case

The first written record of forensic entomology being employed in legal matters dates back centuries toSong Ci (1186-1249) a Chinese forensic medical expert. Song Ci served as a judge on the Chinese high courts and wrote "Collected Cases of Injustice Rectified" in 1248. His book was a summary of several accounts of his own experiences with forensic cases and his personal reflections upon justice. One case in particular relates to the use of forensic entomology to solve a homicide. A man was murdered after suffering several sickle-shaped slash wounds. Since there was no evidence to be found at the scene of the crime, the judge in charge of the autopsy decided to conduct an investigation.

The judge found that the victim had recently been involved in an argument with another man concerning loan money that the victim wanted paid. The judge was able to track down the whereabouts of the suspect along with other evidence. He then issued an area wide confiscation of all the sickles, stating that any man unwilling to comply would be charged with obstruction of justice. Between seventy to eighty sickles were turned in during the investigation in the summer heat.

As the sickles lay out in the sun, flies were attracted to the sickle whose owner just happened to be the man involved in the loan disagreement. The man was later taken into custody and interrogated but would not confess. The judge told the suspect to look at the evidence: the flies were attracted to the remnants of blood on his sickle. This was enough to charge the man with the victim's murder. Song Ci believed in the importance of irrefutable evidence and was strongly opposed to wrongful conviction. As a judge, Song Ci knew that investigations and autopsies needed to be performed under careful scrutiny and stringent protocol to protect the innocent from being unjustly accused.

Danielle Van Dam Murder Trial

A more recent and widely publicized homicide case that employed the use of forensic entomology was the David Westerfield trial. Westerfield was convicted and sentenced to death for the kidnapping and murder of seven-year-old Danielle Van Dam in 2002. Van Dam went missing from her home on the night of February 1, 2002, when her parents thought she was asleep in her bed. After weeks of search efforts, on February 27, 2002, the naked, decomposing body of the seven-year-old was found on the side of a road.

Defendant David Westerfield, who was a neighbour to the Van Dam family in Sabre Springs, California, became a suspect when he was reportedly not at home the morning Danielle went missing. Westerfield had also been spotted at a local dry cleaners dropping off two comforters, two pillowcases, and a jacket. These articles were later examined and tested positive for the blood of the victim.

Once Westerfield was placed under surveillance, the police recovered fiber, hair, and fingerprints that were similar to those of Danielle in the vehicle and the RV of the suspect. Child pornography was also found on his computer. On June 4, 2002, the murder trial began; Westerfield pleaded not guilty. The defense suggested that due to their lifestyle, her parents had put Danielle in danger by being around seedy and untrustworthy people who could have kidnapped her.

The defense lawyers also alleged that the child pornography was downloaded by the son of the accused and pointed out the lack of investigation into searching for other suspects. The prosecution called into evidence the fiber, hair, fingerprint, and blood analysis to support their case. Expert witnesses were able to link fibers found on the body of the victim to the home of the accused. Entomology, however, played the star role in the murder trial. The defense had consulted three separate entomologists to call into question the post mortem interval of Danielle Van Dam.

The prosecution and defense each hired their own forensic entomology expert witnesses. David Faulkner had originally collected the insects from the remains of Danielle at her autopsy and examined maggots, stating that the insects began growing ten to twelve days prior to finding the body. This discovery did not match up with the prosecution since Westerfield was under surveillance during this time and could not have dumped the body. Faulkner was heavily interrogated as to his method for figuring the post mortem interval and important weather factors.

Dr. Neal Haskell also testified for the defense stating that colonization could have occurred February 12 through February 21. Robert Hall believed the body of the victim could have been infested between February 12 and February 23. The prosecution called in Dr. Madison Lee Goff who estimated the last insect infestation occurred February 9 to February 14. Goff also stressed that other factors may have delayed bug arrival such as the possible use of a shroud, but none was found at the scene. In the end, the jury found Westerfield guilty of kidnapping and first degree murder. These two cases illustrate the importance of the education, training and job expertise needed to gain the necessary skills needed in forensic entomology.

Illegal Poaching Case

Forensic entomology is not only applicable in homicide cases, but also in other legal matters. The next case discusses the use of forensic entomology in an illegal poaching case. In July 1995, two baby black bears were found shot to death close to Winnipeg, Canada. Both the bears had their gall bladders removed, most likely to be sold and used as medicine in Asia. Witnesses heard gun shots and spotted a vehicle. Two men were found hiding near the bear's bodies and witnesses were able to confirm the suspects belonged to the vehicle that was sighted earlier. The witnesses recollections were a helpful lead, police officers could not hold the two men solely on suspicion. More evidence was needed in order to connect the two suspects to the crime. Blowfly eggs were found and collected from the bear bodies and sent to entomologist Gail Anderson.

Anderson, as an experienced entomologist, knew that blowfly eggs take twenty-two hours to hatch in the hot summer temperatures the bears were found in. By counting back twenty-two hours and taking into account the weather data for the time the bears were discovered, she was able to find when the fly eggs were first deposited on the bodies. The time Anderson found for the eggs matched up with the time, the two suspects were discovered near the scene of the crime, heard the gun shots, and saw their vehicle.

Forensic entomologists experience a wide variety of opportunities to use their expertise whether in the classroom, the research lab, or in the field. There is an extensive amount of time and energy put into learning the trade, but the job is rewarding in that it gives forensic entomologists the opportunity to impact both the science and social community with ground-breaking research that reaches as far as into the home. While the practice of studying insects as existed for centuries, there are so many areas of the field that remain largely untapped and promising. The innovative ideas of forensic entomologists will continue to emerge over the coming years.

CHAPTER – 9

Management of Plant-Feeding Mites

Around 7000 species of plant-feeding mites are known worldwide, and about half of these are members of the superfamily Eriophyoidea gall, bud, and rust mites. The other half are distributed within the superfamilies Tetranychoidea spider, flat, and peacock mites, Tarsonemoidea (broadand cyclamen mites), and the lesser known bulb mites of the family Acaridae (Astigmata).

In the United States, these groups include about 2000 species. However, recent studies indicate that hundreds of species within the country, have yet to be discovered and described.

Plant-feeding mites play important roles as agricultural pests of timber, fruits, vegetables, forage crops, ornamentals and stored grains. In many instances, lack of information about the correct identity of mites, as well as our lack of adequate knowledge regarding their biology and ecology, have hampered our ability to effectively combat these mite pests.

Their small size and cryptic appearance make mites difficult to detect and thus, infestations are often overlooked. Once established in a new area, certain biological characteristics allow rapid escalation to pest status. These include high egg production, various modes of reproduction (parthenogenesis, paedogenesis, and sexual), short life cycles, a myriad of dispersal techniques, and adaptability to diverse ecological conditions. These traits combined with an exponential increase in world trade have set the stage for potentially devastating situations that may threaten the sustainability of the world's agroecosystems.

PLANT FEEDING MITES

Eriophyoidea

More than 6 000 species of plant feeding (phytophagous) mites are known worldwide. The majority of plant feeding species belong to the obligate plant parasitic Eriophyoidea (e.g. gall mites, erinose mites, bud mites, rust mites) and Tetranychoidea (e.g. spider mites, false spider mites), while a number of species belong to other lineages (e.g. Eupodoidea, Tarsonemidae, and single oribatid mites).

Plant feeding mites form an integral and important part of the natural ecosystem. Some species, especially eriophyoid mites, can be utilised for the biological control of weeds. Many plant feeding mites are of economic importance as pests of crop plants. In South Africa about 65 species cause damage to agricultural crops and ornamental plants.

More than 6 000 species of plant feeding (phytophagous) mites are known worldwide. The majority of plant feeding species belong to the obligate plant parasitic Eriophyoidea (e.g. gall mites, erinose mites, bud mites, rust mites) and Tetranychoidea (e.g. spider mites, false spider mites), while a number of species belong to other lineages (e.g. Eupodoidea, Tarsonemidae, and single oribatid mites).

Plant feeding mites form an integral and important part of the natural ecosystem. Some species, especially eriophyoid mites, can be utilised for the biological control of weeds. Many plant feeding mites are of economic importance as pests of crop plants. In South Africa about 65 species cause damage to agricultural crops and ornamental plants.

- All eriophyoid mites are plant feeding. They are extremely tiny, the majority are less than 300 micron long, and essentially invisible to the unaided eye. They have elongated, worm-like bodies, with only two pairs of legs.
- Eriophyoid mites are commonly known as gall mites, bud mites, rust mites, erineum mites, witches' broom mites, blister mites and so on, referring to the symptoms caused by a particular species. The feeding of almost half of eriophyoid species known, though, does not cause visible damage to their plant hosts.
- The eriophyoid mites belong to three families: Phytoptidae, Eriophyidae and Diptilomiopidae. About 3 400 species are known, but these probably represent only as little as 5 per cent or less of extant eriophyoid species. Most woody and many herbaceous flowering plants, and gymnosperms and ferns most likely host these minute mites. Most eriophyoid species are highly host specific, restricted to one or single closely related plant species.

- In South Africa 25 eriophyid species are regarded as pests.
- Many research activities currently in progress at the ARC-PPRI Arachnology Unit's Acari Section concern this fascinating and economically important group of microscopic organisms.

Spider mites are insect relatives that damage plants by sucking juices, usually from the leaves.These mites have eight legs, except, as very young "larvae", at which time they have only six legs, much like insects. They never possess wings. Some species produce noticeable webbing.

There are many overlapping generations. Their feeding causes chlorosis and ultimately leaf or needle drop when populations are high.

Spider Mite Identification

Spider mites are small, plant-feeding mites that may severely damage plants. Mites pierce the leaf surface, disrupt leaf tissue and extract cell contents. Mite feeding makes a hole in the leaf's protective layer and leaves eventually dry out and turn brown because of water loss through these tiny holes.

Spider mites have eight legs in all stages except larvae which have only six and they develop from egg to adult in as little as two weeks during summer. There can be many generations each year and most spider mites spend winter months as adult females hiding in plant debris at ground level or under bark scales on perennial plants.

Spider mites have many natural enemies but other mites, calledpredator mites, are the most important. Lady beetles, syrphid flies and lacewings also are good predators of spider mites. Spider mite control in gardens and houseplants is relatively simple using the same methods that are used for aphids.

Spruce Spider Mite

For landscape plants called conifers such as arbovitae, spruce, pine, and fir the procedure is a little different. Spruce spider mite (*Oligonychus ununguis*) is the most common spider mite on conifers. Unlike other spider mites, spruce spider mites lay eggs in the fall that won't hatch until the following spring. Other spider mites stop laying eggs by late summer but clusters of the spruce spider mite's red "winter egg" can be found on stems and needles during winter months.

Winter eggs can be effectively controlled by late winterapplications of horticultural or dormant oils. During summer, spruce spider mites can usually be controlled with washing and insecticidal soap as outlined above for other spider mites.

Least-toxic Spider Mite/aphid Control

Scout for pests often during the growing season. Hold a piece of white paper under the leaves where you suspect an infestation. Tap on the branch hard enough to dislodge any mites, but not too hard! If spider mites are present they will appear as tiny, dark flecks, *that are moving,* on the white paper — they are about the size of table salt. Any lighter, and faster mites that you see may be predators. Use your hand lens to get a closer look.

If spider mites are found pick a sunny, warm (about 75-85 ºF) day to apply control measures. In the morning hose off the plants to remove as many mites and eggs as possible. This washing will remove dust, dirt and other debris that favor mites as well. Use enough water pressure to dislodge mites, but be careful not to damage the plant.

Next, mix up a solution of insecticidal soap. Apply spray to all leaf surfaces where mites may be hiding. Do the application in the morning because soap can burn foliage when air temperature is high. Before the soap solution dries rinse it off with a second spray of water. This final step will remove residual soap that might burn tender leaf tissue. Repeat these steps at one to two weeks until you no longer find mites. This procedure will work for houseplants as well.

One final caution: soap solution should be almost clear with a slight milky color when mixed. Don't use the solution if it is milky white or solids form in the container as this is an indication that the soap has "gone bad" and may damage your plants.

ROSES: INSECT AND MITE PESTS AND BENEFICIALS

Roses are among the most intensively managed plants in many home landscapes. Part of this intensive management may include the frequent application of pesticides.

Although insects and mites may attack roses from time to time, many rose enthusiasts are able to maintain vigorous plants and produce high quality blooms with little or no use of insecticides, especially in California's dry interior valleys.

The keys to success are careful selection of varieties, which vary significantly in susceptibility to insect and disease problems, good attention to appropriate cultural practices, and occasional handpicking or using water to forcefully spray away pests. Keep an eye out for rising populations of natural enemies that often rapidly reduce the numbers of aphids, mites, and other pests.

COMMON INSECT AND MITE PESTS

Aphids

Aphids are the most common insect pest on roses . The actual aphid species vary depending on where in the state the roses are grown. These may include the rose aphid, *Macrosiphum rosae,* the potato aphid, *Macrosiphum euphorbiae,* and the cotton aphid, *Aphisgossypii,* among others. Aphids favour rapidly growing tissue such as buds and shoots. Low to moderate levels of aphids do little damage to plants, although many gardeners are concerned with their very presence. Moderate to high populations can secrete copious amounts of honeydew, resulting in the growth of sooty mold, which blackens leaves. Very high numbers may distort or kill buds or reduce flower size. In most areas of California aphids are normally a problem for only about four to six weeks in spring and early summer before high summer temperatures reduce their numbers.

Aphids have many natural enemies including lady beetles, soldier beetles, and syrphid flies, which may rapidly reduce increasing populations. Ants will protect aphid populations for their honeydew against natural enemies. Keep ants out of bushes with sticky barriers, baits, or traps to improve biological control. Lady beetles often increase in number when aphid populations are high. The convergent lady beetle is sold at nurseries for release against aphids and may provide limited control when properly released. Releasing green lacewings against the rose aphid has not been shown to offer significant control in research trials. A naturally occurring disease may control aphids when conditions are wet or humid.

In many landscape situations, knocking aphids off with a forceful spray of water early in the day is all that is needed to supplement natural control. Insecticidal soaps or neem oil can also be used to increase mortality of aphids with only moderate impact on natural enemies.

Soil-applied systemic insecticides, such as imidacloprid (a home garden product with this ingredient is sold under the Bayer label), are effective but are not usually necessary. Use of more toxic products is not warranted in most gardens and landscapes.

Insects that Distort or Discolour Blossoms

Thrips. Western flower thrips, *Frankliniella occidentalis,* and Madrone thrips, *Thripsmadroni,* cause injury primarily to rose flowers, causing blossom petals to streak with brown or become distorted and can be particularly objectionable if attacked early at the bud stage. The tiny yellow or black thrips insects can be found within the blossoms.

Thrips problems are more likely to be severe where many rose bushes located close together provide a continuously blooming habitat. Fragrant, light-colored or white roses are most often attacked and can be severely damaged. Cultivars with sepals that remain tightly wrapped around the bud until blooms open have fewer problems. In most home garden and landscape situations, thrips can be tolerated.

Frequent clipping and disposal of spent blooms may reduce thrips problems. Control with insecticides is difficult because materials are mostly effective on early developmental stages, which are commonly found within buds or flowers where most pesticide applications cannot penetrate. It should be noted that western flower thrips can have a beneficial role as a predator of spider mites.

Insects and Mites that Cause Leaves to Stipple or Yellow

Spider mites, including two-spotted mite, Pacific mite, and strawberry mite, all *Tetranychus* spp., cause leaves to be stippled or bleached, and may cause leaves to dry up and fall off. Some species produce webbing while others do not. They are tiny (about the size of the period at the end of this sentence) and are best seen with use of a hand lens.

Mites usually appear first on the undersides of leaves but move to the upper sides as populations increase. High numbers are usually associated with dry, dusty conditions. Spider mite numbers may greatly increase if their many natural enemies are killed by broad-spectrum insecticides applied for other pests. For instance, applications of carbaryl (Sevin) applied to control other pests are frequently followed by an increase in mite populations.

Conserving natural enemies, providing sufficient irrigation, and reducing dust may all help control mites. Overhead irrigation or periodic washing of leaves with water can be very effective in reducing mite numbers. Releases of predator mites have been used in some situations.

If treatment is necessary, spider mites can be controlled with insecticidal soap, horticultural oil, or neem oil, and sprays should be targeted to insure coverage on the undersides of the leaves. Although, spider mites may be listed on insecticide labels, most insecticides are not very effective against them and can trigger mite flareups as mentioned above. Selective acaricides (miticides) are often difficult to find in the home garden market.

Rose leafhopper, *Edwardsianna rosae,* causes stippling larger than mite stippling but tends to be a problem only in certain localities. Along with stippling, cast skins and the absence of webbing on the underside of leaves are good indications that these pests are present. Plants can tolerate moderate stippling. Use an insecticidal soap if an infestation is severe.

Insects that Cause Canes to Die Back

Flatheaded borers, *Chrysobothris* spp., may kill canes or an entire plant. Larvae are white and up to 1 inch long with enlarged heads. Adult beetles do not significantly damage roses. Eggs tend to be laid on stressed rose plants, especially in bark wounds caused by sunburn or disease. Remove and destroy infested material and keep plants healthy by providing sufficient irrigation and avoiding excessive summer pruning.

Raspberry horntail, *Hartigia cressoni*, larvae are white, segmented caterpillars up to one inch long that can cause tips of canes to wilt and die in spring, reducing second-cycle blooms. Adults appear wasplike, black or black and yellow, and about half an inch long. Inspect canes in spring (mid-April to mid-June) for egg laying incisions or swellings caused by larvae and cut them off below the infestation. Prune off infested canes until healthy pith is found.

Scale insects include the armored scales, *Aulacaspis rosae*, rose scale, and *Quadraspidiotus perniciosus*, San Jose scale. These may cause cane decline or dieback when numbers are high. San Jose scale may spread by wind from almond orchards, and so may be found on roses close to suburbs near the urban-agricultural transition in California's Central Valley. These armored scales can be observed on canes as small, grayish, round to oval encrustations, ranging in size from one-eight to one-four inch. These insects have no legs or antennae for most of their lives and are immobile.

In winter, cut back and destroy infested canes and apply insecticidal oil to remaining infested canes if remaining scale population is high. Scales are attacked by many natural enemies. Look for exit holes in mature scale covers, which indicate parasitization.

A soft scale, cottony cushion scale, *Icerya purchasi*, may also be found on roses. Soft scales produce honeydew which may cause leaves to be sticky and allow sooty mold to colonize leaf surfaces. Washing plants with soap and water may reduce the population. Pruning and application of horticultural oil as for armored scales should provide sufficient control.

Insects Seldom Found in California

Mossy rose gall, *Diplolepis rosae*, causes a spherical spined mass of plant tissue about an inch in diameter to form on year-old rose twigs. At first the deformity resembles moss but becomes hardened as it enlarges. The causal insect is a gall wasp. A related insect causes an elongated stem gall to form, and about forty different kinds of galls can form on rose twigs. These galls are more common in cooler, northern parts of California than in the Central Valley. Pruning should provide sufficient control.

Rose midge, *Dasineura rhodophaga*, was reported infesting roses in a nursery in Petaluma, California, in August 1996. Rose midges are tiny flies that lay their eggs inside the sepals of flower buds or on plant terminals. Hatching larvae move into flower buds to feed, leaving the injured buds to wither, blacken, and die. Pupation occurs in the soil and two to four generations can occur annually. When first reported in 1996, there was widespread fear that this pest would move rapidly through the state, causing severe damage to roses in gardens and commercial nurseries.

However, few midges were found in 1997. The pest has been present in central Oregon and Washington for many years and is not known to be a major pest there. Hopefully it will not become a problem in California. Take any suspected infested material to your county Agricultural Commissioner for identification. Don't confuse the rose midge with the similar looking beneficial midge, *Aphidoletes aphidimyza*, which feeds on aphids. *Aphidoletes* larvae are found on stem, bud, or leaf surfaces feeding within aphid colonies, whereas *Dasineura* larvae re out of view at the base of developing buds in terminals.

BIOLOGICAL CONTROL OF BONESEED WITH THE BONESEED LEAF BUCKLE MITE

The life cycle of the boneseed leaf buckle mite consists of egg, larva, nymph and adult. The duration of the life cycle is unknown, but there is likely to be multiple generations per year. Other eriophyid mites can develop from egg to egg-laying adult in approximately ten days under ideal conditions in the laboratory. Such ideal conditions may occur in summer when plants are healthy and not drought-stressed. Development will take longer during cooler weather (e.g. winter). Adults may live for several weeks and females may lay one or more eggs daily.

Impact

Eriophyid mites have piercing and sucking mouthparts that are used to extract cell contents. All eriophyid mites feed on plants, some induce distorted growth such as galls. Boneseed leaf buckle mite induces the formation of specialized galls called erinea (pl.) or erineum (singular).

These appear as abnormal patches of leaf hairs associated with a distorted area on the leaf. Production of erinea is closely linked to plant growth; they are initiated by boneseed leaf buckle mite feeding on embryonic leaves at the shoot tip. As the young leaf grows, a colony of boneseed leaf buckle mite develops within the erineum.

Eventually many mites may occur in a single erineum. Erinea are present on infested plants throughout the year and new ones develop during boneseed growth flushes. Erinea provide a safe harbor from predators, protection from weather extremes, a plentiful food supply and an environment suitable for breeding. One to a few erinea may develop randomly over the leaf surface.

There is currently little information on the impact of boneseed leaf buckle mite on boneseed. Heavily infested boneseed plants in South Africa are unthrifty and appear to have lower growth rates and reproductive outputs than uninfested plants.

Leaves may become severely distorted and plants may become stunted due to a reduction of photosynthetic tissue. Sometimes lateral buds are entirely converted to a small erineum from which new branch development is prevented.

Integrated Control

Biological control cannot eradicate a weed but can reduce the spread and density of infestations. In some cases, control is achieved to the level where the weed is no longer of concern and no other control is necessary. More commonly, other methods are still required. Biological control should not be considered the complete answer to a boneseed problem. It should be used in conjunction with other control measures in an integrated management program.

Other biological control agents for boneseed have been introduced from South Africa and include the bitou tip moth (*Comostolopsis germana*), the black boneseed leaf beetle (*Chrysolina* sp.), the blotched boneseed leaf beetle (*Chrysolina picturata*), the painted boneseed leaf beetle (*Chrysolina oberprieleri*), the lacy-winged seed fly (*Mesoclanis magnipalpis*) and the boneseed leaf roller moth (*Tortrix* sp.). Although these insects can be destructive on Chrysanthemoides in South Africa, none has yet successfully established in Australia. A contributing factor to establishment failure has been predation by native insects and mites.

MANAGING MITES

The first step in determining the true cause of irritations that may involve mites is to thoroughly inspect the premises and identify any organisms discovered. The simple fact that all mites are tiny creatures, some so small they can be seen only with magnification, often makes inspection and identification difficult. Likewise, mites that affect humans are a diverse group, each with very different habits, all of which investigators should be aware.

Seek medical attention when exposure to mites is suspected as the cause of skin irritation. This is certainly true in the case of scabies infestations that will require medication. In addition, bedding and clothing of scabies-infected persons should be washed regularly.

When mites have been identified, appropriate control measures can be employed. A vacuum sweeper can be a valuable weapon in the mite control arsenal. Infestations of clover mites, rodent and bird mites in and around structures can sometimes be eliminated by vacuuming alone.

Vacuuming may be less effective, but still of value, in controlling various food mites, straw itch mites and dust mites. Note that dust mites are not prevalent in ductwork; therefore, duct cleaning is not recommended for dust mite control. However, a high-efficiency particulate air (HEPA) filter can be installed to help prevent airborne allergens, including dust mite particles.

Moisture control also can be important. Mites transfer air and water through their body walls and are subject to desiccation at low humidity. Dust mite populations, for example, suffer when a relative humidity of 50 per cent or less is maintained. On the other hand, high humidity can cause mite populations to increase exponentially.

Well-ventilated homes in dry climates contain few dust mites. Homes with a relative humidity that consistently rises above 50 per cent can contain more than 100 dust mites per gram of dust. To reduce dust mite numbers, a relative humidity of less than 50 per cent must be *maintained* for several weeks. Any fluctuation in humidity, however brief, seems sufficient for dust mites to remain and reproduce. Daily activities such as air-conditioning and showering, will cause humidity levels to fluctuate in portions of the home. Thus, other means of controlling dust mites should be employed in addition to humidity control.

For dust mites, products containing benzyl benzoate, and possibly abrasive dust formulations, may provide some control when applied to flooring and floor coverings. Bedding, draperies, floor coverings and furniture should be cleaned regularly. Pillows, mattresses and upholstered furniture can be discarded or sealed in plastic covers to help prevent dust mite infestation, and to reduce ongoing infestations and their associated allergens. Persons suffering from allergic reactions or asthma should consult a physician.

Exclusion methods also can be used for certain mites, e.g., clover mites. Structural entry points, e.g., gaps in and around foundations, doors, windows, vents, utility lines, etc., should be sealed. This will help to keep clover mites outdoors along with rats, mice, birds — and the mites these pests bring when they are allowed to nest in structures.

If nests are found, they should be removed and the area around them vacuumed. Other non-chemical methods include maintaining a plant-free border around foundations and reducing the amount of fertilizer applied to lawns – both of which help to keep clover mites away from structures.

Mites Affecting Humans

"Mite" is a term commonly used to refer to a group of insect-like organisms, some of which bite or cause irritation to humans. While some mites parasitize animals, including man, others are scavengers, some feed on plants, and many prey on insects and other arthropods. In fact, there are nearly as many different types of mites as there are insects. Like their relatives, the ticks, mites pass through four stages of development: egg to larva to nymph to adult. All stages have eight legs except the six-legged larva. Most mites never come in contact with humans, but some that do can affect a person's health. Yet, in many situations where mites or other "invisible" arthropods are believed to be biting or "attacking" people, no causative organism is present.

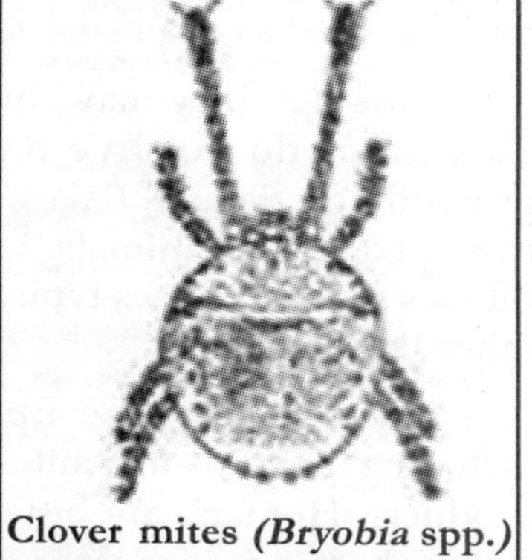

Clover mites *(Bryobia* spp.)

The irritation may be real or imagined: real, due to mechanical, chemical or other inanimate irritants, or imagined due to a psychological disorder.While mites rarely transmit disease to humans in the United States, they definitely impact health in ways that range from simply being a nuisance when they enter homes in large numbers, to inflicting severe skin irritation that can cause intense itching.

This mite sometimes enters homes and other buildings by the thousands, causing panic among residents. Though they do not bite or cause health-related problems, clover mites can be a nuisance. If smashed when they crawl over carpets and drapery, the mites leave a red stain.

Clover mites can be red, green or brown, and have front legs that are about twice as long as their other legs. They feed on clover, ivy, grasses, fruit trees and other plants. Well-fertilized lawns are favored. Clover mites enter homes when their food plants are removed or dry up. They are most active in fall, and will seek refuge in structures as colder weather approaches, when molting (shedding skin) and when laying eggs. Typical of many mite species, all clover mites are females capable of laying viable eggs without fertilization. They have no need for male mites!

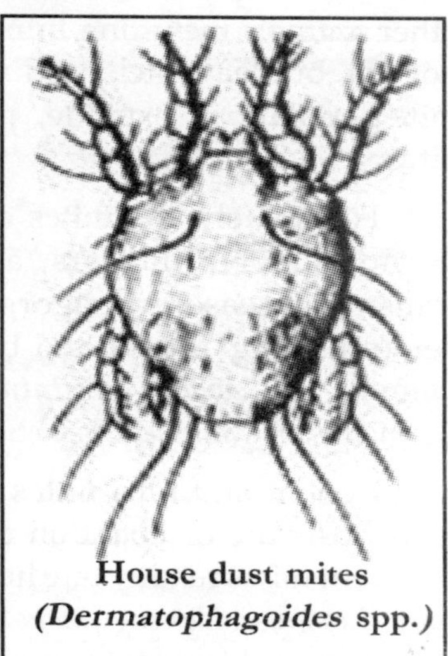

House dust mites
(*Dermatophagoides* spp.)

Much information and misinformation has appeared in recent years about house dust mites. Virtually invisible to the naked eye, house dust mites are nevertheless real. It has been shown that, like cockroaches, dust mites and their feces can become airborne and are one of the most common indoor allergens. That is, most persons diagnosed as being allergic to "house dust" are actually allergic to the dust mites whose bodies and feces are major components of dust.

Roaches and dust mites have also been implicated in triggering asthma attacks. But, unlike rodent mites, itch mites and chiggers, skin irritation is rarely caused by exposure to dust mites.

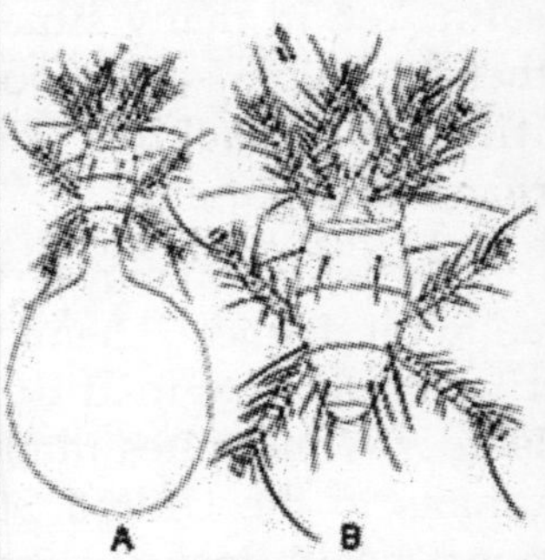

Although they may "hitchhike" on clothing, dust mites do not live on people. They feed primarily on dander, flakes of dead skin that fall from people and animals. Upholstered furniture, pillows and mattresses typically harbor more dust mites than carpeting.

A B

Itch mites (*Pyemotes spp.*)

These mites prey upon insects. Species including the straw itch mite (*P. tritici*) infest stored products. Humans are bitten when they contact straw, hay, grasses, leaves, seeds or similar materials harboring the mites. Another species (*P. herfsi*) also attacks insects living in sheltered locations, including the larvae of midges (gnat-like flies) in leaf galls, and the eggs of cicadas beneath tree bark.

When separated from their insect prey, itch mites may contact and bite other animals including humans.The mites cannot be seen and the bites are not felt, but leave itchy red marks that can resemble a skin rash. When itch mite populations 'explode,' people and other animals may receive numerous bites.

Fortunately, the mites cannot live on humans, do not survive indoors, and are not known to transmit disease. A: engorged itch miteB: female before feeding rodent and bird mites (*Liponyssoides sanguineus, Laelaps echidnina, Ornithonyssus* spp., *Dermanyssus gallinae, Cheyletiella* spp.)

Tropical Rat Mite

Rodent and bird mites may bite people when their hosts die or abandon their nests. Three types of rodent mites readily bite humans: the house mouse mite *(Liponyssoides saguineus)*, spiny rat mite *(Laelaps echidnina)* and tropical rat mite *(Ornithonyssus bacoti)*. The house mouse mite prefers to suck the blood of mice, but also will bite rats and people, often causing a rash around the bite. They prefer warm places (e.g., around pipes and furnaces) where rodents live. The spiny rat mite feeds on rats at night and hides by day in cracks and crevices around rat nests and resting places. The tropical rat mite's bite is painful and causes skin irritation and itching.

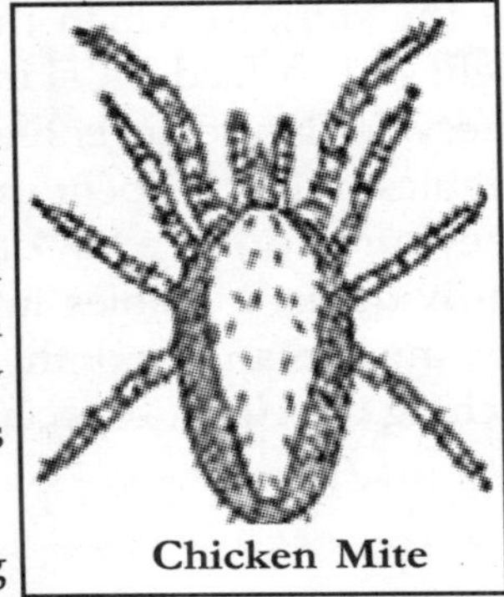
Chicken Mite

Mites that normally infest birds also bite people. The northern fowl mite (*Ornithonyssus sylviarum*) and chicken mite (*Dermanyssus gallinae*) primarily infest chickens, but also pigeons, starlings and sparrows. The northern fowl mite cannot survive for more than a month off its host, while the chicken mite hides in cracks and crevices near bird nests during the day and feeds by night. *Cheyletiella* mites infest both birds and mammals.

They may prey on other mites and insects living on the host's skin. They can cause a mange-like condition in pets, and itching in people who handle infested pets. They do not stay long on humans.

Chiggers *(Eutrombicula spp.)*

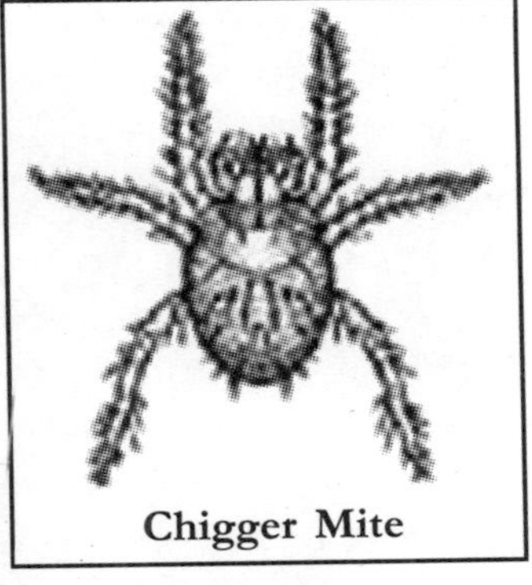
Chigger Mite

Two species of chigger mites attack humans and other mammals, birds and reptiles. The nymph and adult stages prey on insects. It is the six-legged larval stage that typically feeds on rodents or ground dwelling birds but will bite people when they are available. Chigger larvae are red to yellow in color and appear as scarcely visible specks.

When they detect the carbon dioxide exhaled by an animal, they climb on soil or vegetation and wave their front legs to contact it, then grasp it with their mouthparts. They do not suck blood but cut into the skin, inject skin-digesting saliva and suck up the liquefied skin. If not dislodged, the chigger will feed for several days. The bite becomes inflamed, hardens and itches.

Chiggers spend most of their lives in cracks in the soil. They are typically found in rural, less disturbed areas, but can persist for years on soil in new sub-divisions.

Sarcoptes scabiei are mites that infest mammals, including man. Most human infestations result from person-to-person contact. Although they can transfer from animals to humans and vice versa, several types of scabies mites exist, each having a preferred host species on which it reproduces.

In dogs, scabies mites cause mange. Scabies is the most common and important condition resulting from mite infestation of humans. Unlike other mites, scabies mites actually *burrow* and roduce tunnels one centimeter or more in length just below the surface of the skin, in which they lay eggs. The mites are believed to feed on skin and secretions. The entire lifecycle (ten to seventeen days for human-infesting scabies mites) is spent on their host. Without a host, they survive only a few days. In previously unexposed individuals, a scabies infestation may go unnoticed for more than a month. Then, severe irritation and itching develops, especially at night.

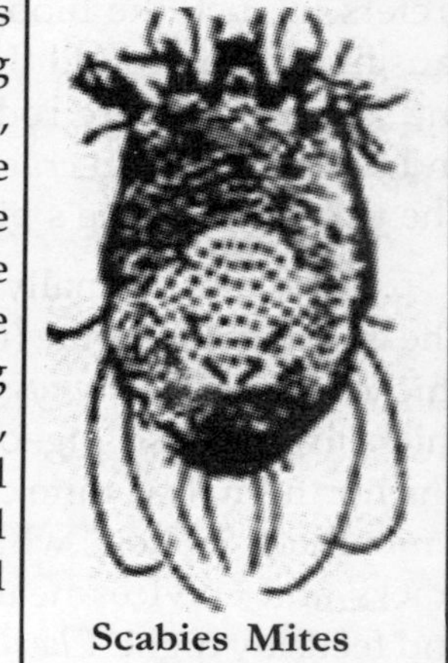
Scabies Mites

CHAPTER – 10

Host-plant Resistance and Pesticides

The prospects for major contributions to protecting world food and fiber production through crop resistance and tolerance to nematodes are truly exciting. Agricultural scientists consistently identify plant resistance as the highest research priority for nematode pest management. The advantages and benefits of breeding crop plants resistant to injurious parasitic nematodes, and growing them on infested land, are many and varied.

Resistant crops provide an effective and economical method for managing nematodes in both high- and low-cash value cropping systems. In annual cropping systems, resistant crops can reduce nematode populations to levels that are non-damaging to subsequent crops, thereby enabling shortening and modification of rotations.

They are environmentally compatible and do not require specialized applications, as opposed to most chemicals and, apart from preference based on agronomic or horticultural desirability, do not require an additional cost input or deficit. In less developed countries and in low-cash crop systems, plant resistance is probably the most viable solution to nematode problems.

Understanding the genetic diversity of the nematode population will require continued effort in introducing new resistance gene sources as virulent biotypes are selected.

Nematode Management

The current availability and/or use of resistant cultivars and rootstocks for nematode management reflect the success to date of research efforts in identifying and evaluating resistance sources, incorporating them into commercially acceptable crop selections, and implementing them in management programmes. The relatively few crop and nematode combinations where plant resistance or tolerance to nematodes are in use is probably less a reflection of the difficulty of the task and more a reflection of limited research emphasis.

The potential for success in this area seems enormous in light of the essentially untapped sources of resistance to nematodes in a broad range of botanical groups, and the rapid technical advances such as in-embryo rescue, somatic hybridization, and direct gene transfer that should promote a more efficient genetic transfer across conventionally difficult biological barriers (e.g., sexual incompatibility, polyploidy, unacceptable gene linkages).

Plant resistance has been found and incorporated mainly to the highly-specialized parasitic nematodes such as Globodera, Heterodera, Meloidogyne, Rotylenchulus, Tylenchulus, and Ditylenchus; these nematodes have sedentary endoparasitic relationships with their host at least for a portion of their lifecycle.

Resistance in a given cultivar or rootstock may be conferred to nematode species of different genera, to more than one species from the same genus, to a single species, or to certain within-species variants. With few exceptions, such as *Xiphinema indexresistance* in grapevines, resistance to ectoparasitic nematodes has not been identified, although many examples of non-hosts (immunity) exist.

Utilization Strategies for Nematode Host Plant Resistance

Resistance can be important for annual crops in two major respects:

1. Firstly, self-protection by a resistant cultivar is achieved in many cases because resistance genes also impart tolerance to nematode injury. Thus, these cultivars yield well under moderate to heavy infection without input of other management tactics (e.g., processing tomatoes).
2. Secondly, cultivars with genes carrying moderate to high resistance block nematode reproduction significantly, resulting in decreases in nematode population levels in soil. This reduces the damage potential for the next crop in rotation. In tomato, this can result in complete protection of a following cotton or bean crop. Thus, rotational value of resistant cultivars can be enormous.

   Rotational aspects are of less concern in most perennial crops. Most important is tolerance to injury associated with resistance, and traits such as limited tissue damage (i.e., root galling or lesions) that will reduce potential for root rots and other diseases resulting from secondary infection of nematode-disrupted tissue.

Beginning of Agriculture Pests

Since the beginning of agriculture pests have caused problems, but the coexistence of pest and crop plant had resulted in traditional farming systems that generally kept damage to a minimum. However, intensification, including changes of cultivars, crops and cultivation patterns, have often created conditions more favourable to pests. Migration or introduction of pests to new areas may also call for control where it was not previously needed. The classical example is grapes, where treatments are now required for diseases in Europe that were introduced from another continent in the last century.

Changes in cultivation and the use of new varieties as in rice production in Southeast Asia have changed the agricultural situation completely, in the process making pests much more difficult to control. Land shortage and lack of inputs have increased the speed of rotations and decreased fertility in the Sahel of Africa, leading to favourable conditions for the parasitic weed Striga. A relatively new development is the spread of noxious weeds (e.g. Imperata) that appear to be resistant to most herbicides.

Migratory pests have been the scourge of crops since times memorial (one of the ten plagues of Egypt were locusts). In the 1980s, population growth of the four species of locusts found in sub-Saharan Africa assumed threatening proportions for the first time in fifty years. The FAO Emergency Centre for Locust Operations was set up to coordinate the international control efforts. The campaign was successful. It revealed a need for new strategies which are being sought in an FAOUNDP research programme on desert locust control.

Protecting Crops from Pests

Ways and means to protect crops from pests are many and varied. Numerous organisms have the capacity to become major pests but most of these are controllable by combinations of cultural measures, host plant resistance and biological control.

Pesticides are used where these other control mechanisms do not keep pests below an acceptable level. For control of weeds, labour scarcity or cost has prompted a gradual shift from manual and mechanical means to use of chemicals.

Pesticide use has, however, led to a number of new problems: biological control agents may also be eliminated, or the pests may become resistant to the pesticide. Excessive or overly liberal use of pesticides may also harm human health and the environment. Lack of knowledge, risk-avoiding behaviour and aggressive sales techniques often result in a misuse or overuse of pesticides.

FAO promotes research to prevent and decrease pest damage. Such research covers the reduction of the pest population, the use of cultural methods, enhancement of host plant resistance and, where appropriate, the identification and use of biological control agents. Research to discover new pesticides, research on application techniques and research on the relationship between pesticides and the environment are also of major importance. An example of biological control is "the sterile insect technique" (SIT).

Plant Protection and Pest Management

In promoting plant protection and pest management, FAO especially emphasizes the role of integrated pest management (IPM). One example of a recent successful project is the development and application of integrated pest control in rice growing in south and southeast Asia. Field trials were made to define appropriate IPM technology in farming areas of the participating countries. These trials involved the identification of natural enemies of the major insect pests, and the choice of effective methods of pest surveillance and of forecasting insect attack severity during the growing season.

Such projects vary in the level of science and technology required or used. Some serve to establish national or regional research capabilities while others stimulate the extension of appropriate methodologies to farmers. A major FAO-executed programme presently under development is the application of IPM in vegetable production. The Organization's work on all aspects of IPM is directly related to sustainable agriculture.

The International Plant Protection Convention covers the field of plant quarantine. FAO serves as the secretariat of the Convention and as an information exchange on pest distribution and pesticide legislation and regulations. The 1989 Conference of FAO recommended that work be done on harmonization of the principles of plant quarantine legislation, of the principles of scientific evidence for plant quarantine measures, and of plant quarantine procedures.

Single Gene Resistance

This has received the most attention so far in HPR research and application. Single, dominant genes for resistance are often most convenient to select and to use in breeding programmes. For example, tomato lines which contain the Mi gene exhibit effective resistance to root-knot nematodes in the field and produce normal yields even in fields severely infested by these nematodes.

Single genes are also desirable for molecular engineering studies because they are easier to identify and manipulate than multiple genes with additive effects and quantitative expression. Thus, major advances in gene cloning, and formation of transgenic plants, will most likely involve single gene systems in the forseeable future. However, a negative aspect of single gene HPR is vulnerability to circumvention by aggressive isolates of nematodes arising through directional selection during frequent exposure to resistant host plants.

A well-characterized example of single-gene resistance is provided by cultivars of tomato that are resistant to root-knot nematodes (e.g., *Meloidogyne* spp.). These nematodes penetrate the host near root tips and cause many changes in root morphology and physiology. Changes include formation of galls and development of specialized "giant cells" for support of nematode development and egg production.

A hypersensitive response consisting of localized cell necrosis at the infection site is characteristic of single gene resistance to many plant pathogens including viruses, bacteria, nematodes, and fungi. These resistance genes appear to involve specific recognition by the plant of some feature of the invading parasite. Often recognition is limited to particular strains or isolates of the pathogen and is believed to be mediated by single genes called avirulence genes in the pathogen, giving rise of gene-for-gene complementarity between host and pathogen.

While avirulence genes have been cloned from bacterial pathogens, less progress has been made in the identification of plant resistance genes. Reasons for this include the high complexity of plant genomes as well as lack of any knowledge about resistance gene products. No definitive information on the tissue localization and level of expression of resistance gene products is available. Whether resistance gene products are induced by pathogens or are constitutively expressed remains an open question. Also, it is not known if the resistance gene products act directly or indirectly in pathogen recognition or in triggering the hypersensitive response.

Identification and selection of genetic sources of HPR to nematodes will require cooperative efforts between nematologists and plant breeders. In addition to collaboration, research needs in this area should focus on the search for gene sources in wild plant gene pools and the selection of traits through classical breeding approaches. Traditional breeding involves the introgression of selected traits into breeding lines and further selecting through recurrent backcrossing programmes to develop resistant cultivars or rootstocks.

Research efforts must be expanded in the isolation and cloning of desirable traits of HPR and tolerance to facilitate understanding of mechanisms of resistance and host-parasite recognition. Cloned genes will enable direct transfer of resistance into crop plants that are unrelated to the gene donor plant. Success in transfer will depend upon adequate, non-disruptive expression of the desired HPR trait in the transgenic plants. The use of novel transfer techniques, including tissue culture, cell and protoplast fusions, embryo cultures, and embryo cloning techniques may help to overcome incompatible plant barriers.

In conjunction with transfer of natural resistance genes, the use of novel sources of resistance (derived through induced mutations and somatic and somaclonal variations) can be explored, as well as incorporation of toxin-producing genes or inhibitors into plants.

Multiple Gene Resistance

Multiple gene resistance is less well understood and usually much more difficult to identify, select, and transfer through classical breeding programmes. Little or no work in nematology on multiple resistance has been attempted at the molecular level, and inheritance studies and basic genetic characterizations are limited thus far. This represents an area where more research emphasis is desirable. Generally, multiple gene HPR is considered more durable than single gene resistance and, thus, may well be of greater long-term value to agriculture.

Because multiple gene resistance is broad-based, and may involve multiple mechanisms, resistance-breaking biotypes may not be readily selected, although studies with multigenic potato lines and the potato-cyst nematode suggest this is not necessarily always the case. Recently, the use of DNA markers has been helpful for breeding complex traits into plants, such as soluble solids into tomato.

Host-plant Tolerance

Tolerance of plants to nematode infection is highly desirable. It is often conferred by genes for resistance, but not always (hypersensitivity can be a problem). Tolerance can also be selected for, independent of genes for resistance, but it is very labor- intensive and programmatically expensive to select for in most cases, requiring large amounts of greenhouse and field plot facility. Research on identifying simple, linked markers for tolerance is required, which could be morphological, physiological, biochemical, or molecular in nature and that would aid in screening, selection, and breeding efforts.

Research Needs – Host Plant Resistance

Key needs in the area of genetic resistance and plant breeding include cooperation with, and support for, classical plant breeding programmes, and research dollar support in the following areas:

1. natural and novel gene source identification and development;
2. classical and novel gene transfer techniques;
3. genetic studies on HPR, tolerance traits, nematode parasitism, and virulence factors;
4. bioengineering studies to facilitate molecular approaches to gene study;
5. transfer and expression of foreign genes in plants; and
6. certain other potential areas such as microtoxin use in vitro, and immunization systems.

Development of a statewide computerized database is also needed to allow access to information on plant susceptibility to nematodes and on management techniques. Longer-term research needs include the development of resistant plants using germplasm from wild species, development of transgenic plants, understanding nematode genetics and its impact on stability of HPR, and understanding the mechanisms of HPR.

A considerable amount of ongoing research in molecular biology is directed toward understanding the nature of control and inheritance of HPR, but it is still unclear how the resistance traits are expressed relative to the nematode and how they are integrated into the physiology of the whole plant.

1. What is the effect of the expressed gene on nematode behaviour, feeding, and reproductive habits?
2. How does expression of the gene affect the growth, fruitfulness, or longevity of the plant?
3. When is the gene expressed?
4. What environmental conditions influence or constrain the expression of the gene?

For example, the expression of resistance conferred by the Mi gene of tomato is not thermostable. The resistance breaks down at soil temperatures above 28° C, which could be a serious constraint in warm environments or at certain times of the year.

In addition to understanding the ramifications of HPR in whole plants, it is also necessary to understand the subtleties of its expression under field conditions. Critical to this understanding is genetic variability of nematode populations, which is not readily measured and is not well documented.

Some interesting lessons have been learned already about the impact of employing single gene resistance against nematodes in whole fields of plants. For example, single genes have been incorporated into soybeans to confer resistance to the soybean-cyst nematode, *H. glycines*. Repeated culture of the resistant varieties selects for variants in the nematode population so that resistance-breaking biotypes become predominant. Consequently, the resistant cultivar is no longer effective in that field, and new sources of resistance are needed.

Similar examples exist for the cyst-nematode parasites of potatoes and cereals in Europe. In another example, a gene for resistance to the root-knot nematode, *M. incognita*, has been incorporated into tobacco varieties grown in the southeastern United States. As a result, *M. arenaria* (another root-knot nematode more virulent than *M. incognita*) has now been selected for in that region.

The solution to the problem of selection for aggressive biotypes or species of a nematode pest by using resistant cultivars may lie in what Vanderplank (1984) described as "stabilizing selection." The underlying principle assumes that genes for aggressiveness to a resistant cultivar may not confer any advantage to the biotype of the nematode in the absence of the selection pressure imposed by the resistance.

In other words, the original biotype or species of the pest was probably predominant because it was well adapted to that environmental situation and ecological niche, and was probably a better competitor for resources than the variants.

Consequently, removal of the selection pressure, by growing a susceptible cultivar, will remove any advantage provided for the new biotype or species and allow selection for the better-adapted, original genotype.

The superior competitive abilities of the original genotype should result in a decline of the new genotype. Obviously, this could lead to reversion to the original problem, so a delicate balance of rotating resistant and susceptible cultivars must be achieved to keep both genotypes below damaging levels.

The implementation of stabilizing selection to preserve the longevity and utility of HPR, based on single-gene sources, requires both the study and measure of a number of epidemiological and population genetics parameters:

- Should the same question be addressed in reverse for the susceptible cultivar?
- What is the frequency of the new genotype in the population?
- What is the appropriate rotation of resistant cultivars, susceptible cultivars, and non-host crops to minimize crop damage, maximize yields and profits, and to preserve the usefulness of the resistant cultivar for that field?

- How rapidly does the frequency of the new genotype increase, and the frequency of the old genotype decrease when the resistant cultivar is grown?

Clearly, in addressing these questions, the planning horizon for nematode management is extended from a single crop season to multiple growing seasons. Also, the perception of management of genotype frequencies of nematode populations in a field over time is introduced, as opposed to merely controlling the numbers of nematodes to a low level prior to planting.

PLANT RESISTANCE TO INSECTS AND DISEASES

Selecting a plant variety that has resistance or tolerance to insects or diseases makes it possible to avoid or lessen the use of pesticides or other management tactics. Seed catalogues and cooperative extension publications should be examined carefully to find varieties of plants that have resistance, or at least some level of tolerance, to the important pests in your area. Our own experiences in the field should also help you decide what varieties to grow in the future, and what ones to avoid because of their susceptibility to insect and disease pests. Plant resistance should be considered a cornerstone for pest management for organic growers.

It may not be feasible to find varieties of plants resistant to all insects and diseases in a specific area, so it is important to identify the pests that are the most damaging in your area and find suitable varieties resistant to them.

Successful breeding for insect and disease resistance has occurred in many different crop types, including vegetables, fruits, field crops and ornamentals. Because field crops are considered low value crops compared with fruits and vegetables, control costs must be minimized and it is in these crops that host plant resistance breeding has had the most attention and success.

Even as far back as the late 1700s wheat varieties resistant to the Hessian fly were used in commercial plantings and host plant resistance remains a major tactic for insect control in field crops. Disease resistance has also become the standard method of controlling fungal and viral pathogens in corn, wheat and other field crops, as well as many of the important vegetable crops.

There are many similarities in breeding for disease and insect resistance, including the ability of pests to overcome the resistance. Plants and pests interact on a physical, chemical and molecular level and changes in the genetics of either the plant or the pest may affect their interaction. In the case of resistance this results in a constant battle in which the pest evolves to overcome whatever resistance the plant may have. Depending on the complexity of the interaction between the pest and the plant, plant resistance may break down rapidly or be long-lived.

Plant resistance to pests is based on the plant genetics and the consequential molecular interactions that occur between host and pest organism. There are three general types of mechanisms for resistance based on how the pest and plant interact.

Antibiosis is defined as the adverse effect that a plant may have on the pest because of chemicals or structures the plant possesses. Plants contain a wealth of chemicals some of which may be toxic to a pest or cause it to grow more slowly. The chemical commonly referred to as DIMBOA is antibiotic to the European corn borer and occurs in corn, rye and wheat varieties. There are dozens of plant chemicals that have some antibiotic effect on insects, including botanical pesticides such as rotenone and pyrethrum.

Some of the chemicals, such as jasmonic acid, may be produced by plants when first attacked by insects or pathogens. However, their levels are sometimes too low to provide adequate protection. Likewise, plants may possess structures such as hairs or trichomes that may impede insects or secrete chemicals that ensnarl them and thus have an antibiotic effect.

Antixenosis resistance involves behavioural factors that cause an insect not to choose the plant for feeding or laying its eggs. This lack of selection could be the result of chemicals or colors or even the presence of structures on the plant. An example of antixenosis is the chemical coumarin, which is produced by sweet clover and deters feeding by the vegetable weevil and several other insect pests.

Tolerance is a characteristic of some plants that enable them to withstand or recover from insect or disease damage. An example of breeding for tolerance is the development of corn plants with vigorous root systems that can compensate when they are attacked by corn rootworms.

Another example is breeding sweet corn with husks that inhibit the ability of insects to damage the ear. Tolerance to disease is commonly found against plant viruses, where a plant can be infected with a virus, but show few symptoms and the infection has little if any effect on yield.

Vertical Resistance

Vertical resistance is more commonly a form of disease resistance and is generally controlled by a single gene, referred to as an R-gene. These R-genes can be remarkably effective in controlling disease and can confer complete resistance. However, each R-gene confers resistance to only one race of the pathogen. Thus, depending on the race of the pathogen present in your area a variety may appear strongly resistant or completely susceptible. Many varieties contain multiple R-genes against the same pathogen; for example, many bell pepper varieties have resistance known as X3R that confers resistance to three races of Xanthomonas (the pathogen that causes bacterial leaf spot).

Horizontal resistance is also known as multi-gene resistance because this type of resistance is controlled by many genes. Because of the large number of genes involved, it is much more difficult to breed varieties with horizontal resistance. Unlike vertical resistance, horizontal resistance generally does not completely prevent a plant from becoming damaged. For pathogens, this type of resistance may slow the infection process so much that the pathogen does not grow well or spread to other plants. Additionally, horizontal resistance is generally effective against all races of a pathogen.

In 1965, it was noted that 65 of 300 crop cultivars registered in the US contained some disease resistance, while only six per cent contained significant levels of insect resistance. This difference can be attributed to the general tendency for multiple plant genes to be involved in insect resistance and the increased difficulty breeding such polygenic resistance requires.

Plant breeders, and the plant pathologists and entomologists with whom they collaborate, constantly look for new sources that can be utilized to develop resistant plants. Sources of plant material that can be tapped for resistant germplasm include the USDA, international research centers, foreign seeds banks, private individuals and seeds companies.

Resistance to pesticides in arthropod pests is a significant economic, ecological and public health problem. Although extensive research has been conducted on diverse aspects of pesticide resistance and we have learned a great deal during the past 50 years, to some degree the discussion about 'resistance management' has been based on 'myths'. One myth involves the belief that we can manage resistance.

We will maintain that we can only attempt to mitigate resistance because resistance is a natural evolutionary response to environmental stresses. As such, resistance will remain an ongoing dilemma in pest management and we can only delay the onset of resistance to pesticides.

'Resistance management' models and tactics have been much discussed but have been tested and deployed in practical pest management programmes with only limited success. Yet the myth persists that better models will provide a 'solution' to the problem.

The reality is that success in using mitigation models is limited because these models are applied to inappropriate situations in which the critical genetic, ecological, biological or logistic assumptions cannot be met.

It is difficult to predict in advance which model is appropriate to a particular situation; if the model assumptions cannot be met, applying the model sometimes can increase the rate of resistance development rather than slow it down. Are there any solutions? I believe we already have one. Unfortunately, it is not a simple or easy one to deploy.

It involves employing effective agronomic practices to develop and maintain a healthy crop, monitoring pest densities, evaluating economic injury levels so that pesticides are applied only when necessary, deploying and conserving biological control agents, using host-plant resistance, cultural controls of the pest, biorational pest controls, and genetic control methods.

As a part of a truly multi-tactic strategy, it is crucial to evaluate the effect of pesticides on natural enemies in order to preserve them in the cropping system. Sometimes, pesticide-resistant natural enemies are effective components of this resistance mitigation programme. Another name for this resistance mitigation model is integrated pest management (IPM). This complex model was outlined in some detail nearly 40 years ago.

To deploy the IPM resistance mitigation model, we must admit that pest management and resistance mitigation programmes are not sustainable if based on a single-tactic strategy.

Delaying resistance, whether to traditional pesticides or to transgenic plants containing toxin genes from Bacillus thuringiensis, will require that we develop multi-tactic pest management programmes that incorporate all appropriate pest management approaches.

As pesticides are limited resources, and their loss can result in significant social and economic costs, they should be reserved for situations where they are truly needed—as tools to subdue an unexpected pest population outbreak. Effective multi-tactic IPM programmes delay resistance (= mitigation) because the number and rates of pesticide applications will be reduced.

PESTICIDES: A CODE FOR DISTRIBUTION AND USE

An important recent development has been the adoption by the FAO Conference (1985) of an International Code of Conduct on the Distribution and Use of Pesticides, amended in 1987 to include the principle of prior informed consent. The pesticides industry, through the International Group of National Associations of Agrochemical Manufacturers (GIFAP), and UNEP in regard to the prior informed consent clause, agreed to assist FAO in the implementation of the provisions of the code. Environmental groups use the code as a yardstick to evaluate pesticide management in developing countries.

The code is supported by a set of guidelines prepared with the cooperation and advice of experts from FAO member countries. These guidelines cover such topics as registration and control (legislative and monitoring) of pesticides; efficacy data needed for registration; environmental criteria; residue data; labeling, packaging and storage; and disposal of waste pesticides and pesticide containers.

An activity complementary to the code is the provision of technical assistance to strengthen national and regional pesticide control schemes, to establish the necessary analytical facilities, and to give guidance on the safe and efficient use of pesticides.

In cooperation with WHO, FAO proposes maximum residue limits and tolerable levels of intake over time, based on toxicology data provided by governments and industry and reviewed by FAO/WHO expert groups. More than 150 different pesticides have been evaluated, resulting in the adoption by the Codex Alimentarius Commission of more than 2 000 maximum residue limits on specific commodities.

Quality control standards have been prepared for 25 pesticide active ingredients. These standards are used by national governments in the formulation of their legislation and for establishing import controls. They have also found use in international trade.

BIOLOGICAL CONTROL FOR MANAGEMENT OF INSECT PESTS OF TURFGRASS

Insects feeding on endophyte infected plants are sometimes less susceptible to insect-parasitic nematodes and the alkaloids present in endophyte-infected plants can influence the efficacy of biological controls. Research has also shown that fertility can influence the concentration of defensive compounds present in endophyte-infected plants and that the degree to which fungal endophytes protect their plant symbiont from insect herbivory can vary with fertility.

However, the relationship between fertility, endophyte-mediated resistance, and biological controls has not been explored. As a results, turfgrass fertility programmes have not been optimized for use with modern alternative pest management strategies. Implementation of alternative management strategies has been slow in turfgrass systems because it is unclear how basic turfgrass management practices may interact with cultural and biological alternatives.

Fertility, a basic component of turfgrass management, may be very important in this regard because of the profound influence it can have on ecosystem structure and function. Unfortunately, the relationship between fertility, host-plant resistance and biological controls has not been examined in this system.

In order to identify and prioritize the arthropod pests and natural enemies associated with Indiana turfgrass and determine how management practices influence the abundance and diversity of these arthropods, lawn care operators will be asked to rank a complete list of turfgrass insects in terms of their potential for causing damage.

This will be followed by a biological survey of residential lawns in Tippecanoe Co., IN. Property owners will be recruited and asked to provide baseline information about their lawn management practices. Lawns will be classified according to management intensity and turfgrass species composition, insects, weeds, arthropod natural enemies, entomo-pathogenic nematodes, and plant nutrition will be measured.

Additional descriptive data (lot size, age of the lawn, previous land use, slope and direction of slope, shading, overall quality and satisfaction, cutting height, fate of clippings, thatch depth and soil properties) will also be collected. Data analysis will be performed using MANCOVA and correlation analysis. Principle component analysis will be used to determine which combinations of factors best describe the variation in measured responses. To describe how interactions between soil fertility and fungal endophytes influence plant growth and resource allocation, alkaloid production, insect herbivore performance and susceptibility to biological and biorational controls, a series of laboratory and greenhouse experiments will be performed. Endophyte-infected and uninfected tall fescue will be grown in the greenhouse and supplied with nutrient solutions containing different levels and sources of nitrogen or different levels of phosphorus.

Plant growth and resource allocation, alkaloid production, insect herbivore performance, and insect susceptibility to biological/biorational controls (nematodes, Bt, spinosad) will be measured. Analysis of variance (ANOVA) will be used to determine how the different fertility treatments influence response variables. Additionally, graphical comparisons of the statistical models describing each response variable will used to determine levels of fertility where combinations of measured parameters are optimized.

Using information gathered through completion of objective 1, a series of field experiments will be performed to develop and evaluate management strategies for key insect pests based on the integration of fertility management, endophyte-mediated resistance, and biological/biorational controls.

Plots of tall fescue containing high and low levels of endophyte infection will be fertilized with different levels and sources of nitrogen or different levels of phosphorus and inoculated with key insect pests. Plots will be treated with entomopathogenic nematodes, *Bt*, or spinosad. Insect populations and their damage will be sampled and rated. Plant growth and resource allocation and alkaloid production will also be measured. Soil cores will also be taken at several times during the year to evaluate the abundance and diversity of beneficial soil arthropods. Data will be analyzed using ANOVA, but additional statistical techniques will be employed as appropriate.

NOVEL EVOLUTIONARY CHANGES

Adaptation to novel evolutionary challenges such as pesticides or new habitats often imposes a fitness cost, which is a reduction in fitness relative to susceptibles in the absence of the selective agent. Fitness costs are commonly enhanced or more easily detected in stressful environments: e.g. under high competition; in low nutrient conditions; or during overwintering. Thus, costs may be reduced when environmental conditions are benign or when resource quality is high, perhaps because physiologically less stressed organisms may be able to rely on compensatory mechanisms to mask physiological deficiencies. Host-plant defences can represent a significant source of stress and mortality for herbivores.

Moreover, the magnitude and genetics of fitness costs of resistance to the bacterium *Bacillus thuringiensis* (*Bt*) can be altered by plant defence compounds and may be greater on crop plants that are better defended against herbivore attack. If the fitness costs of resistance to pesticides can vary predictably with food-plant defences, these characteristics may be important tools in resistance management. Conversely, high resource quality (e.g. escape from competition) may be generally important for the spread of novel adaptations through a population.

We hypothesized that fitness costs to a lepidopteran host associated with resistance to *Bt* should increase on better-defended food plants. Our study species, the diamondback moth, *Plutella xylostella L.*, has repeatedly evolved resistance to Bt. This bacterium is widely used as a bio-pesticide (e.g. DiPel) and Bt genes expressing insect-specific toxins are commonly incorporated into genetically modified crops.

MATERIAL AND METHODS

Insects, Plants and Selection Protocols

Two resistant populations of P. xylostella were collected from Malaysia in 2001 and 2002, respectively, from Chinese cabbage, *Brassica pekinensis*, farms 200 km apart that are regularly sprayed with DiPel. The strains differ in their mode of inheritance of resistance: incompletely recessive in Karak; semi-dominant in Keluang, although the mechanism of resistance has only been described for Karak. Revertant strains, i.e. previously selected strains that had lost resistance to *Bt*, were produced by long-term culture on Chinese cabbage *B. pekinensis;* resistant strains were selected periodically with Cry1Ac (the predominant crystal toxin in DiPel) as described previously. Prior to experiments, resistance levels to Cry1Ac were checked using leaf-dip bioassays.

The common cabbage, *Brassica oleracea L.*, var. 'Wheelers Imperial', and the Chinese cabbage, *B. pekinensis*, var. 'One Kilo, S.B', were used in this study at eight and five weeks old, respectively. *B. oleracea* has defences against lepidopteran attack (waxiness, toughness and glucosinolate levels) that are much reduced in B. pekinensis. Plants were grown in a climate-controlled glasshouse maintained at 20±1°C with supplementary lighting (400 W sodium and halide lamps: min. incident radiation 300 W m^2).

Performance of Revertant and Resistant Populations on Two Plant Species

Cry1Ac resistant and susceptible revertant strains from the Karak and Keluang populations were used in a full-factorial experiment with plants of both Brassica species. Individual plants (n=9–10) were randomly allocated to treatments. We added 45 and 35 freshly emerged neonates to each *B. oleracea* and *B. pekinensis* plant, respectively. Mean mass and number of larvae on each plant were recorded after five days. After one week, plants were checked daily and pupae removed and weighed.

Female fecundity was measured by rearing up to three individual pairs from each plant in 50 mm diameter Petri dishes (one dish per pair) with access to 20% honey solution for five days. The means of data from each plant were used in analyses to avoid pseudo-replication.

Stability of Resistance on *B. oleracea* and *B. pekinensis*

This experiment tested whether variation in plant-associated fitness costs in the Karak population would lead to different rates of decline of resistance in culture. Each replicate was initiated with 200 neonates from the resistant Karak population with four plants per replicate cage and four cages per treatment. Thereafter, each generation was propagated with 40-50 pupae.

Replicates were reared in individual culture cages (at 25±1°C, 50-60 per cent RH, 16 h photophase) for three generations. Thereafter, all populations were reared for a single generation on B. pekinensis in order to control for plant-based maternal effects and bioassayed in the following generation (N=35-40 larvae per dose and six doses).

Data Analysis

Statistical analysis was carried out in R using analysis of variance and generalized linear modelling. Proportional data were logit-transformed and models were scaled to correct for overdispersion, where appropriate.

The stability experiment was analysed with a mixed model analysis of covariance, with replicate as a random effect and bioassay dose nested within replicate. In the mixed model, mortality data were arcsine transformed and doses log-transformed.

HOST PLANT RESISTANCE

Host plant resistance pertains to a plant's ability to resist damaging insect invasions. Some plants use their physical appearance as a deterrent such as plants that have hair covering their leaves or plants with a thick leaf cuticle. With biotechnology, came a new form of host plant resistance.

The ability to insert genes into plants, creating transgenic hybrids, gave a whole new meaning to plant resistance. Plants that previously had no resistance mechanisms now are able to resist damaging insects. This is the case with the development of the YieldGard® corn traits. The first YieldGard on the market was developed for plant resistance against European corn borer. It used the Cry1Ab protein from Bacillus thuringiensis to control the European corn borer.

This protein is specific to the insect order Lepidoptera and can only be activated in the gut of the larva (caterpillar). The same concept for creating this type of host-plant resistance was used for YieldGard® Rootworm. YieldGard Rootworm was developed to allow corn plants to have resistance to damaging corn rootworm larvae.

Yield Gard Rootworm contains *Bt* (*Bacillus thuringiensis*) that is specifically targeted to affect the corn rootworm. The Bt protein inserted into YieldGard Rootworm corn is Cry 3Bb and can only be activated inside the corn rootworm gut to cause death.

Additional research has been conducted to determine effects on other non-target organisms. YieldGard Rootworm has been found to pose minimal risk to mammals, birds, fish, and other non-target insects including lady beetles and monarch butterflies.

Mode of Action

The use of *Bt* as an insecticide is an effective, plant delivered approach to controlling certain insects. There are three criteria that need to be met for an insect to be affected by Bt. First, the correct Bt protein must be used against the specific insect that is susceptible. For example, YieldGard® Corn borer contains the *Bt* protein that will control corn borer but will not control corn rootworm.

The second criterion that must be met is for the insect to have the correct pH within the gut system to activate the Bt protein. The third criterion requires that the insect targeted by the *Bt* protein, have the appropriate midgut receptor. If an insect does not have the correct receptors, there is no binding site for the protein and therefore, no toxic activity will take place inside the insect.

Advantages

There are many advantages to using transgenic hybrids including reduced exposure to insecticides, ease of use, and proven product performance. The handling practices required when using transgenic hybrids, such as YieldGard, minimize exposure to pesticides. Since the insect resistance is contained within the plant and is not applied on the outside, there is never any contact with insecticides for the producer.

Transgenic hybrids are very easy to use, as well. These hybrids can be planted using the same equipment and plant populations as non-transgenic hybrids. The insect protection technology is in the seed, therefore eliminating any need to calibrate insecticide application equipment.

Proven product performance can be seen through examples such as improved crop harvestability and the ability of the corn hybrid to reach its maximum yield potential. The hybrid is protected season long from CRW damage due to the internal insect protection offered by YieldGard, therefore reducing the possibility of lodging. In addition, the plants' chances of producing the maximum amount of grain have increased since the adverse affects of CRW feeding have been drastically reduced.

Disadvantages

There are disadvantages to using transgenic hybrids including possible development of insecticide resistance, the limited spectrum of the transgenic hybrid, harvested grain channeling, and unnecessary use of transgenic technology. Insecticide resistance occurs when the insect becomes resistant to the management option, in this case, the transgenic hybrid. This can occur in a number of different ways and should be closely monitored. More on insecticide resistance management is discussed in the next section.

The limited spectrum disadvantage pertains to the transgenic hybrids ability to only control one insect, CRW. YieldGard Rootworm is only able to protect itself from corn rootworm larvae. Therefore, if another root damaging insect is present, such as the white grub, YieldGard will not provide plant protection. In these cases another method of management will have to be implemented.

The third disadvantage of using transgenic hybrids is the difficulty in which the producer may have in marketing the grain after harvest. Some grain elevators and export markets will not accept YieldGard Rootworm grain. The producer must then determine where the grain can be stored and ultimately into which market it can be sold.

Finally, the disadvantage of using transgenic hybrids when not needed can directly affect producers' profit. The insecticide technology is always in the plant whether or not the target insect is present. Producers must pay a fee to use this technology when purchasing the seed. Therefore, in the event of low insect pressure, the producer who planted transgenic seed has unnecessarily applied insecticide to the field.

CHAPTER – 11

Insect Morphology

The morphology of insects enables the phenomenal success of this class of arthropods. The sheer quantity and diversity of its taxa are matched by a large variation of modifications in its body structure. The high rate of speciation, short generations and long lineage have caused insects to evolve in many ways resulting in very large variations in morphology.

These modifications allow insects to occupy almost everyecological niche, utilise a staggering variety of food sources and possess diverse lifestyles. Insect body sizes range from 0.3 mm in the case ofmymarid wasps which parasitise insect eggs to the 30 cms wingspan of the American owlet moth *Thysania agrippina* (family Noctuidae).

Insects are by far the most successful group in the Arthropoda. They differ in significant ways from the other classes of Hexapoda, such as Protura, Collembola and others who are now considered by some authorities to be more basal than insects.

Due to paucity of paleontologicalrecord, morphology was the main source for inputs for constructing insect phylogeny but was invariably beset with conjecture and conditionality. A stable and reliable phylogeny of insects is slowly developing due to the advent of DNA genome analysis. This has reduced the importance of morphology in evolutionary studies. However morphology still plays a great part in understanding how insects adapt and cope with their myriad lifestyles on planet Earth.

PRINCIPLES OF INSECT MORPHOLOGY

RE Snodgrass first published *Principles of Insect Morphology in* 1935. Several reprints and 70 years later, this text still is useful and interesting for a student of entomology, and is a wonderful reference for any entomologist to have.

Yes, it does not have the molecular information that one would find in more recent works such as Chapman's Insects: Structure and Function. At one point Snodgrass refers to the germ cells as "the carriers of inheritance, whatever that may be". Modern understanding of inheritance through DNA was not discovered until the middle part of the last century.

However, the drawings are excellent, and our understanding of basic structures of the insects such as the general body plan, the sclerites, muscles, wings, digestive tract, etc, have not changed much since this book was published. The writing and explanation of the figures is also excellent, and Snodgrass' hypotheses for the evolution of the insect ground plan are still in use today.

Snodgrass was a very meticulous, ordered and organized character. His daily habits were regular, he would fill his coffee cup to the same exact line every day at the same time and walk the same thirty some steps down the hallway to his office. This understanding of order and attention to detail shows very well in his drawings. His particular style of work was to reduce figures to the smallest necessary number of lines to convey proper understanding of structures. Those of you who have worked in biology labs before understand that too much detail in a reference figure obscures understanding of the position and structure of the very parts which you are using as reference. By reducing lines, Snodgrass effectively conveyed the exact message he wished to with his drawings, rather than putting us in awe of his artistic work and scrambling to understand what goes where.

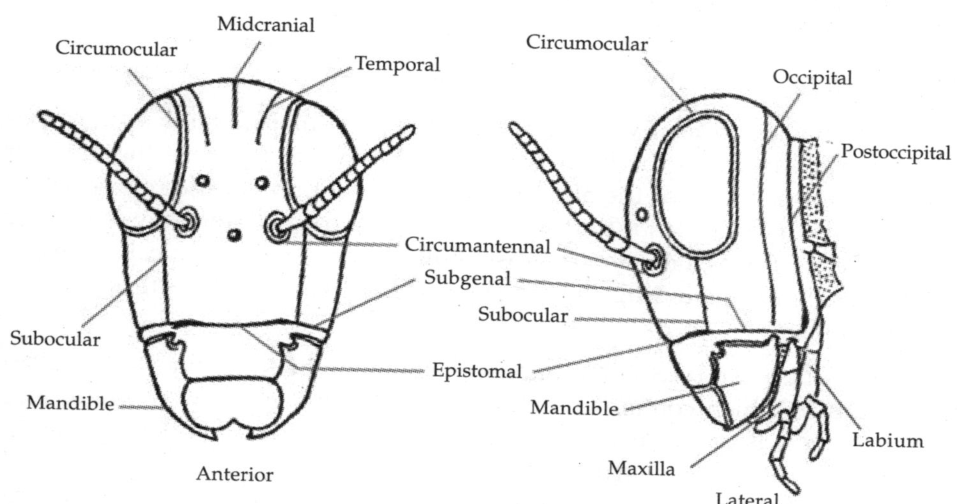

Generalized Head of an Orthopteroid Insect Showing Major Sulci or "Sutures"

An example of Snodgrass' drawing style. Note the lack of stipling except to differentiate membrane from sclerotized regions.

INSECT ANATOMY

Because of the great diversity of form exhibited by the insects any introduction to anatomy like this is only going to be able to cover the basics, within each order and family these familiar themes are replayed in a myriad of different ways creating what might seem to be a bewildering array of different body plans.

A closer look will reveal the same basic plan in all insects, at least in the adult forms. Below are described some of the basic parts that make up an insects body.

An insect body has a hard exoskeleton protecting a soft interior, it is divided into three main parts (the head, thorax and abdomen) each of which is in turn composed of several smaller segments.

Pete the Grasshopper

The Integument

The amazing success of the insects must in part lie with the incredible mixture of flexibility and strength of the integument (that is the part of an insect that makes up the hard exoskeleton) that allows the insects their freedom of movement without loss of defence and protection. It is made up of three parts, the most visible of which is the outer 'cuticle' and its attendant bristles and hairs, below this are the 'epidermis' and the 'basement membrane'

The Cuticle

The cuticle is a relatively thin layer of non-cellular material which lines the external surface of the body as well as lining the tracheae the anterior and posterior sections of the alimentary canal and parts of the reproductive system. It is flexible, elastic and white when first formed and stays this way in many larval forms, however in most adults it undergoes chemical processes which result in hardening and darkening and which are referred to as 'sclerotization'.

The cuticle can be divided into two layers, a very thin outer layer called the epicuticle which contains no chitin and is highly resistant to water and other solvents. Beneath this is the much thicker procuticle which can again be divided into two distinct layers, an outer 'exocuticle' which lies immediately below the 'epicuticle' and an inner 'endocuticle' which consists of a large number of layers of protein and chitin fibres laid down in a laminated pattern such that the individual strands in each layer cross each other thus creating an extremely tough and flexible substance.

Below the cuticle lie the other two components of the integument, the 'epidermis' which is a single layer of secretary cells and the 'basement membrane' which is an amorphous layer about 0.5 micrometres thick.

The head

The insect's head is sometimes referred to as the head-capsule, and is the insects feeding and sensory centre, and supports the eyes, antennae and jaws of the insect,. The upper-mid portion is called the 'frons' below this is the 'clypeus' and below this the 'labrum' to either side of which may be seen the edges of the 'mandibles' in some insects various aspects of the 'maxilliary' palps may extend beyond and or below these even when viewed from front on.

The 'frons' that area of the face below the top two 'ocelli' and above the 'frontoclypeal sulcus' (if and when this is visible) and in between the two 'frontogenal sulci', it supports the 'pharyngeal dilator' muscles and in immature forms it bears the lower two arms of the ecdysial cleavage lines.

The 'clypeus' that are of the face immediately below the frons (with which it may be fused in the absence of the frontoclypeal sulcus) and the fc. sulcus. It supports the 'cibarial dilator' muscles and may be divided horizontally into a 'post.' and 'anteclypeus'.

The 'labrum' is equivalent to the insects upper lip and is generally moveable, it articulates with the clypeus by means of the 'clypeolabral suture'.

The rest of the front of the head, that bit which is above the frons is known as the 'epicranium'.

The Antennae

The antennae are primarily non-visual sense organs, though in some are instances they have become adapted for seizing prey items (i.e. the larva of *Chaoborus* sp.) or holding females during mating (i.e. the males of *Meloe* sp.) Not all insects possess antennae, they are absent from the Protura.

In most insects, the antennae possesses a mechanosensory organ on the pedicel (the second antennal segment) called 'Johnston's organ'; Also only basal antennal segment contains intrinsic muscles, however in two orders (Diplura and Collembola) the antennae lack a 'Johnston's organ' and all but the last segment contains intrinsic muscles, thus allowing far greater controlled movement of the antennae as demonstrated in the rolling and unrolling of the antennae observed in the Collembola Tomocerus longicornus.

Antennae come in a wide variety of shapes and sizes, generally the first segment is known as the 'scape' the second segment as the 'pedicel' and the rest as the flagellum. It is quite usual that the males of a species have more elaborate antennae than the females, this is because it is normally the males who have to find the females. The greater the surface area of the antennae the more dilute scents they can detect, thus male insects with feathery antennae, such as those seen in many moths, are far more sensitive than the purely filamentous ones of crickets and cockroaches.

The Eyes

Though some species of insects have been shown to be able respond to light stimulus through their cuticle, most light sensitivity occurs through one or more of a series of eyes. Insects possess two different sorts of eyes, the usually large and obviously visible compound eyes, and two varieties of ocelli or simple eyes.

Compound Eyes

Compound eyes are so named because the cornea is composed of a number of individual facets or lenses (called ommatidia), rather than a single lens as in ocelli. The number of separate visual elements or ommatidia varies greatly between species as well as between the larger taxa, so that while worker ants of different species may have between 100 and 600 ommatidia per single eye, adult male Odonata may have more than 28,000 per single eye.

This creates a considerable difference in the presentation of light stimulus to the insect brain, however the ability of insects to navigate the world by means of visual stimuli suggest that they have overcome the problems inherent in this multi-faceted perception. Much like our eyes, the eyes of insects, can be divided into four basic parts: the supportative material that keeps all the parts together; a light gathering part (the lens and the auxilary lens called a 'crystalline cone'); a light receptor that converts the recieved light into electrical energy; and the nerves that carry the electrical impulses to the brain for analysis. In the compound eyes of insects these parts are repeated numerous times side by side in a space saving hexagonal pattern. See above.

The lens is formed by a transparent and colourless cuticle and it is usually biconvex. Beneath this is the crystalline cone (which is comprised of four cells called 'Semper cells' after the man who first described them). Normally this functions as a secondary lens.

The receptive parts of an insect's eye are the 'retinula cells'. Each ommatidium normally has eight retinula cells arranged to leave a central core space in the centre of the ommatidium, into which each retinula cell projects a series of microvilli (like very small fingers). These microvilli are the actual light detecting part of the cells and are collectively referred to as the rhabdomere (think cornea). The eight (or occasionally 7 or 9) rhabdomeres (sets of microvilli) form a rhabdom.

The corneal lens is supported by 'primary pigment cells' and the retinula cells and associated rhabdoms are supported by 'secondary pigment cells'. The retinula cells are connected to axons at the base of the eye, it is these which carry the information collected by the lenses and converted into electrical impulses by the rhabdom to the brain, thus allowing the insect to see.

Simple Eyes

Ocelli are present in most insects to some degree, though as with all aspects of insect anatomy there is a great deal of variety in form and even in relative function. Generally they consist of five separate parts the 'cornea', the 'corneagen layer', the 'retina', the 'pigment cells', and the 'central nervous connections'.

(a) *The Cornea* this is a thickened area of generally transparent cuticle to the outside of the ocellus which serves as a lens.

(b) *The Corneagen Layer* this is a single layer of specialised transparent and colourless epidermal cells which secrete the cornea.

(c) *The Retina* this is a group of primary sensory cells which convert light into an electrical stimulus and transfer it to the; the cells are called 'retinula' cells and they are arranged in circular groups with each member of the group contributing to its portion rhabdomere to the group rhabdom. The rhabdom is the light sensitive pigment, or the part of the ocellus that converts the light into an electrical stimulus.

(d) *The Central Nervous Connections* which link to the 'protocerebrum' and hence to the 'Corpora pedunculata' (the brain).

(e) *The Pigment Cells* this is a group of highly pigmented (coloured) cells variably distributed around the ocellus whose main roll would appear to be the exclusion of light from parts of the ocellus other than the cornea.

The function of the corneal lens is obscure, although it does project an image into the ocellus this image forms below the level of the light-sensitive cells, or rhabdom. Therefore the ocellus can generate no image information, however it is very sensitive to low levels of light and to changes in light intensity and scientists believe that the ocelli are useful in allowing the insect to detect the horizon, to respond quickly to changes in light intensity.

Two different forms of ocelli have been described for insects, *Dorsal ocelli* and *Lateral ocelli*. Dorsal ocelli occur mostly in adult insects and are situated on the front of the insects face in the area of the 'frons' and or the 'epicranium', lateral ocelli generally occur on the sides of the insect head and are the form of eye most common in larval forms; there are a number of concrete differences between the two forms which can be be found explained in any competent entomological text book such as Imm's 1984.

Hearing and Other Senses

Ears

Many but not all insects can hear sounds, some even hear sounds that we can't hear ourselves. Insects hear through one of four different ways, the most common of which is the tympanum. Tympanal organs always occur as paired organs, they are composed a thin cuticular membrane (the tympanum) stretched across an air space of some sort and some form of connection to the nervous system. In the Orthoptera (Grasshoppers and Crickets) tympanum are common, though situated in different places in different species, i.e. on the third thoracic segment in the Locusts Locusta migratoria and on the front legs in the House Cricket Acheta domesticus.

Tympanal organs also occur in the Cicada (Cicadidae, Hemiptera) and some families of the Lepidoptera, (i.e. Noctuidae, Geometridae, and Pyralididae). The other three forms of hearing organs are:

(a) Johnston's Organ, via the movement of hairs on the antennal scape i.e. the Mosquito Aedes aegypti.

(b) Auditory Hairs these occur on some Lepidopteran larvae as well as on some Orthoptera.

(c) The Pilifer this is a unique auditory organ found only in the head of certain species of Hawk Moths of the subfamily Choerocampinae its optimum frequency is between 30 and 70 kHz.

Smell

Most insects communicate using smell or chemoreception and it is not surprising that they have evolved a large variety of ways of detecting the molecules involved. Insects do not have noses like us which concentrate all our sense of smell in one place, instead they have a lot of small sensory bodies scattered over their body, though they tend to have a concentration of them on their antennae.

We can recognise several different common forms of chemoreceptor though these are not the only forms they can take by any means:

(a) Sensilla trichoidea, hair-like structures commonly found on the feet of flies and the antennae of many insects, they are the most common form of chemoreceptor found.

(b) Sensilla basiconica and Sensilla styloconica, these are peg-like or cone-like and are thicker and more solid than trichoid sensilla, these are commonly found on the antennae, though they also occur on the maxillary palps of Lepidopteran larvae and the ovipositor of the Blowfly Phormia regina.

(c) Sensilla coeloconica or pit-peg organs these are always situated in a pit as their common name suggests, unlike the previous two which project above the insects cuticle. They are common on a variety of insect antennae and and in Apis mellifera (the Honey Bee) they detect Carbon Dioxide.

(d) Sensilla placodea these differ from the first three in that they consist of a flat plate of cuticle, they occur on the antennae of various Aphids and Apis mellifera (the Honey Bee).

Touch

Touch is an extremely important sense to insects and like smell insects have developed many different ways to detect mechanical stimulus, these all involve some form of physical change in the receptor, the most common are hairs attached to nerves which react when the hairs are moved, these are called *Trichoid sensilla.*

Another common type looks more like a drum with something pressing up against the skin of the drum from beneath, these are called *Campaniform sensilla.* Mechanoreceptors detect not only the physical interaction with another body but also air movements, changes in air pressure and also changes in the stresses being applied to the insects cuticle, thus allowing it to better control its movements and maintain balance.

Insects also use modified forms of the various sensory detectors described above to detect, changes in temperature, humidity and also in some cases to detect infra red radiation, x-ray radiation and the Earth's magnetic field.

THE MOUTHPARTS

The insect mouth articulates (moves) from side to side in a horizontal plane, rather than vertically as do ours. It consists of a number of parts which starting from the foremost are called:

(a) The Labrum

(b) The Mandibles

(c) The maxillae

(d) The Labium

(e) The Hypopharynx or tongue.

The Mandibles

The mandibles, with the maxillae, the labial palps and in some species the hypopharynx constitute the moveable aspects of the insect mouth, the mandibles and the maxillae are the equivalent of jaws with the exception that they move transversely (from side to side). The mandibles show great variety within the insect orders and like our more familiar teeth they are hard and show variation in accordance with diet, thus they are sharp edged in carnivores, being extremely sickle like in the ant Aceton burchelli, whilst being adapted for crushing and chewing in herbivores.

They have become a secondary sexual characteristic and are extremely large in some Beetles (i.e. in the genus Chiasognathus and Lucanus [Stag Beetles]).

In other orders they have become residual as in the adults of some Lepidoptera, or entirely absent as in the adults of the rest of the Lepidoptera, Trichoptera, Ephemeroptera and the Diptera. Mandibles are are used not only for feeding but also for attack and defence, becoming extremely exaggerated in various species of termites ants (i.e. *Atta texanus*), and for manipulation of materials as in the nest building insects particularly the Hymenopteran Bees, ants and wasps.

The Maxillae

The maxillae are a pair of modified limbs which work behind the mandibles and in front of the labium as a pair of accessory jaws. They are composed of the following parts:

- The Cardo, this is the piece nearest the head capsule and in some species of insect it is the only part of the maxillae that is connected to the head.
- The Stypes this is central bulk of the maxillae and supports;
- Palpifer, which in turn supports;
- Maxilliary palp, which has one to seven segments and is mainly used as a sensory organ.
- The Lacinia is situated at the distal end of the Stypes, is often serrated or toothed and serves to aid the eating process both by holding and masticating the food. It is boarded distally (to the far side in relation to the overall body);
- The Galea and proximally (to the near-side in relationship to the body); and
- The Subgalea for more information on which I would recommend a specialist text on insect morphology (body shape) such as those by 'Snodgrass'.

The Labium

It results from the fusion of a pair of limbs and serves a purpose similar to our lower lip for the insects. The main body of the labium is divided into three parts the central 'mentum' which is boarded on either side by the 'submentum' proximally which hinges with the head, and the prementum distally.

The prementum supports two pairs of lobes known as the 'glossae' and to the outside of them the 'paraglossae', and a pair of labial palps which are primarily sensory in function. The glossae and paraglossae may be fused, with one or the other considerably reduced, in which case the whole thing is known as the 'ligula'.

The hyper-pharynx or tongue is found behind the mouth, and has the salivary ducts at its base, in most Diptera (true flies) and Hemiptera (true bugs) it has become highly modified and serves as the main feeding organ, in many cases combining with the rest of the mouthparts to form a stylette or piercing organ.

The Thorax

The thorax is the main engine room of the insect. It like the Abdomen is built up of a series of concave upper integumental plates known as 'tergites' and convex lower integumental plates known as 'sternites', the whole being held together by a tough yet stretchable membrane.

The thorax can be conveniently divided into three separate and normally easily visible sections called from the front, the 'prothorax' the 'mesothorax' and the 'metathorax'.

In the adult insects as well as in the nymphs of those insects with an 'incomplete metamorphosis' (those whose life cycle lacks the production of a pupa), each of these sections supports a pair of legs. In the pterygote (winged) insect orders the first two sections support a pair of wings, except in the Diptera (true flies) where the second or hind wings have become modified into a pair of club-like balancing organs called 'halteres'.

The Legs

The typical insect leg consists of six main sections:

1. The Coxa, this is the most basal aspect of the insect leg and articulates with the 'sternites'.
2. The Trochanter is usually small and serves as a joint between the 'coxa' and the 'femur'.

3. The Femur is usually long and stouter than the other segments and contains the main muscles used in running, jumping and digging.
4. The tibia is also generally long serving to increase the length of the leg, as well as adding an extra joint and thus extra flexibility the underside of the tarsal segments may possess pads.
5. The Tarsus is the foot of the insect leg and can consist of between one and five segments.
6. The Claws are situated at the end of the 'tarsus' and serve to assist the insect in holding onto the substrate or to its prey. Between the claws may be found a special pad known as an 'arolium' and which acts using suction developed by large numbers of minute tubular hairs to help hold the insect to smooth substrates.

As in all aspects of insect anatomy their is an amazing diversity of form to be found it the insect leg three examples.

The Wings

Unlike legs, wings only occur in the adult forms of those insects which possess them, in those insects with 'incomplete metamorphosis' small wing buds are visible in the place the wings will occupy in the adult.

Generally speaking wings are thin flat structures consisting of two fine membranes supported by a series of sclerotized veins. In many small insects the veins may be absent and in some very small insects the wings consist of a central midrib supporting a series of fine hairs, these look more like feathers. Wings are not totally stiff but bend and flex in an amazing manner during flight greatly improving their aerodynamics. Most species of winged insect have two pairs of wings and in many of the more advanced orders these two wings are held together by a variety of mechanisms to form a single, larger, functionally wing.

Insect wings are soft and shapeless when the adults first emerge, but are immediately inflated with blood pressure through the veins before they are hardened and darkened by contact with the air.

Though most insect wings appear bare to the naked eye many are dotted with minute hairs and in some cases such as the 'Trichoptera' (Caddis Flies) completely clothed in fine hairs, or as in the 'Lepidoptera' (Moths and Butterflies) completely covered in tiny scales. Though insect wings are primarily concerned with flight they serve a number of purposes, in the 'Coleoptera' (Beetles), and some 'Hemiptera' (True Bugs) the fore wings have become highly sclerotized and act as armour protecting the insect concerned. While some very small parasitic 'Hymenoptera' use their wings to swim through the water to their hosts.

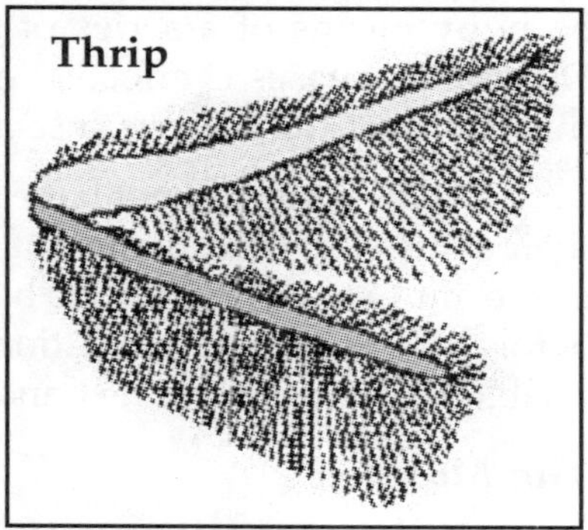
Thrip

The bright colours of many insect wings are there for mating purposes and allow males and females to recognise each other, in others the colours perform a role in camouflage hiding the insect from its predators, and in others they perform a thermodynamic role, the different colours reflecting and absorbing different wave lengths of light allowing the insect to control its internal temperature. In some insects, the wings may perform two or more of these functions simultaneously. In two orders of insects one pair of wings has become completely reduced to small balancing organs and they provide no power of lift during flight at all. The most common of these are the Flies (House Flies, Dung Flies etc.) which have the hind wing reduced. Much less commonly seen but just as interesting are the Stylopids which have the forewing reduced.

In many insects the hind wings are reduced to some extent and thus smaller than the forewings, in others, the forewing has become stiffened to form a protective function the hind wing is often larger than the forewing, and therefore needs to be folded up when it is not in use. Grasshoppers and Crickets fold their wings longitudinally, while Beetles, and Earwigs the wings are folded both longitudinally and laterally. In Staphylinid betles and Earwigs the forewings are very short and the degree of folding of the hindwings is truly amazing.

The Abdomen

The insect abdomen contains the insects digestive tract and reproductive organs, it consists of eleven segments in most orders of insects though the eleventh segment is absent in the adult of most the higher orders. In the 'Collembola' (Springtails) the abdomen has only six segments.

Unlike other Arthropods the the insects possess no legs on the abdomen in the adult form, though the 'Protura' do have rudimentary leg-like appendages on the first three abdominal segments. Many larval insects particularly the 'Lepidoptera' and the 'Symphyta' (Sawflies) have appendages called 'pseudo' or prolegs on their posterior abdominal segments as well as their more familiar thoracic legs these allow them to grip onto the edges of plant leaves as they walk around.

Inside the Insect

Breathing

Insects have no lungs! Most insects breath passively through their spiracles (special openings in the side of there cuticle) and the air reaches the body by means of a series of smaller and smaller pipes called 'Tracheae'. Diffusion of gases is effective over small distances but not over larger ones, this is one of the reasons insects are all relatively small.

Insects which do not have spiracles and tracheae breath directly through their skins, also by diffusion of gases. Here is a lovely drawing of the trachea of the ant Lasius flavus done by the Russian artist and physiologist Nasonov before the the great revolution in that country, unfortunately I have been unable to decipher the text and so the labels are missing.

The Muscles

Like us Insects need muscles in order to move the various different bits of their bodies around, however insects have their muscles attached to the inside of their skeleton because like all the arthropods they have their skeletons on the outside of their body. The inside of an insect's exoskeleton has special contours and bits and bobs on it which project inwards and allow for muscles to be attached and to help give them leverage, these projections are called 'apodemes'.

The musculature of even the smallest insect can be as complicated as our own and makes for a fascinating study of design in miniature. The muscles of insects are generally light grey or translucent, unlike ours which appear red. This is because insects lack both the blood system that we have and the haemoglobin that makes our blood and hence our muscles red.

The Heart and the Blood

The haemolymph (blood) of insects flows freely around the inside of their bodies. Because an insect's haemolymph is not responsible for the transmission of oxygen to its cells and therefore does not contain haemoglobin, it is not red. Normally it is a watery green colour, though it is pigmented (coloured) in some species.

This haemolymph is a sort of soup rich in nutrients that flows around the inside of the insects body allowing the various organs to get at whatever resources they need and into which they dump their waste products. These waste products are later removed from the haemolymph by the Malpighian tubules. Because insects do not have veins and arteries like us and the rest of the vertebrates, (they do not need to), they do not have a complicated heart like ours either.

The insect heart it is basically a tube, sealed at one end, which runs along their back. It beats regularly thus swishing the blood in and out and around the body. You can get some idea how the heart of an insect works by cutting the nozzle off the top of an empty washing-up-liquid bottle and taking it into the bath with you. Hold it under the water and squeeze it a few times and watch how the water swirls around.

Here is a lovely drawing of the internal organs of an ant by the same Russian scientist mentioned that it is very large and if you have a slow link you might like to see the smaller sectioned drawings below it instead though they have lost some clarity in resizing.

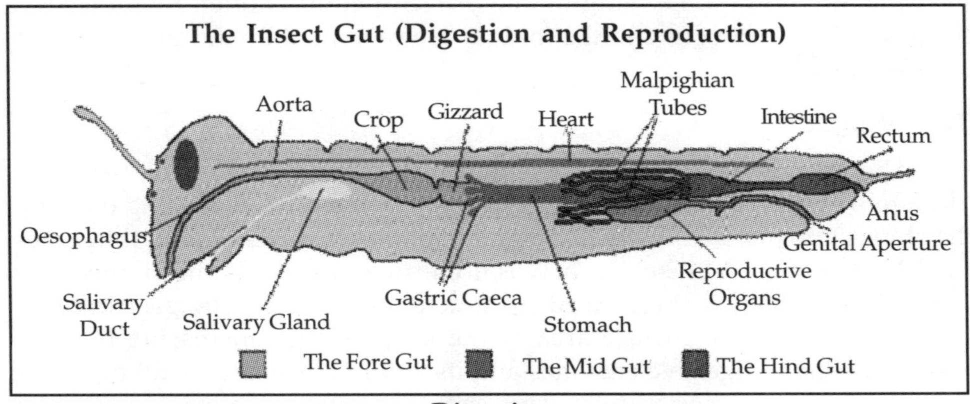

Digestion

The digestive system of an insect is usually a long straight tube running from the mouth to the anus, it is often divided into the 'foregut', the 'midgut' and the 'hindgut'. Immediately behind the mouth are the Salivary Glands, in most species these secrete saliva, generally a watery fluid that lubricates the food and contains a few enzymes to begin the processes of digestion. However, in some carnivorous insects the saliva is composed entirely of digestive enzymes, this applies particularly to those with external digestion of the food. In other insects the salivary glands have become modified for purposes that have nothing to do with digestion. In Lepidopteran caterpillars and Caddisfly larvae they have been converted to the production of silk, while in the Queen Honey Bee they are called the mandibular glands and secrete hormones.

The Foregut

The foregut is generally considered to consist of four sections, the Pharynx, the Oesophagus, the Crop and the Proventriculus. It is also known as the Stomodaeum.

The pharynx is the first part of the foregut and apart from being a tube that connects the interior of the mouth area (sometimes known as the 'Buccal Cavity) with the more inward parts of the gut it sometimes serves as a pump to suck up the liquefied food of those insects which feed by means external digestion. The Oesophagus is basically a tube leading to the midgut via the crop and the proventriculus.

The crop is simply a storage area and the proventriculus is a muscular extension of the crop. In those insects which feed on solid foods it is used to grind the food up into smaller particles, it can also serve as a filter to keep oversized particles out of the main digestive tract and as a valve controlling the flow of food into the midgut. The proventriculus is often referred to as the gizzard. The foregut and the midgut are separated by the 'stomodeal or cardiac valve'.

The Midgut

The midgut (called the Mesenteron in some books) runs from the 'digestive or gastric caeca', a series of stubby pointed tubes leading off from the stomach to just before the Malpighian tubules, a series of long thin tubes (which are orange in Pete). In between the two of these is the stomach, or ventriculus, which is the area of most active digestion. The gastric caeca serve to increase the surface area of the midgut, thus increasing both its ability to secrete digestive enzymes and its ability to extract useful products from the partially digested food. The useful proteins, vitamins and fats that are released by the digestive processes pass across the wall of the midgut into the body cavity.

The Malpighian tubules (named after Malpighi who discovered them) are not really to do with digestion at all but with elimination. They act like our kidneys and extract metabolic waste products (mostly nitrogenous ones such as urea, and uric acid) from the circulating body fluid called the haemolymph and excrete them into the intestines which is the first part of the hingut.

The midgut is lined by a semipermeable membrane composed of protein and chitin, like the cuticle, which allows the passage of liquids and dissolved substances to the midgut wall while preventing the passage of solid food particles, it is continually worn away by the passage of food through the gut and replaced by the epithelial cells of the midgut wall. The midgut and the hindgut are separated by the 'proctodeal valve'.

The Hindgut

From the midgut the food passes to the hindgut (called the Proctodaeum in some books). The hind gut comprises the 'intestines' which is where much of the diffusion into the the insects body occurs. The 'rectum' which compresses the undigested food and waste products, extracts more water from this if necessary before it is passed out through the 'anus' as faeces.

Though insects possess a large number of digestive enzymes, they are often helped by the presence of symbiotic microorganisms, such as protozoa in the case of the termites and some primitive cockroaches which feed on wood, and bacteria in the wax moth Galleria mellonella which feeds on the wax that honey bees Apis mellifera uses to make the combs in its hives.

Reproductive Structures

Most insect species are bisexual, i.e. there are males and females in most species, these often look very different and have even been mistaken for different species in the past, some species are capable of reproduction without males, the eggs are unfertilised but develop and hatch into nymphs or larvae that are always female themselves, this is called 'parthenogenesis'.

Externally the sexual organs, called genitalia, of a female insect generally consist of an 'ovipositor' which is often encased in a pair of filaments called a 'sheath' and is which is used to by the female to put her eggs where she wants. Its form very greatly throughout the Insecta (i.e. the whole order of insects).

The ovipositor of the Diptera (True Flies) is functionally similar i.e. it is used to lay eggs, but is morphologically distinct i.e. it arises or is made from different parts of the insects anatomy and should be called a 'pseudovipositor'. The median part of the oviduct which receives the aedeagus during mating is called the 'vagina'.

Externally the sexual organs of the male, also called genitalia, consist of a pair of 'claspers' which the male uses to hold onto the females genitalia and an intromittant organ called the 'aedeagus' which is the means by which the male passes the sperm onto the female.

Internally the female reproductive organs consist of a pair of ovaries which contain the ovarioles which is where the eggs or ova are formed, the bursa copulatrix which is where the sperm is first received)in those insects which have it) and a spermatheca which is where the sperm is stored.

There are also various tubes down which the ova travel on their way from the ovaries to the outside world, fertilisation occurs in the common oviduct after the the egg has received its shell or the 'chorion'. To facilitate this the shell contains a very small opening at one end called the micropyle which allows the sperm to enter. As well as tubes there are several important glands some of which (spermathecal glands) allow the female to keep the sperm alive and viable for a long time, as much as two decades in some social insects (Ants and Bees); and some of which (collaterial glands) secrete the substances which allow the female to stick the eggs where she wants then to stay i.e. underneath a leaf, or to protect the eggs as in the ootheca produced by the cockroaches and mantids.

Internally the male reproductive organs consist of a pair of 'testes' containing the 'testicular follicles' where the spermatozoa are made, the 'vas deferens' which is the tube down which the sperm travels, a 'seminal vesicle' which is where the sperm is stored prior to mating, and accessory glands which supply seminal fluid for additional volume and to nourish the sperm before and during their journey.

The Nervous System

The insect nervous system consists of a 'brain' (the result of three pairs 'ganglia' (a) collection of neurons or nerve cells] fused together) and a pair of slender nerve cords called 'connectives' which run from it to the end of the insects abdomen, these are joined at intervals where a series of pairs of 'ganglia' (singular ='ganglion') occur the transverse fibres that connect the ganglia are called 'commissures'.

There is usually one pair of ganglia per body segment, thus, as the head is made up out of six fused body segments it contains six pairs of ganglia, these are collected into two groups each of three ganglia the foremost of which is called the brain and the hindmost which is called the 'subesophageal ganglion'.

The ganglia function to coordinate the activities of the body segment they represent, there are usually 3 thoracic ganglia and 8 abdominal ganglia but in some insects such as the Hemiptera (True Bugs) and some Diptera (True flies) the abdominal ganglia tend to fuse and have moved towards the most forward part of the abdomen.

Circulatory System

Insect blood or haemolymph's main function is that of transport and it bathes the insect's body organs. Making up usually less than 25 per cent of an insect's body weight, it transports hormones, nutrients and wastes and has a role in, osmoregulation, temperature control, immunity, storage (water, carbohydrates and fats) and skeletal function. It also plays an essential part in the moulting process.

An additional role of the haemolymph in some orders, can be that of predatory defence. It can contain unpalatable and malodourous chemicals that will act as a deterrent to predators. Haemolymph contains molecules, ions and cells; regulating chemical exchanges between tissues, haemolymph is encased in the insect body cavity or haemocoel. It is transported around the body by combined heart (posterior) and aorta (anterior) pulsations which are located dorsally just under the surface of the body. It differs from vertebrate blood in that it doesn't contain any red blood cells and therefore is without high oxygen carrying capacity, and is more similar to lymph found in vertebrates.

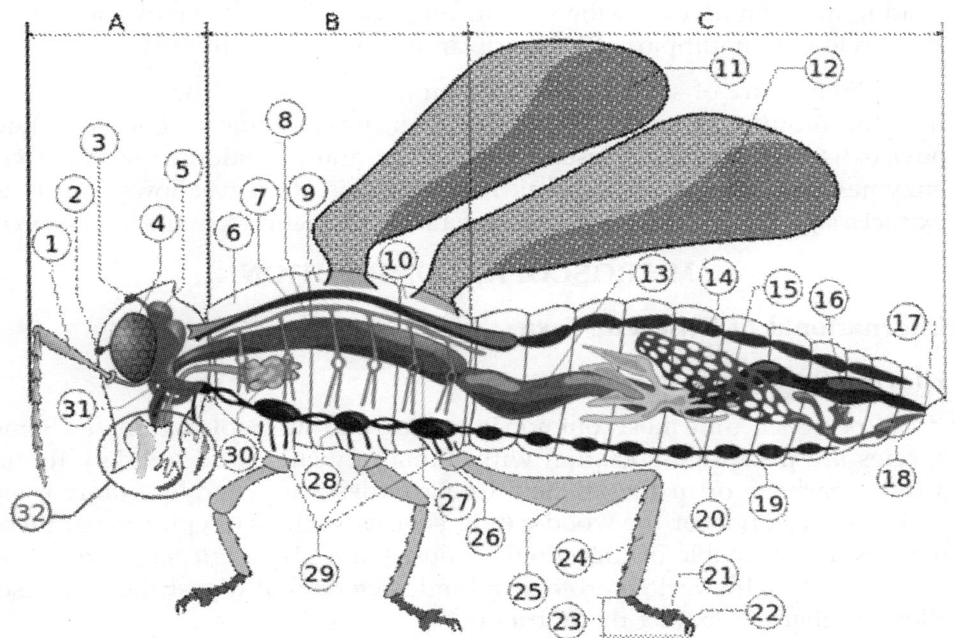

A - Head **B** - Thorax **C** - Abdomen

1. *antenna;* 2. *ocelli* (lower); 3. Ocelli (upper); 4. *Compound eye;* 5. Brain (cerebral *ganglia*); 6. *prothorax;* 7. Dorsal Blood Vessel; 8. *Tracheal* Tubes (trunk with *spiracle*); 9. *Mesothorax;* 10. *Metathorax;* 11. *Forewing;* 12. *Hindwing;* 13. Mid-gut (stomach); 14. Dorsal Tube (Heart); 15. Ovary; 16. *Hind-gut* (intestine, rectum & anus); 17. Anus; 18. Oviduct; 19. Nerve Chord (abdominal ganglia); 20. *Malpighian Tubes;* 21. Tarsal Pads; 22. Claws; 23. *Tarsus;* 24. *Tibia;* 25. *Femur;* 26. *Trochanter;* 27. Fore-gut (crop, gizzard); 28. Thoracic Ganglion; 29. *Coxa;* 30. Salivary Gland; 31. *Subesophageal Ganglion;* 32. *Mouthparts*

Body fluids enter through one way valved ostia which are openings situated along the length of the combined aorta and heart organ. Pumping of the haemolymph occurs by waves of peristaltic contraction, originating at the body's posterior end, pumping forwards into the dorsal vessel, out via the aorta and then into the head where it flows out into the haemocoel.

The haemolymph is circulated to the appendages unidirectionally with the aid of muscular pumps or accessory pulsatile organs which are usually found at the base of the antennae or wings and sometimes in the legs, with pumping rates accelerating with periods of increased activity. Movement of haemolymph is particularly important for thermoregulation in orders such as Odonata, Lepidoptera, Hymenoptera and Diptera.

Endocrine System

The salivary glands in an insect's mouth produce saliva. The salivary ducts lead from the glands to the reservoirs and then forward through the head to an opening called the salivarium, located behind the hypopharynx. By moving its mouthparts the insect can mix its food with saliva.

The mixture of saliva and food then travels through the salivary tubes into the mouth, where it begins to break down. Some insects, likeflies, have extra-oral digestion. Insects using extra-oral digestion expel digestive enzymes onto their food to break it down. This strategy allows insects to extract a significant proportion of the available nutrients from the food source.

MICROSCOPIC COMPOSITION

International of Different Texa

Blattodea

Cockroaches are most common in tropical and subtropical climates. Some species are in close association with human dwellings and widely found around garbage or in the kitchen. Cockroaches are generally omnivorous with the exception of the wood-eating species such as Cryptocercus; these roaches are incapable of digesting cellulose themselves, but have symbiotic relationships with variousprotozoans and bacteria that digest the cellulose, allowing them to extract the nutrients.

The similarity of these symbionts in the genus *Cryptocercus* to those in termites are such that it has been suggested that they are more closely related to termites than to other cockroaches, and current research strongly supports this hypothesis of relationships. All species studied so far carry the obligate mutualistic endosymbiont bacterium *Blatta bacterium,* with the exception of *Nocticola australiensis,* an Australian cave dwelling species without eyes, pigment or wings, and which recent genetic studies indicates are very primitive cockroaches.

Cockroaches, like all insects, breathe through a system of tubes called *tracheae*. The tracheae of insects are attached to the spiracles, excluding the head. Thus cockroaches, like all insects, are not dependent on the mouth and windpipe to breathe.

The valves open when the CO_2 level in the insect rises to a high level; then the CO_2 diffuses out of the tracheae to the outside and fresh O_2 diffuses in. Unlike in vertebrates that depend on blood for transporting O_2 and CO_2, the tracheal system brings the air directly to cells, the tracheal tubes branching continually like a tree until their finest divisions, tracheoles, are associated with each cell, allowing gaseous oxygen to dissolve in the cytoplasm lying across the fine cuticle lining of the tracheole. CO_2 diffuses out of the cell into the tracheole.

While cockroaches do not have lungs and thus do not actively breathe in the vertebrate lung manner, in some very large species the body musculature may contract rhythmically to forcibly move air out and in the spiracles; this may be considered a form of breathing.

Coleoptera

The digestive system of beetles is primarily based on plants which they for the most part feed upon, with mostly the anterior midgut performing digestion. Although, in predatory species (e.g., Carabidae) most digestion occurs in the crop by means of midgut enzymes. In Elateridae species, the predatory larvae defecate enzymes on their prey, with digestion being extraorally. The alimentary canal basically comprises a short narrow pharynx, a widened expansion, the crop and a poorly developed gizzard. After there is a midgut, that varies in dimensions between species, with a large amount ofcecum, with a hingut, with varying lengths. There are typically four to six Malpighian tubules.

The nervous system in beetles contains all the types found in insects, varying between different species. With three thoracic and seven or eight abdominal ganglia can be distinguished to that in which all the thoracic and abdominal ganglia are fused to form a composite structure.

Oxygen is obtained via a tracheal system. Air enters a series of tubes along the body through openings calledspiracles, and is then taken into increasingly finer fibers. Pumping movements of the body force the air through the system.

Beetles have hemolymph instead of blood like other insect species, the open circulatory system of the beetle is driven by a tube-like heart attached to the top inside of the thorax. Some species of diving beetles (Dytiscidae) carry a bubble of air with them whenever they dive beneath the water surface.

This bubble may be held under the elytra or it may be trapped against the body using specialized hairs. The bubble usually covers one or more spiracles so the insect can breathe air from the bubble while submerged.

An air bubble provides an insect with only a short-term supply of oxygen, but thanks to its unique physical properties, oxygen will diffuse into the bubble and displacing the nitrogen, called passive diffusion, however the volume of the bubble eventually diminishes and the beetle will have to return to the surface.

Different glands specialize for different pheromones produced for finding mates. Pheromones from species of Rutelinea are produced from epithelial cells lining the inner surface of the apical abdominal segments or amino acid based pheromones of Melolonthinae from eversible glands on the abdominal apex. Other species produce different types of pheromones. Dermestids produce esters, and species of Elateridae produce fatty-acid-derived aldehydes and acetates. For means of finding a mate also, fireflies (Lampyridae) utilized modified fat body cells woth transparent surfaces backed with reflective uric acid crystals to biosynthetically produce light, or bioluminescence. The light produce is highly efficient, as it is produced by oxidation of luciferin by the enzymes luciferase in the presence of ATP (adenosine triphospate) and oxygen, producing oxyluciferin, carbon dioxide and light.

A notable number of species have developed special glands that produce chemicals for deterring predators. The Ground beetle's (of Carabidae) defensive glands, located at the posterior, produce a variety of hydrocarbons, aldehydes, phenols, quinones, esters, and acids released from an opening at the end of the abdomen. While African carabid beetles (e.g., Anthia and Thermophilium) employ the same chemicals as ants: formic acid. While Bombardier beetles have well developed, like other carabid beetles, pygidial glands that empty from the lateral edges of the intersegment membranes between the seventh and eighth abdominal segments. The gland is made of two containing chambers.

The first holds hydroquinones and hydrogen peroxide, with the second holding just hydrogen peroxide plus catalases. These chemicals mix and result in an explosive ejection, forming temperatures of around 100° C, with the brake down of hydroquinone to $H_2 + O_2$ + quinone, with the O_2 propelling the excretion.

Tympanal organs or hearing organs, which is a membrane (tympanum) stretched across a frame backed by an air sac and associated sensory neurons, are described in two families. Several species of the genus Cicindela (Cicindelidae) have ears on the dorsal surface of the first abdominal segment beneath the wing; two tribes tribes in the family Dynastinae (Scarabaeidae) have ears just beneath the pronotal shield or neck membrane.

The ears of both families are to ultrasonic frequencies, with strong evidence that they function to detect the presence of bats via there ultrasonic echolocation. Even though beetles constitute a large order and live in a variety of niches, examples of hearing is surprisingly lacking in species, though it is likely that most are just undiscovered.

Dermaptera

The neuroendocrine system consist of what typical insect would. There is a Brain, a subesophageal ganglion, three thoratic ganglia, and six abdominal ganglia; a ganglion being a mass of neurons. Strong neuron connects connect the neurohemal corpora cardiaca to the brain and frontal ganglion, where the closely related median corpus allatum produces Jeuvenile hormone III in close proximity to the neurohemal dorsal arota. The digestive system of earwigs is like all other insects: consisting of a fore-, mid-, and hindgut, albeit, earwigs lack gastric caecae which specialize in many species of insects for digestion. Long, slender (extratory) malpighian tubules can be found between the junction of the mid- and hind gut.

The reproductive system of females consist of paired ovaries, lateral oviducts, spermatheca, and agenital chamber. The lateral ducts are where the eggs leave the body, while the spermatheca is where sperm is stored. Unlike other insects, the gonopore, or genital opening is behind the seventh abdominal segment. The ovaries are primitive in that they are polytrophic; or the nurse cells andoocytes alternate along the length of the ovariole. In some species these long ovarioles branch off the lateral duct, while in others, short ovarioles appear around the duct.

Diptera

The genitalia of female flies are rotated to a varying degree from the position found in other insects. In some flies this is a temporary rotation during mating, but in others it is a permanent torsion of the organs that occurs during the pupal stage. This torsion may lead to the anus being located below the genitals, or, in the case of 360° torsion, to the sperm duct being wrapped around the gut, despite the external organs being in their usual position. When flies mate, the male initially flies on top of the female, facing in the same direction, but then turns round to face in the opposite direction. This forces the male to lie on its back in order for its genitalia to remain engaged with those of the female, or the torsion of the male genitals allows the male to mate while remaining upright. This leads to flies having more reproduction abilities than most insects and at a much quicker rate. Flies come in great populations due ir ability to mate effectively and in a short period of time especially during the mating season.

The female lays her eggs as close to the food source as possible, and development is very rapid, allowing the larva to consume as much food as possible in a short period of time before transforming into the adult. The eggs hatch immediately after being laid, or the flies are ovoviviparous, with the larva hatching inside the mother. Larval flies, or maggots, have no true legs, and little demarcation between the thorax and abdomen; in the more derived species, the head is not clearly distinguishable from the rest of the body. Maggots are limbless, or else have small prolegs.

The eyes and antennae are reduced or absent, and the abdomen also lacks appendages such as cerci. This lack of features is an adaptation to a food-rich environment, such as within rotting organic matter, or as anendoparasite. The pupae take various forms, and in some cases develop inside a silk cocoon.

After emerging from the pupa, the adult fly rarely lives more than a few days, and serves mainly to reproduce and to disperse in search of new food sources.

Lepidoptera

In reproductive system of butterflies and moths, the male genitalia are complex and unclear. In females there are three types of genitalia based on the relating taxa: monotrysian, exoporian, and dytresian. In the monotrysian type there is an opening on the fused segments of the sterna 9 and 10, which act as insemination and oviposition. In the exoporian type (in Hepaloidae and Mnesarchaeoidea) there are two separate places for insemination and oviposition, both occurring on the same sterna as the monotrysian type, 9/10.

In most species the genitalia are flanked by two soft lobes, although they may be specialized and sclerotized in some species for ovipositing in area such as crevices and inside plant tissue. Hormones and the glands that produce them run the development of butterflies and moths as they go through their life cycle, called the endocrine system. The first insect hormone PTTH (*Prothoracicotropic hormone*) operates the species life cycle and diapause.

This hormone is produced by corpora allata and corpora cardiaca, where it is also stored. Some glands are specialized to perform certain task such as producing silk or producing saliva in the palpi. While the corpora cardiaca produce PTTH, the corpora allata also produces jeuvanile hormones, and the prothorocic glands produce moulting hormones.

In the digestive system, the anterior region of the foregut has been modified to form a pharyngialsucking pump as they need it for the food they eat, which are for the most part liquids. An esophagusfollows and leads to the posterior of the pharynx and in some species forms a form of crop.

The midgut is short and straight, with the hindgut being longer and coiled. Ancestors of lepidopteran species, stemming from Hymenoptera, had midgut ceca, although this is lost in current butterflies and moths. Instead, all the digestive enzymes other than initial digestion, are immobilized at the surface of the midgut cells. In larvae, long-necked and stalked goblet cells are found in the anterior and posterior midgut regions, respectively. In insects, the goblet cells excrete positive potassium ions, which are absorbed from leaves ingested by the larvae. Most butterflies and moths display the usual digestive cycle, however species that have a different diet require adaptations to meet these new demands.

In the circulatory system, hemolymph, or insect blood, is used to circulate heat in a form ofthermoregulation, where muscles contraction produces heat which is transferred to the rest of the body when conditions are unfavorable. In lepidopteran species, hemolymph is circulated through the veins in the wings by some form of pulsating organ, either by the heart or by the intake of air into the trachea. Air is taken in through spiracles along the sides of the abdomen and thorax supplying the trachea with oxygen as it goes through the lepidopteran's respiratory system. There are three different tracheae supplying oxygen diffusing oxygen throughout the species body: The dorsal, ventral, and visceral. The dorsal tracheae supply oxygen to the dorsal musculature and vessels, while the ventral tracheae supply the ventral musculature and nerve cord, and the visceral tracheae supply the guts, fat bodies and gonads.

CHAPTER – 12

Mites of Ornamental Plants

Description

Mites differ from insects in that they have 8 legs and 2 body regions whereas insects have 6 legs and 3 body regions. There is one exception however, young mites or nymphs have only 6 legs in their early stages and gain the 4th pair of legs as they mature. Mites also vary greatly in color as their appearance is a function of the host plant on which they are feeding. Most of the coloration of spider mites results from the accumulation of food material and waste in the body. Consequently, coloration is more pronounced just prior to molting in nymphs and in more mature adults.

Fig. 12.1: **Leaf Blister Mite Damage on Pear**

The spruce mite is quite small (1/60 inch) and usually a dark reddish color. In some cases, the mite may be dark green. The legs and front part of the body are buff or tan colored. Large quantities of "spider-like" webbing are usually produced during feeding the process. European red mites are bright to brownish-red and unspotted. The body is quite elliptical in outline and about 1/75 inch in length. There are four rows of long curved spines down the back, each borne on a whitish tubercle. The two-spotted spider mite is about 1/60 inch long and ranging in color from pale yellow through green to brown to orange. The male is smaller with a narrower body and pointed abdomen. Two dark spots, composed of food contents, show through the transparent body wall. The mites are oval in shape and sparsely covered with spines.

Life History

Most mites have a similar life cycle however, certain species overwinter either as eggs or adults. The spruce and European red mites overwinter as eggs while the honeylocust spider mite overwinters as a mature female. The overwintering sites vary (ie. spruce mites and two-spotted spider mites on the foliage, honeylocust spider mites in bark cracks and crevices of the host plant and European red mites on twigs and smaller branches). Once mites hatch from the egg, they begin feeding on the foliage rupturing the cells and withdrawing the contents. The result is the presence of tiny chlorotic flecks and a bronzing of the foliage. Extensive feeding will result in stippling, and a yellow and white cast to the leaves.

Fig. 12.2: **European Red Mite Damage on Apple**

Mites are very prolific and populations can build up quite rapidly. Most mites are active throughout the growing season, however the spruce spider mite is a cool season mite and is more prolific in late spring/early summer and late summer/early fall. During hot dry weather, they tend to hibernate. However, the damage caused by their feeding usually coincides with the first hot dry spells of summer.

Damage

Damage from mite infestations can be quite pronounced and significantly reduce the vigor and growth of affected plants. Webs are usually present as well as a graying of the foliage particularly on evergreens. Close examination of the needles and webs reveals tiny flecks or particles which are usually the mites themselves. Holding a light sheet of paper under a branch and shaking the branch vigorously will dislodge them and facilitate a correct diagnosis.

DAMAGE BY ERIOPHYID MITES

Introduction

There are hundreds of species of eriophyid mites. They are commonly divided into groups of gall, bud, rust, and blister mites, depending on the type of damage they cause. Their microscopic size makes their identification difficult. They are identified by their host plant or by the damage they produce. Most eriophyid mites are not considered to be serious pests because the damage is generally only aesthetic and rarely kills the plant.

Do not equate eriophyid mites with other species of mites that damage plants. Eriophyid mites are much different and smaller, and their infestation is usually less damaging – see Biology on page three.

Damage

Eriophyid mites are considered plant parasites because they seldom kill plants. They are host-specific, with each species usually feeding on a particular plant or plant part. The relationship between the host and the mite reflects a degree of specialization between the two.

Eriophyid mites penetrate plant cells and suck up the cellular contents, causing visible deformation or abnormalities. The response of the plant is specific to the species of mite feeding on it. When present, they may cause some plants to form stem or leaf galls. Other common symptoms are russeting, folding, or blistering of leaves or flower petals.

Gall mites cause abnormal growth of leaf and stem tissues by injecting growth regulators into the tissues. The galls that the plant develops provide a protective pocket in which the mites can feed and reproduce (Fig. 12.3). There is an exit hole at the bottom of each gall. Galls may develop on the underside of leaves as hairy mats called erinea (Fig. 12.3). The leaf hairs provide the mites with food and protection. Feeding by the mite may distort the upper leaf surface. Most galls are on the leaves of plants, but they may occur on flowers, petioles, stems, and roots of plants. Galls are generally most abundant early in the year on new growth, foliage, and near the trunk.

Bud mites invade developing buds and fruits of particular plants. Partial or total arrest of bud development or swelling of the buds (referred to as "big bud") may result from an infestation in the bud tissue. The buds die after the mites leave.

Fig. 12.3: **Erineum Mites Cause Leaves to Develop Mats on the Undersides Leaves (above). Damage by Maple Bladder Gall Mite on Sugar Maple (below).**

Rust mites are generally not as damaging as other eriophyid mites, but do cause a bronzing, browning, or silvering of the leaf surface as a result of their feeding on the leaf's cellular contents. Rolling and folding of leaf edges may also result. Rust mites are often on the undersides of leaves, but may feed on both leaf surfaces.

Damage by *blister mites* is similar to the injury caused by gall mites, but the pocket is formed in the internal leaf tissue (mesophyll) rather than on the outer surface. This internal damage causes an external deformity of the leaf and is expressed as a discolored blister.

The blisters dry out in the summer, leaving dead areas on the leaf blades.

Flower galls dwarf stalks by causing the shortening of stem internodes, or they may stimulate secondary development of leaf hairs.

Eriophyid mites may also cause "witches broom," which is a cluster of brushlike growth of stunted twigs or branches on trees and shrubs.

Eriophyid Mites in Nevada

Poplar bud gall mite (*Eriophyes parapopuli*) is one species prevalent in Nevada. Various species of poplars, cottonwoods, and aspens are hosts to this mite. It prevents leaf buds from developing into normal leaves and stems and produces galls near the ends of new growth that are wrinkled and less than one inch in diameter. They are irregular, lumpy, solid masses of plant tissue. The galls develop on one side of the twig, but eventually encircle the base of the bud or shoot. Young galls are greenish, but older galls are red to brown. Galls from previous years are gray-black. Lower branches are usually more heavily infested and may become crooked or stunted. Infestations may cause stress in the tree and make it more prone to other problems. Another species, *E. populi*, causes multiple, irregular buds to be produced in poplars and cottonwoods.

The leaf gall caused by *Phyllocoptes didelphis* may also be found in Nevada. This mite infests quaking aspen (*Populus tremuloides*) and produces circular, shallow galls protruding from the upper surface of the leaf blade. The underside of the leaf is open and filled with solid, yellowish, irregular tissue. The mites reside within the nooks of the growth or partially on the surface of the gall. Lower shaded branches of the tree are more likely to be affected than limbs in the upper canopy in full sun.

Ash flower gall mites (*Eriophyes* fraxiniflora) damage male trees by feeding on the blooms and causing galls to form. The galls are large, blackened, irregular masses. These aesthetically damaging mites are common in southern Nevada.

Biology

Eriophyid mites are more closely related to spiders and ticks than to insects. They are long, ringed (annulate), and worm-like. Most other mites have four pairs of legs, but eriophyid mites only have two pairs, located near their heads. At less than 1/100 of an inch long, eriophyid mites are among the smallest of mites and a hand lens or microscope is required for examination. They are poor crawlers, but their small size facilitates travel between hosts by wind, water, insects, birds, and people.

Eriophyid mites reproduce rapidly. Fertilization occurs when females come in contact with sperm sacs left on the host by males. Females can lay as many as 80 eggs in one month under favorable conditions.

Most eriophyid mites have a simple life cycle in which they develop through three growth stages: egg, first and second nymphs, and adult. Some species have a more complicated life cycle. They alternate between a generation of only overwintering females called deutogynes, and a male-female generation, where the females are called protogynes. Alternating generations is more common in eriophyids that feed on deciduous, woody plants, and appears to be an adaptation based on the seasonal changes of the hosts. Adults live for about one month, and there are as many as six to eight generations per year where seasons are long (southern Nevada).

Management

Detecting eriophyid mites requires a thorough diagnosis of the plant's symptoms. Galls, blisters, or leaf bronzing are common symptoms of their presence, but other pests may cause similar tissue damage. Eriophyid mites usually do not cause serious injury, even large populations can be tolerated by plants, but the damage may be unsightly. Examining plants early in the season will allow quick detection and removal. Look for any color changes or abnormalities in the leaves or buds. Closely inspect the foliage. To avoid problems with eriophyid mites, plant resistant varieties or keep uninfested plants away from susceptible varieties.

It is fairly easy to control eriophyid mites in ornamental plants. Infected leaves and twigs can be pruned off to eliminate adult mites and remove unattractive tissues. Burn or bag and dispose of infested tissues in the trash. Trees should be pruned in early spring when the tree is dormant and the mites are overwintering. All infected branches should be removed or else there is a great possibility of reinfestation.

Heavy infestations can be controlled with insecticides, but spraying plants will not get rid of the galls or erinea once they have been produced. Apply insecticides just after bud break in early spring. Dormant oil, carbaryl, dicofol, horticultural oils, and insecticidal soaps may be effective. Carbaryl is highly toxic to bees and should not be applied when they are active. Exposed mites are easily controlled, but most pesticides do not kill the mites living within galls. Caution: applying chemicals to control eriophyid mites may also kill beneficial insects.

Bibliography

Agosta, Salvatore J.; Janzen, Daniel H. (2004). "Body Size Distributions of Large Costa Rican Dry Forest Moths and the Underlying Relationship Between Plant and Pollinator Morphology". *Oikos* 108 (1): 183-193.

Campbell, N.A. (1996) Biology (4th edition) Benjamin Cummings, New Work. p. 69 ISBN 0-8053-1957-3.

Capinera, JL (Editor). 2008. Encyclopedia of Entomology, 2nd Edition. Springer. ISBN 1-4020-6242-7.

Chown, S.L.; S.W. Nicholson (2004). Insect Physiological Ecology. New York: Oxford University Press. ISBN 0-19-851549-9.

Dunlop, J.A. 1996. Evidence for a Sister Group Relationship Between Ricinulei and Trigonotarbida. Bull. Brit. Arachnol. Soc. 10: 193-204.

Eggleton, P. (2001). Termites and Trees: A Review of Recent Advances in Termite Phylogenetics. *Insectes Sociaux* 48: 187-193.

Eisemann, WK *et al.* (1984). "Do Insects Feel Pain? — A Biological View". Cellular and Molecular Life Sciences 40: 1420-1423.

Gerald W. Krantz & D.E. Walter, ed (2009). A Manual of Acarology (3rd ed.). Texas Tech University Press. ISBN 978-08-9672-620-8.

Gerald W. Krantz & D.E. Walter, ed (2009). A Manual of Acarology (3rd ed.). Texas Tech University Press. ISBN 978-08-9672-620-8.

Gilliott, Cedric (August 1995). Entomology (2 ed.). Springer-Verlag New York, LLC. ISBN 0-306-44967-6.

Hoell, H.V., Doyen, J.T. & Purcell, A.H. (1998). Introduction to Insect Biology and Diversity, 2nd ed. Oxford University Press. pp. 493-499. ISBN 0-19-510033-6.

Johnston, D.E. 1982. Acari. In: Parker, S.P.(ed.) Synopsis and Classification of Living Organisms. McGraw-Hill, New York, p. 111.

Kapoor, V.C.C. (January 1998). Principles and Practices of Animal Taxonomy. 1 (1 ed.). Science Publishers. p. 48. ISBN 1-57808-024-X.

Kethley, J.B., Norton, R.A., Bonamo, P.M. and Shear, W.A. 1979. A Terrestrial Alicorhagiid Mite (Acari: Acariformes) from the Devonian of New York. Micropaleontology 35: 367-373.

Lighton J.R.B. & Lovegrove B.G. (1990) "A Temperature-induced Switch from Diffusive to Convective Ventilation in the Honeybee, " Journal of Experimental Biology, Vol. 154, pp. 509-516.

McGavin, G.C. (2001). "Essential Entomology; An Order by Order Introduction". New York: Oxford University Press.

Merritt, RW, KW Cummins, and MB Berg (2007). An Introduction to the Aquatic Insects of North America. Kendall Hunt Publishing Company. ISBN 0-7575-4128-3.

Meyer, John R. (17 February 2006). "Circulatory System". NC State University: Department of Entomology, NC State University. pp. 1. Retrieved 2009-10-11.

Meyer, John R. (5 January 2007). "External Anatomy: WINGS". Department of Entomology, NC State University. Retrieved 2011-03-21.

Nation, James L. (November 2001). "15". Insect Physiology and Biochemistry (1 ed.). CRC Press. pp. 496. ISBN 0-8493-1181-0.

Spieth, HT (1932). "A New Method of Studying the Wing Veins of the Mayflies and Some Results Therefrom (Ephemerida)". Entomological News.

T. Woolley (1988). Acarology: Mites and Human Welfare. New York: Wiley Interscience. ISBN 0-47-104168-8.

Triplehorn, C.A.; Johnson, N. F. (2005). "Borror and DeLong's Introduction to the Study of Insects". Brooks/Thomson Cole: Brooks/Thomson Cole.

Walter & H.C. Proctor (1999). Mites: Ecology, Evolution and Behaviour. University of NSW Press, Sydney and CABI, Wallingford. ISBN 0-86840-529-9.

Williams, C.M. 1947. Physiology of Insect Diapause. II. Interaction Between the Pupal Brain and Prothoracic Glands in the Metamorphosis of the Giant Silkworm "Platysamia Cecropia". Biol. Bull. 92: 89-180.

Index